FreeHand Graphics Studio 7

AUTHORIZED

MACROMEDIA
PRESS

FreeHand Graphics Studio 7 Authorized
Macromedia, Inc.

 Published by Macromedia Press, in association with Peachpit Press,
a division of Addison Wesley Longman.

Macromedia Press
2414 Sixth Street
Berkeley, CA 94710
510/548-4393
510/548-5991 (fax)
Find us on the World Wide Web at:
http://www.peachpit.com
http://www.macromedia.com

ISBN: 0-201-68832-8

Printed and bound in the United States of America

 Printed on recycled paper

9 8 7 6 5 4 3 2 1

CREDITS

Producer
Karen Tucker, Macromedia

Authors and Instructional Designers
Thomas Faist and the team at Datrix Media Group: Lori Faist, Craig Faist, Kevin Walsh, and Diane Faist

Artwork
Julia Sifers, Glasgow & Associates
Thomas Faist and Craig Faist, Datrix Media Group

Production
Rick Gordon, Emerald Valley Graphics
Myrna Vladic, Bad Dog Graffix

Editor
Judy Ziajka

Indexer
Steve Rath

Thanks to
Rocky Angelucci, Macromedia
Monica Dahlen, Macromedia
Darcy DiNucci, To the Point Publishing
Joel Dreskin, Macromedia
Joanne Watkins, Macromedia

table of contents

LESSON 2 COMBINING TEXT AND GRAPHICS

LESSON 3 WORKING WITH PATHS AND POINTS

introduction

Macromedia's FreeHand Graphics Studio 7 combines Macromedia FreeHand 7, a powerful and comprehensive drawing and layout program, with three other professional-level applications: Fontographer for creating and editing fonts, xRes for working with digital images, and Extreme 3D for creating three-dimensional illustrations and animations. Together, these applications provide a complete set of tools for creating dynamic graphics and page designs in print and on the World Wide Web.

This Macromedia Authorized training course introduces you to the major features of FreeHand and the other applications in the FreeHand Graphics Studio by guiding you step by step through the development of several sample projects. This 15-hour curriculum includes these lessons:

Lesson 1: FreeHand Basics
Lesson 2: Combining Text and Graphics
Lesson 3: Working with Paths and Points
Lesson 4: Using Layers and Styles
Lesson 5: Designing Multiple-Page Documents
Lesson 6: Advanced FreeHand Techniques
Lesson 7: Creating Custom Fonts
Lesson 8: Preparing Art for Extreme 3D
Lesson 9: Adding a Third Dimension
Lesson 10: Creating Shadows and Textures
Lesson 11: Putting It All Together
Lesson 12: Shocking Artwork for the Web

Each lesson begins with an overview of the lesson's content and learning objectives, and each is divided into short tasks that break the skills into bite-size units.

Each lesson also includes these special features:

Tips: Shortcuts for carrying out common tasks and ways to use the skills you're learning to solve common problems.

Boldface terms: New vocabulary that will come in handy as you use FreeHand and work with graphics.

Menu commands and keyboard shortcuts: Alternative methods for executing commands in the FreeHand Graphics Studio. Menu commands are shown like this: Menu › Command › Subcommand. Keyboard shortcuts (when available) are shown in parentheses after the first step in which they can be used; a plus sign between the names of keys means you press keys simultaneously: for example, Ctrl+Z means that you should press the Ctrl and Z keys at the same time.

Appendices A and B at the end of the book provide a quick reference to shortcuts you can use in Windows and Macintosh systems, respectively, to give commands in FreeHand.

As you complete these lessons, you'll be developing the skills you need to complete your own designs, layouts, and illustrations for print, multimedia, and the Internet. At the end of this course, you should have mastered all the skills listed in the "What You Will Learn" list on the last page of this introduction.

All the files you need for the lessons are included in the Lessons folder on the enclosed CD-ROM. Files for each lesson appear in their own folders, titled with the lesson name. You can use the lesson files directly from the CD-ROM, or you can copy the Lessons folder to your hard drive for quicker access.

Each lesson folder contains three subfolders—Complete, Media, and Start. The Complete folder contains completed files for each project so you can compare your work or see where you are headed. The Media folder contains any media elements you need to complete each lesson, such as graphics or text required to complete a layout. The Start folder contains any prebuilt files you will need to complete the lesson. The completed, media, and starting files you will need are identified at the beginning of each lesson. (Some lessons may not require starting files or media elements, so in some lesson folders, these subfolders will be empty.)

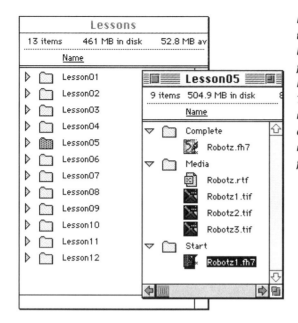

Files for each lesson appear in their own folders titled with the lesson number. The Complete folder contains completed FreeHand files for each lesson. The Media folder contains the media elements you need to complete each lesson. If a lesson requires a prebuilt file, you will find it in the Start folder.

Each book in the Macromedia Authorized series includes the complete curriculum of a course taught at Macromedia's Authorized Training Centers. The lesson plans were developed by some of Macromedia's most successful trainers and refined through long experience to meet students' needs. We believe that Macromedia Authorized courses offer the best available training for Macromedia programs.

The instructions in this book are designed for graphic artists, illustrators, designers, and others interested in creating stunning graphics, typography, and layouts for print, multimedia, and the World Wide Web. This course assumes you are a beginner with FreeHand but are familiar with the basic methods of giving commands on a Windows or Macintosh computer, such as choosing items from menus, opening and saving files, and so on. For more information on those basic tasks, see the documentation provided with your computer.

Finally, the instructions in this book assume that you already have FreeHand 7 and the other FreeHand Graphics Studio applications installed on a Windows or Macintosh computer, and that your computer meets the system requirements listed on the next page. This minimum configuration will allow you to run FreeHand 7 and open the training files included on the enclosed CD-ROM. Lessons 8 through 12 in this course explore the creation of a project that requires the use of Fontographer,

Extreme 3D, and xRes along with FreeHand. If you do not own FreeHand 7 or the FreeHand Graphics Studio, you can use the training version of the software on the CD-ROM provided with this manual. You will be able to complete all the lessons with the training version of the software, but you will not be able to save your work. Follow the instructions in the Read Me file on the enclosed CD-ROM to install the training version of the software.

note *Three TrueType font families included on the FreeHand 7 software CD-ROM you received when you purchased the FreeHand Graphics Studio are used throughout the lessons in this course. To accurately reproduce the projects with the original fonts, install the News Gothic T, URW Garamond T, and Vladimir Script font families on your system before starting the lessons. Windows 95 users should drag those font files into the Fonts folder in the Control Panel. Macintosh users should drag those font files into the Fonts folder in the System Folder.*

If you do not install these specific fonts, simply choose other fonts available on your system and adjust type size and formatting as needed to make your projects similar in appearance to the lesson files. Working without the original fonts installed will not interfere with your ability to complete the lessons.

Welcome to Macromedia Authorized. We hope you enjoy the course.

WHAT YOU WILL LEARN

By the end of this course you will be able to:

Create, combine, and transform graphic elements in FreeHand

Incorporate graphics and text into your projects

Create single- and multiple-page layouts

Take advantage of powerful and easy-to-use special effects features

Import and export files for easy integration with other applications

Create custom fonts with Fontographer

Add a third dimension to artwork with Extreme 3D

Combine objects and enhance images with xRes

Use the four FreeHand Graphics Studio applications together in a project

Use Shockwave to prepare graphics and images for use on the World Wide Web

MINIMUM SYSTEM REQUIREMENTS

Windows	Macintosh
486/50 or Pentium processor (Pentium recommended)	68040 or PowerPC processor (Power PC recommended)
16 MB available RAM (24 MB recommended)	16 MB available RAM (24 MB recommended)
25 MB available disk space	25 MB available disk space
CD-ROM drive	CD-ROM drive
Windows 95 or Windows NT	System 7.1 or higher

For Lesson 12, you will need Shockwave, Afterburner (for FreeHand and xRes), and a browser that supports Shockwave (see Macromedia's Web site at http://www.macromedia.com for more information).

basics

FreeHand

FreeHand's drawing and layout tools can be used to develop everything from the simplest illustrations to the most complex designs. Its extensive control over graphics, colors, type, and imported artwork make FreeHand a powerhouse for any graphic design project.

LESSON 1

This simple robot figure is constructed from a series of shapes created with FreeHand's basic shape tools. You will see how in this lesson.

FreeHand is an object-oriented drawing program. Object oriented means that your document is created from graphic objects, or shapes, rather than from individual pixels as with a bitmap drawing tool. Object-oriented graphics are also known as vector graphics. Unlike bitmap graphics, object-oriented graphics can be scaled to any size or output resolution with no loss of quality.

In this lesson, you will create a simple drawing of a robot using groups of these simple graphic objects, created using FreeHand's basic shape tools—Rectangle, Ellipse, and Line—and the Pointer tool.

If you would like to review the final result of this lesson, open Robot.fh7 in the Complete folder within the Lesson 1 folder.

WHAT YOU WILL LEARN

In this lesson you will:

Create a new document

Identify and organize tools and controls

Customize application settings

Create basic shapes such as rectangles, ellipses, and lines

Change the way elements look on the page by adding color and changing line thickness and moving and aligning objects.

Group objects together

Create additional copies of existing elements

Transform elements by reflecting them and rotating them

APPROXIMATE TIME

It usually takes about 1 hour to complete this lesson.

LESSON FILES

Media Files:

None

Starting Files:

Lesson01\Start\Robot1.fh7 (optional)

Completed Project:

Lesson01\Complete\Robot.fh7

CREATING A FOLDER ON YOUR HARD DRIVE

Before you begin building anything, you will create a folder to hold all the projects you will create as you work through the lessons in this book. If you are using the training version of FreeHand Graphics Studio provided on the CD-ROM that came with this book, you do not need to create this folder because you will not be able to save files.

1] Create a folder called *MyWork* on your hard drive.

You will save all of your work in this folder.

Now you are ready to begin.

CREATING A NEW DOCUMENT

To begin working on a new project, you must first launch FreeHand and either create a new document or open an existing document.

1] Open the FreeHand application.

Open the application by double-clicking the FreeHand icon. The FreeHand toolbox, toolbars, and menu bar appear, but without an open document window.

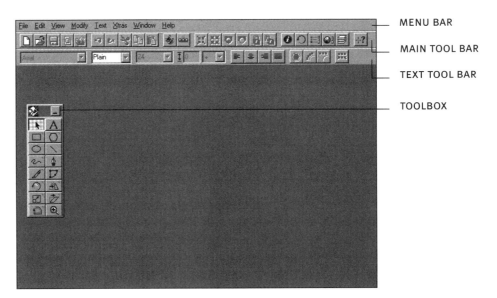

MENU BAR

MAIN TOOL BAR

TEXT TOOL BAR

TOOLBOX

2] Create a new document by choosing File › New (Windows Ctrl+N, Macintosh Command+N).

A new document appears in a document window. The page is sitting on FreeHand's **pasteboard**, which is a work surface that contains all of the pages in your document. The pasteboard initially contains one page. The 222-inch × 222-inch pasteboard can hold more than 675 letter-sized pages. You will be creating a robot illustration in this window later in this lesson.

You will be learning about the elements on this screen throughout this lesson.

tip   *If you cannot see the entire page, choose View > Fit To Page.*

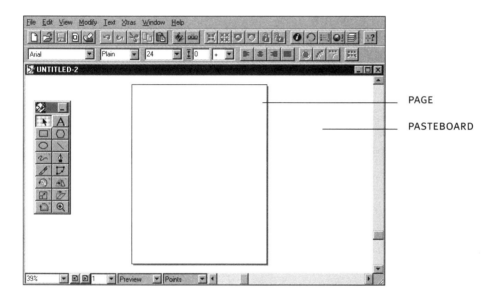

EXPLORING THE CONTROLS

1] Move the cursor over the main and text toolbars across the top of the screen. Rest the cursor over a button to see its name.

The **main toolbar** contains many of the basic functions of FreeHand. The **text toolbar** contains buttons and menus for the most frequently used text commands. When you point to a button and hold the mouse still for a few moments, the button's name will appear.

tip   *If the main and text toolbars do not appear on your screen, you can display them by selecting Window > Toolbars.*

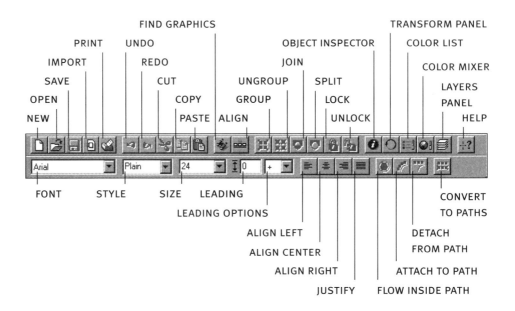

2] Look at the toolbox at the left side of your screen.

The **toolbox** contains FreeHand's drawing and transformation tools. You select a tool in the toolbox by clicking the desired tool once. Move the cursor into the document window to use the tool.

tip   *If the toolbox does not appear on your screen, you can display it by selecting Window > Toolbars > Toolbox.*

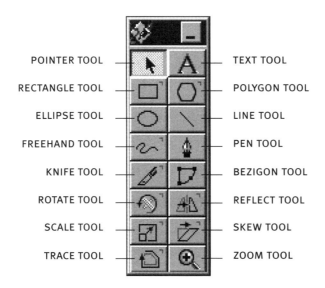

POINTER TOOL — TEXT TOOL

RECTANGLE TOOL — POLYGON TOOL

ELLIPSE TOOL — LINE TOOL

FREEHAND TOOL — PEN TOOL

KNIFE TOOL — BEZIGON TOOL

ROTATE TOOL — REFLECT TOOL

SCALE TOOL — SKEW TOOL

TRACE TOOL — ZOOM TOOL

CUSTOMIZING APPLICATION PREFERENCES

FreeHand lets you set a wide array of preferences for customizing your working environment. You can customize the way elements are displayed, the number of Undo levels, and the way text and graphics can be edited, among many other settings.

Before beginning to work with FreeHand, you will change two preference settings that will make it easier to learn the program and see your results clearly.

1] Choose File › Preferences to display the Preferences dialog box.
In the Preferences dialog box that appears, you choose a category of preferences from a list on the left side. The options on the right side of the dialog box change with the category you select on the left.

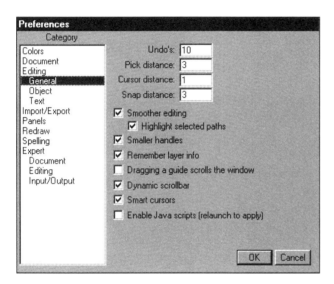

2] Select Object from the left side of the dialog box, under Editing. Turn off (uncheck) the option Changing Object Changes Default.
Turning off this option ensures that when you apply a color to a graphic, it will not change the color of the next elements you create. The default settings of the other options in the Object Editing preferences are shown here.

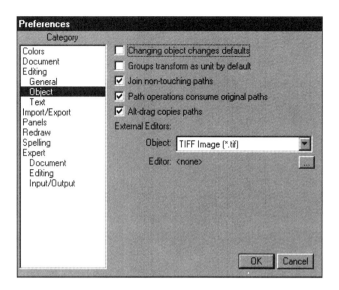

3] Now select Redraw from the left side of the dialog box. Make sure that the option Better (but Slower) Display is turned on (checked).

This will give you a better screen display of gradient fills (transitions between two or more colors) and should not significantly slow down most computer systems. Another option in the Redraw group is High-Resolution Image Display, which allows FreeHand to display imported images with much greater clarity, but it can slow down screen redrawing significantly when you are working with very-high-resolution images. Leave this option off (unchecked) at this time. These two options apply only to the display and do not have any effect on your printed results. The default settings of the other options in the Redraw preferences are shown here.

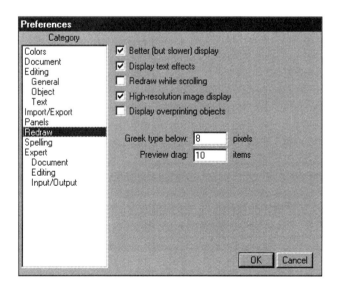

4] Click OK to close the Preferences dialog box.

You will not see the results of these preference changes until you start working with elements on the page.

WORKING WITH PANELS

Many FreeHand drawing settings can be set in **panels**, floating collections of tools and formatting controls that you can open, close, customize, and move around on your desktop. Unlike dialog boxes, FreeHand's panels can remain on the screen as you work for quick and easy editing of document settings. In this section, you'll be introduced to some of the most useful panels: the Inspectors, Color Mixer, and Color List. You will use these panels often in the lessons that follow.

1] Display the Object Inspector by clicking the Inspector button on the main toolbar or by choosing Window > Inspectors > Object.

OBJECT INSPECTOR

FreeHand's Inspector panels are grouped together by default; when you open the Object Inspector, you see the Stroke, Fill, Text, and Document inspectors as well. These panels display current information regarding selected objects and allow you to change the characteristics of those objects.

No information is displayed in the Object Inspector at this time, since no element is selected.

tip *The five Inspectors (Object, Stroke, Fill, Text, and Document) contain important controls for editing FreeHand graphics. Virtually every FreeHand drawing task involves one or more of these Inspectors. These Inspectors are on movable panels and can be arranged to suit your individual preference.*

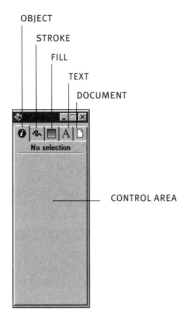

OBJECT
STROKE
FILL
TEXT
DOCUMENT

No selection

CONTROL AREA

2] Click the tab for the Document Inspector to activate that set of controls (bringing that Inspector to the front of the group).

The Document Inspector contains controls for specifying page size and orientation, and for adding or removing pages from the document. You will work with each of these controls in later lessons.

You can change to any of the other Inspectors by clicking its tab at the top of the panel group.

3] Display the Color Mixer by clicking its button on the main toolbar.

COLOR MIXER

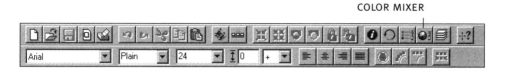

The Color Mixer enables you to create and modify colors and tints that can be applied to elements throughout the document. You will see how this tool works later in this lesson.

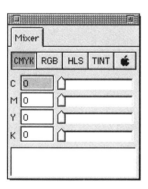

4] Display the Color List by clicking its button on the main toolbar.

COLOR LIST

The Color List appears, showing the names of the colors that have been defined for this document. Adding colors to the Color List makes it easy to apply those colors to other elements in the document without having to redefine them in the Color Mixer for each use.

The Color List is initially grouped with the Layers panel. The Layers tab can be seen at the top of this panel group. Two or more panels combined in this way are called a **panel group**.

5] Click the Layers tab at the top of the Color List panel group.

The Layers panel comes to the front of the group, hiding the Color List. In an upcoming lesson, you will use Layers to organize artwork in a more complex illustration than the robot drawing you create in this lesson.

6] Drag the Layers panel out of this panel group by pointing to the name *Layers* in the tab at the top of the panel and dragging the tab out onto the pasteboard. Then release the mouse.

Layers now appears as a separate panel, so you can access the Color List at the same time as Layers. You have ungrouped these two panels.

 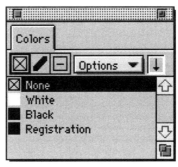

7] Drag the Layers tab onto the Color List panel and release the mouse.

This combines the two panels into a panel group again. As you can see, panels can be
separated or combined by dragging their tabs.

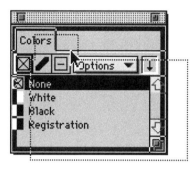

8] Hide the Color List by clicking the button on the main toolbar again.

Display and hide panels as needed using the toolbar. You can also display any of
FreeHand's panels by selecting Window > Panels and choosing the panel you
want to use.

ORGANIZING THE WORKSPACE

Next you will see how you can align panels to one another and connect panels
together to customize your working environment. The Inspectors and Color Mixer
should still appear on your screen as you begin this task.

1] Display the Color List panel again by clicking the button on the main toolbar.

FreeHand has built-in capabilities to help you align panels to keep your working
environment organized.

**2] Move the top of the Color List panel toward the bottom of the Color Mixer panel
by dragging the header bar at the top of the Color List panel.**

Notice that as you move the Color List close to the Color Mixer, it **snaps** into
position so that the two panels are aligned. These panels are not connected together,
but are neatly aligned at the edges. When you drag a panel or group by its header bar
to within 12 pixels of another panel or group, FreeHand will automatically align
them with one another. Panels will snap to the top, bottom, and sides of other panels
when you move any edge of a panel to within 12 pixels of another panel.

You can also align panels to the edge of your workspace by dragging them to within
12 pixels of the monitor border or to the border of the application (this last option
applies only to Windows when the application window does not fill the screen).

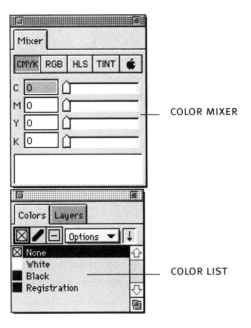

COLOR MIXER

COLOR LIST

3] Move the Color List away from the Color Mixer and release the mouse. Then hold down the Shift key and move the Color List back toward the Color Mixer. Release the Shift key.

The panels do not snap together. Pressing Shift while dragging a panel (Shift+drag) temporarily disables snapping. Panels will automatically snap to one another when you move panels without holding down the Shift key.

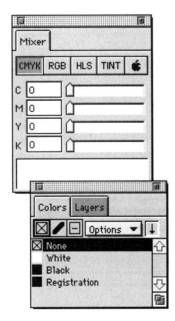

4] Move the top of the Color List toward the bottom of the Color Mixer by dragging the Color List's header bar while holding down the Control key.

This **docks** the panels, connecting them together so they behave as if they are one. Unlike a panel group, docked panels are all displayed at the same time. Notice the **panel dock**, a small bar connecting the two panels together.

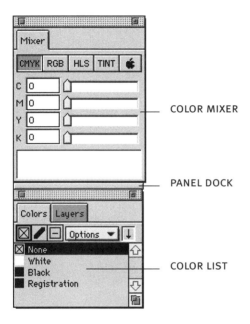

COLOR MIXER

PANEL DOCK

COLOR LIST

5] Try moving one of the docked panels. Then collapse one of the docked panels by clicking the Minimize button (Windows) or Zoom box (Macintosh).

Docked panels move and collapse together, making it easier to work with several panels at once.

6] Expand the collapsed panels, and then undock the panels by clicking the panel dock between the two panels.

The panels are now independent again. You can also undock the panels by holding down the Control key while dragging the header bar of a docked panel away from its adjacent panel.

7] Close all open panels.

As you work with FreeHand, you can position, group, dock, and collapse panels as desired. Remember that you can also show and hide panels quickly with the buttons on the main toolbar.

The flexibility that FreeHand offers with panels makes it easy for you to organize the controls in a way that is comfortable for you.

CHANGING THE VIEW

FreeHand offers several features for viewing your artwork on the screen.

1] Select the Zoom tool at the bottom right of the toolbox by clicking it once. Then point to a corner of your page and click to zoom in on that spot.

Clicking with the Zoom tool magnifies the spot where you click. Another way to zoom in is to hold down the mouse button and drag the Zoom tool cursor to surround the desired area with a **marquee**, a dotted line that surrounds the area you define by dragging the mouse; when you release the mouse, FreeHand will zoom in to the surrounded area.

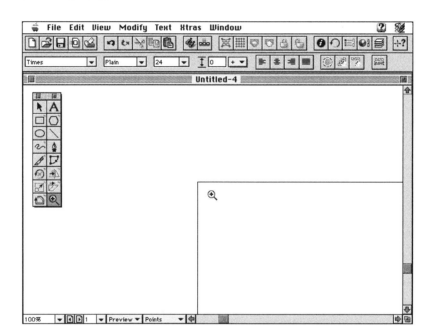

2] Press and hold the Alt (Windows) or Option (Macintosh) key and click with the Zoom tool to reduce the view.

The Zoom tool displays a plus or minus sign to indicate whether it will magnify (+) or reduce (–) the view. If the magnifying glass cursor appears without either a plus or minus sign, you are zoomed in or out as far as possible. FreeHand supports a zoom range of from 6 percent to 25,600 percent of the drawing size, so you shouldn't see the empty cursor very often. Notice that the magnification value appears in the lower-left corner of the screen.

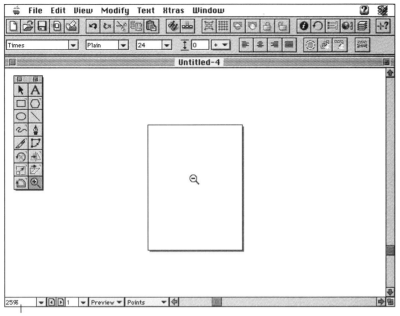

MAGNIFICATION LEVEL

3] Use the View › Fit To Page command to see the entire page again (Windows Ctrl+Shift+W, Macintosh Command+Shift+W).

The top three choices on the View menu allow you to change your view of the page immediately with specific results. Fit Selection zooms to fill the document window with any selected element (or elements), Fit To Page resizes the view so you can see the entire page, and Fit All reduces the view so you can see all of the pages in your document at once. (Right now, Fit All and Fit To Page would have the same results, since you have only one page in your current document.)

4] Point to the arrow at the lower-left corner of the document window and hold down the mouse button to display the magnification menu. Select 100% and release the mouse button.

This menu contains popular preset magnification values. Instead of typing a value in the magnification value field, you can select a value from this menu.

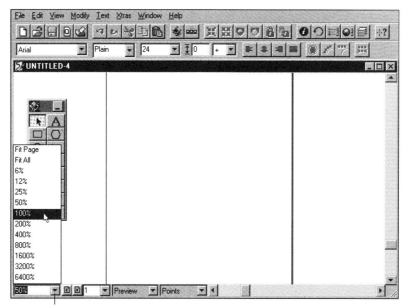

CLICK HERE TO ACCESS THE MAGNIFICATION MENU

As you can see, FreeHand offers several ways for you to achieve the same results, so you can work in the way that is most convenient for you.

CREATING BASIC SHAPES

Now you will begin creating the basic elements needed to construct your first project: a simple drawing of a robot. This lesson will introduce concepts you will use in every FreeHand project.

If you prefer to re-create the robot more closely, you can work from the template provided. Use the File > Open command and open Robot1.fh7 in the Start directory for Lesson 1. Remember, though, the important point in this lesson is to learn to use the drawing tools, not to match the sample exactly. Don't worry if your version of the robot looks a little different from ours.

You will start by creating a rectangle for the body.

1] Choose the Rectangle tool by clicking it once in the toolbox.

Always select a tool from the toolbox by clicking on it once and then releasing the mouse.

2] Position your cursor where you want the upper-left corner of the rectangle; choose a spot near the center of the screen. Then hold down the mouse button and drag diagonally downward and to the right to create a vertical rectangle. Release the mouse when you are pleased with the size of the rectangle.

The rectangle appears on the page with a border and no fill. (If your rectangle looks different, don't worry. You will be changing its characteristics shortly.)

Small boxes appear at the corners, called **selection boxes**, which indicate that this element is selected.

tip *Zoom in to see the artwork clearly as you work.*

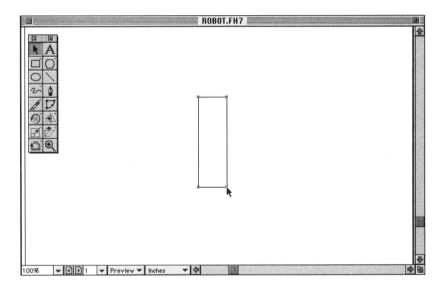

3] Select the Pointer tool in the toolbox. Position the tip of the pointer on one of the corner selection boxes of your rectangle, hold down the mouse button, and drag to resize the rectangle as necessary to create the body of the robot. If you decide you prefer the size of the rectangle before it was resized, choose Edit › Undo to undo the change.

FreeHand supports multiple levels of Undo. The default setting is 10 levels of Undo, but you can specify the number of Undo operations by selecting File > Preferences > General.

4] **Create another rectangle above the body for the shoulders. Make this rectangle horizontal. Then use the Pointer tool to move the shoulder element by pointing to the edge of the rectangle (not on a selection box), holding down the mouse button, and dragging. Visually position the shoulders over the body.**

Don't worry if your elements are not centered perfectly above one another. You will fix that shortly.

tip *To move this element, point to the border of the element (without pointing to a selection box) and drag. Since this rectangle is empty, there is nothing to grab inside the border when you want to move the object.*

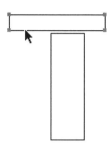

5] **Select the Ellipse tool and use this tool to create a perfect circle for the head by holding down the Shift key as you drag diagonally. Then move the circle into position over the shoulders using the Pointer tool.**

Holding the Shift key enables you to draw perfect circles with the Ellipse tool and perfect squares with the Rectangle tool and constrains lines created with the Line tool to 180-, 90-, and 45-degree angles. Make sure that you release the mouse button *before* you release the Shift key.

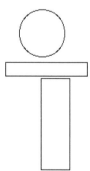

6] Draw a smaller horizontal rectangle below the body for the hips of the robot. Then use the Line tool to draw a vertical line connecting all of these shapes; this is the spine of the robot. Make sure to hold down the Shift key to keep the line vertical.

You now have five elements on your page.

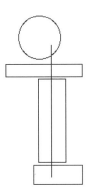

SAVING THE DOCUMENT

Saving your work frequently is a good habit. You should save at least every 15 minutes or each time you finish a task. This will prevent you from losing hours of work if a power outage or computer malfunction occurs.

1] Choose File › Save to display the Save As dialog box (Windows Ctrl+S, Macintosh Command+S). Alternatively, you can click the Save button on the toolbar.

Since this is the first time you have saved this document, FreeHand will ask for a location and name for the file.

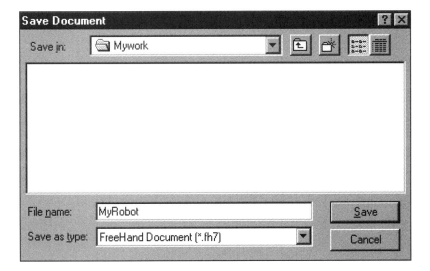

2] Select a location where you want to save this document. In this case, choose the MyWork folder you created on the hard drive.

If you are using the training version of FreeHand Graphics Studio supplied on the CD-ROM that came with this book, you will not be able to save your work.

3] Enter a name for the document, such as *MyRobot,* and press the Enter key (or click the Save button).

When FreeHand is finished saving the file, the name you entered will appear in the title bar at the top of the document window.

> **tip**   *Always choose the location before entering a name for a document. This will ensure that you always know exactly where you have saved your document.*

APPLYING FILLS AND STROKES

The circle and rectangles you have created are empty shapes with thin black outlines. In this task, you will fill in each of these empty shapes with one or more colors or shades. Applying colors to the inside of an element is called applying a **fill**. You will also change the border, or **stroke**, of each element.

1] Open the Color Mixer by choosing Window › Panels › Color Mixer or by clicking the Color Mixer button on the main toolbar.

You will use the Color Mixer to create new colors to apply to elements in your document. You can also create **tints**, which are lighter shades of a color, expressed as a percentage of the base color. (Tints are also referred to as **screens**.)

2] Click the Tint button at the top of the panel and select Black from the color menu below the Tint button.

This displays a strip of tints, in small squares called **swatches**, in 10 percent increments of the base color—in this case, black. This panel also provides a custom tint control (with an entry field and slider) for creating other tint values.

You can drag and drop any swatch from the Color Mixer panel onto a desired element in your document. You will use this technique to fill the shapes in the robot.

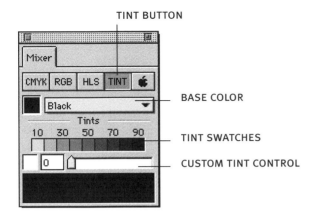

TINT BUTTON

BASE COLOR

TINT SWATCHES

CUSTOM TINT CONTROL

3] Drag the 30 percent swatch and drop it inside the shoulder rectangle of your robot.
You can drop a color inside any closed shape to apply a basic (solid) fill. Open shapes, like the line you drew, cannot be filled. If the stroke changes instead of the fill, you dropped the swatch on the stroke; choose Edit > Undo and try again.

tip *It is often easier to drop color inside a small shape if you first zoom in on the element.*

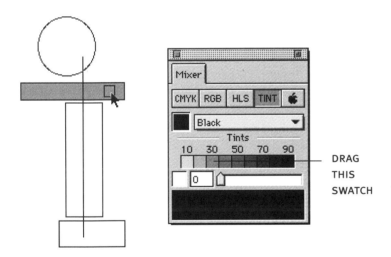

DRAG
THIS
SWATCH

4] Drop the 60 percent swatch on the bottom rectangle (the hips). Then drag the black swatch from the top of the panel onto the body rectangle and drag the 40 percent swatch onto the circle.

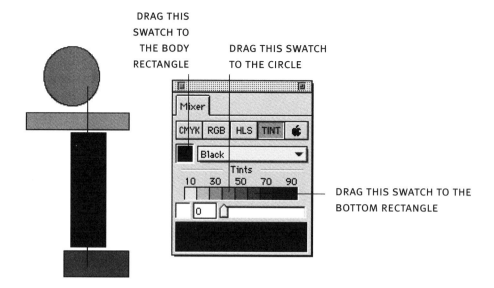

DRAG THIS SWATCH TO THE BODY RECTANGLE

DRAG THIS SWATCH TO THE CIRCLE

DRAG THIS SWATCH TO THE BOTTOM RECTANGLE

Next you will change the thickness of the robot's spine.

5] Select the spine line with the Pointer tool. Select the Stroke Inspector by choosing Window › Inspectors › Stroke or Modify › Stroke. Alternatively, you can select the Stroke Inspector by clicking the Inspector button on the toolbar and then clicking on the Stroke tab.

The Stroke Inspector appears. With this Inspector, you can control the stroke (line) characteristics of the selected object.

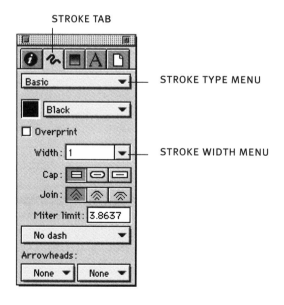

STROKE TAB

STROKE TYPE MENU

STROKE WIDTH MENU

6] At the top of the panel, make sure that the Basic and Black stroke options are selected. Change the width to 4 points either by entering 4 in the width field or selecting 4 from the adjacent menu.

The selected line should now appear thicker, representing the increased stroke width.

7] Select the body with the Pointer tool. Hold down the Shift key and click the head, shoulder, and hip elements. In the Stroke Inspector, change the stroke from Basic to None in the Stroke Type menu. Then press the Tab key to deselect all elements.

You have now removed the outlines from the robot elements.

You can add to a selection by holding down the Shift key and clicking additional objects. By selecting four elements together, you were able to change the stroke for all four at once.

You can apply a thick or thin stroke to any selected graphic, or remove the stroke instead.

You will now change the fill inside two of the elements from a solid shade, called a **basic** fill, to one that changes from one shade to another, called a **gradient** fill.

8] Select the body with the Pointer tool. Click the Fill tab in the Inspector panel group to display the Fill Inspector. Alternatively, you can choose Window › Inspectors › Fill or Modify › Fill.

The Fill Inspector appears. With this Inspector, you can control the characteristics of the fill inside a closed shape.

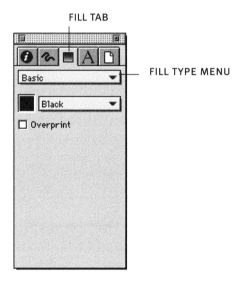

FILL TAB

FILL TYPE MENU

9] In the Fill Inspector, select Gradient from the Fill Type menu. Drag the 40 percent tint from the Color Mixer Tints panel and drop it on the white color swatch at the bottom of the Fill Inspector. Change the direction of the gradient by dragging the direction control in the Inspector.

The rectangle is now filled with a linear gradient fill that changes from a solid black to a 40 percent tint of black.

A linear gradient changes color in a straight line across a graphic, in the direction specified with the direction control.

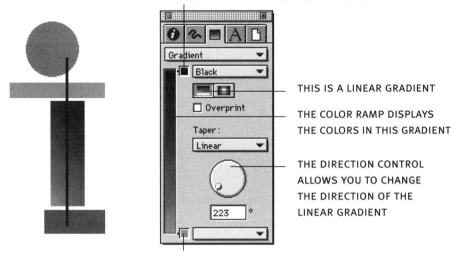

THE GRADIENT STARTS WITH THIS COLOR

THIS IS A LINEAR GRADIENT

THE COLOR RAMP DISPLAYS
THE COLORS IN THIS GRADIENT

THE DIRECTION CONTROL
ALLOWS YOU TO CHANGE
THE DIRECTION OF THE
LINEAR GRADIENT

THE GRADIENT ENDS WITH THIS COLOR

10] Select the robot's head (the circle) and change the fill to Gradient in the Fill Inspector. Then click the Radial button in the Fill Inspector. Move the center of the radial fill up and to the right by dragging the center point in the Fill Inspector.

A radial fill changes color from a center point outward in all directions; a linear fill changes color in a straight line across an element. When you click the Radial button, the options in the Fill Inspector change to enable you to reposition the center point of the radial fill.

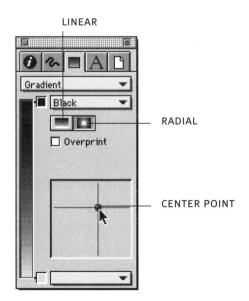

LINEAR

RADIAL

CENTER POINT

Your robot should now look similar to the following illustration.

tip *A radial fill in a circle like this can create the illusion that this is a three-dimensional sphere, instead of a flat circle.*

11] Save the document with File › Save.

tip *Remember to save frequently as you work.*

ARRANGING, ALIGNING, AND GROUPING ELEMENTS

FreeHand arranges elements on the page in the order that they are created, which is why the spine of the robot is in front of the other body parts. You will rearrange the elements to make the robot look better.

1] Select the spine with the Pointer tool and choose Modify › Arrange › Send to Back.
The spine is now behind all of the other elements. The Arrange submenu offers four commands you can use in different situations. Use Send to Back or Bring to Front to move an object behind or in front of all of the other elements. Move Forward and Move Backward move a selected object forward or backward one element at a time.

Next get all the elements in your robot into proper alignment so the body looks symmetrical.

2] Select all of the elements with the Edit › Select All command (Windows Ctrl+A, Macintosh Command+A). Choose Window › Panels › Align or Modify › Align.
The Align panel appears. This panel provides several choices for both horizontal and vertical alignment.

tip   *Alternatively, click the Align button on the main toolbar.*

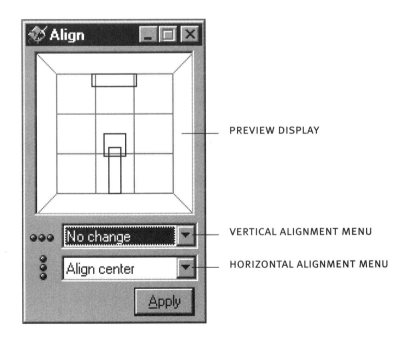

PREVIEW DISPLAY

VERTICAL ALIGNMENT MENU

HORIZONTAL ALIGNMENT MENU

3] In the Vertical Alignment menu, select No Change. In the Horizontal Alignment menu, select Align Center.

The preview display in the Align panel should show the desired results: elements centered left and right and not aligned up or down.

4] Click Apply at the bottom of the Align panel to align your elements.

All five elements are now aligned accurately. To keep them in this arrangement and prevent accidental changes, you can group the elements.

5] With all five elements still selected, choose Modify › Group (Windows Ctrl+G, Macintosh Command+G).

This ties all the selected elements together into one group. One set of selection boxes now appears around the group, instead of individual selection boxes around each element. Now you can move, resize, and modify all of these elements as one.

6] Save your work.

ADDING OTHER ELEMENTS

Next you will add arms and legs to complete the robot. The two arms are identical, so you can create one and make a copy for the second. The legs are identical also, but the feet point in opposite directions. For this effect, you will **reflect** a copy to mirror the two legs.

First create an arm. Then you will perform a simple copy and paste to create the second arm.

1] Choose the Ellipse tool and position the cursor about halfway up the left edge of the shoulder. Hold the Alt (Windows) or Option (Macintosh) key and the Shift key and draw a circle just a bit larger than the height of the shoulder box. Fill the circle with 50 percent black using the Tint subpanel in the Color Mixer, and set the stroke to None in the Stroke Inspector.

Holding Shift creates a perfect circle. Holding Alt or Option draws an object from the center. Notice that the cursor changes from the standard crosshair to a crosshair in a circle to indicate that you are drawing the circle from the center. These keys work the same way for the Rectangle tool.

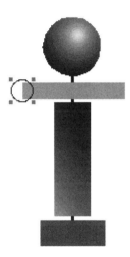

tip *Remember that you can choose Undo if you do not like your first attempt. Also, once the ellipse is on the page, you can use the Pointer tool with the Shift and Alt or Option key to resize the circle from the center.*

2] Draw a vertical line from the middle of the circle downward to form the arm. Using the Stroke Inspector, change the width of this line to 8 points.

For this robot, the arm should not reach as low as the hips.

3] Bring the circle to the front by selecting the circle and choosing Modify › Arrange › Bring to Front (Windows Ctrl+F, Macintosh Command+F).

The arm is almost ready to be duplicated, but it would be easier to work with if the two elements were grouped together.

4] Select the circle and the line at the same time by clicking either element with the Pointer tool. Then hold down the Shift key and click the other element.

Holding down Shift and clicking additional elements allows you to select multiple objects. Shift-clicking a selected item deselects it, while leaving all other selected elements selected.

5] Group the selected elements by using the Modify › Group command.

Now you can work with the arm as if it were a single element.

6] With the arm still selected, choose Edit › Copy.

This puts an electronic copy of the selected artwork onto the clipboard.

7] Choose Edit › Paste to paste a second copy of the arm on the page.

FreeHand will paste the duplicate arm on the page in the center of your screen.

You now need to move the duplicate arm into position.

8] Use the pointer to move the second arm into position on the other shoulder. Then select both arm groups and use the Align panel to align both arms vertically.

Use Edit > Undo if something goes wrong.

9] Repeat steps 1 through 5 to create one leg by drawing a circle and a line. Fill the circle with any fill and set the stroke of the line to 8 points.

You will add a foot in the next task before duplicating this leg.

10] Save your work.

CUSTOMIZING TOOL SETTINGS

The feet in the robot are rounded rectangles, which you can draw after making an adjustment to the way the Rectangle tool works. Notice that the Rectangle tool in the toolbox is one of several tools that has a small mark in the upper-right corner. This mark indicates that preferences can be set for this tool. Double-clicking these tools displays a dialog box where you can change the settings.

RECTANGLE TOOL

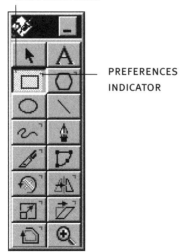

PREFERENCES
INDICATOR

1] Double-click the Rectangle tool in the toolbox.

A dialog box appears where you can specify a radius for rounded corners. The default radius of zero means that the tool will draw rectangles with sharp, right-angle corners and no rounding.

2] Set the radius to 9 points by dragging the slider or entering a value in the radius field. Then click OK.

The radius value determines how rounded the corners of your rectangle will be. A radius value of zero creates rectangles with angled corners; increasing the value makes larger curves at each corner of the rectangle. If you specify a value larger than half the length of any sides of your rectangle, those entire sides will be curved.

3] Draw a small rounded rectangle at the bottom of the robot's leg and fill it with any tint of black.

Notice the rounded corners on the rectangle. Reposition the foot as needed with the Pointer tool.

4] Complete the leg by selecting all three pieces and grouping them together with Modify › Group.

Remember that you can select several elements at the same time by holding down the Shift key.

5] Save your work.

The robot is nearly complete.

CLONING, REFLECTING, AND ROTATING ELEMENTS

Duplicating the leg is a bit more challenging than duplicating the arm because the copy must face the opposite direction.

Your first step will be to **clone** the leg. Cloning creates a duplicate of the selected object directly in front of the original object. (It's like Copy and Paste, but it always positions the new copy directly in front of the original selection.) This is important since you will then reflect the *clone* to the opposite side of the body, leaving the original leg in its current position.

1] Select the grouped leg and choose Edit › Clone to make a duplicate that is positioned precisely in front of the original leg.

Since the duplicate is sitting directly in front of the original, it may appear that nothing has happened. The clone is now selected, instead of the original object.

You will see in the next steps how cloning an object can be a useful technique when you want to keep the new element aligned with the original.

2] With the clone still selected, choose the Reflect tool from the toolbox.

You will use the Reflect tool to horizontally flip the selection, so that the feet on both legs point away from the center of the body.

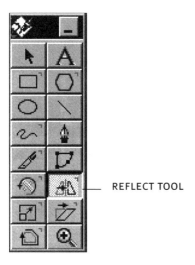

— REFLECT TOOL

3] Position the cursor on the spine of the robot. Hold down the Shift key while pressing the mouse button and move the mouse down slightly, until the reflection axis that appears is perfectly vertical. Then release the mouse.

The clone is positioned on the other side of the body, so your robot now has two legs.

The reflection axis works as a mirror, reflecting a selected item an equal distance on the opposite side of the axis. Holding Shift limits the reflection axis to 45-degree angles. In this case, you held Shift and moved the mouse downward to display the reflection axis as a vertical line. This is why the clone of the leg was reflected straight across the body to the correct position at the opposite end of the hips.

tip *The robot's spine is in the exact center of the figure. Positioning the cursor here to perform the reflection ensures that the new leg is the same distance from the spine as the old leg.*

4] Reposition the new leg with the Pointer tool, if necessary.

The artwork should be in the correct position already, if you followed the instructions in the previous steps accurately. Make any adjustments now as needed.

The robot is so happy to have all of its parts—now help it kick up its heels. You will use the Rotate tool to swing the leg up

5] Select one of the legs. Choose the Rotate tool in the toolbox and position the cursor in the center of the circle at the top of the leg. Don't press the mouse button yet!

The position of the cursor when you begin rotating sets the center of rotation. The selection will rotate around that spot. Be careful when rotating to hold down the mouse button the entire time, until the artwork appears to be in the desired position.

6] Begin rotating the leg by holding down the mouse button and sliding the mouse several inches to the right along the horizontal line that appears while the mouse button is held down. Then move the mouse slowly upward to swing the foot out to the right. When the leg is in the desired position, release the mouse.

This line is like a lever. Once you have moved the mouse away from the center of rotation, you can swing the lever up, down, or around to rotate the selection. The farther out along the lever you move, the more precise control you will have over the rotation. If you do not like your first attempt, remember the Undo feature.

You can hold the Shift key to constrain the rotation to 45-degree angles. When you are satisfied with the position of the robot's leg, your artwork is complete.

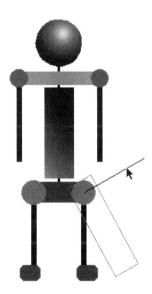

7] Save your document.

Congratulations. You have just created your first piece of original art with FreeHand.

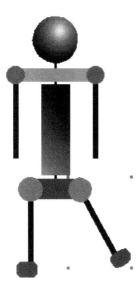

ON YOUR OWN

There will be times when you just cannot remember a specific technique and need a quick and easy resource for more information. In addition to the manuals that come with the application, FreeHand offers an online help system for quick reference while you're working. For assistance in FreeHand, click the Help button on the main toolbar. Experiment with the help system by looking up some topics in the help index or searching for help on a particular command or feature.

HELP

WHAT YOU HAVE LEARNED

In this lesson you have:

Opened FreeHand and created a new document [*page* **8**]

Been introduced to FreeHand's tools, toolbars, and panels [*page* **9**]

Customized application and tool preferences [*page* **11**]

Worked with panels and organized the workspace [*page* **13**]

Created basic shapes with the Rectangle, Ellipse, and Line tools [*page* **22**]

Applied basic and graduated fills and adjusted stroke width [*page* **26**]

Aligned and grouped elements together [*page* **33**]

Duplicated elements with the Copy and Paste commands and the Clone command [*page* **37**]

Transformed elements using the Reflect and Rotate tools [*page* **41**]

and graphics

combining text

LESSON 2

The basic drawing tools you used in the last lesson are good for more than drawing playful robots. In this lesson, you will use the same tools, along with FreeHand's text tool, to create a graphic identity for a corporate letterhead. You will use the same basic shape tools you worked with in Lesson 1: the Rectangle, Ellipse, and Line tools. Here you will combine the elements in new ways, apply color for fills and strokes, and add text to create the completed design.

This corporate letterhead was created from scratch using FreeHand's drawing and text tools.

Designed by Julia Sifers of Glasgow & Associates.

If you would like to review the final result of this lesson, open World.fh7 in the Complete folder within the Lesson02 folder.

WHAT YOU WILL LEARN

In this lesson you will:

Set a custom page size

Specify measurement units

Create and combine more basic shapes

Change the appearance of objects

Practice rotating elements

Design the layout for printing with two ink colors

Practice aligning and grouping elements

Enter and format text

Import another FreeHand graphic

APPROXIMATE TIME

It usually takes about 1 hour and 30 minutes to complete this lesson.

LESSON FILES

Media Files:

Lesson02\Media\Plane.fh7

Starting Files:

None

Completed Project:

Lesson02\Complete\World.fh7

CREATING A NEW DOCUMENT WITH A CUSTOM PAGE SIZE

In this lesson, you will design the letterhead for New World Shipping. You will create this letterhead for an Executive-size page, which measures 7.25 by 10.5 inches. Your first task is to create a page with these dimensions.

1] Choose File › New to create a new document (Windows Ctrl+N, Macintosh Command+N).

A new document window will appear containing one page on the pasteboard.

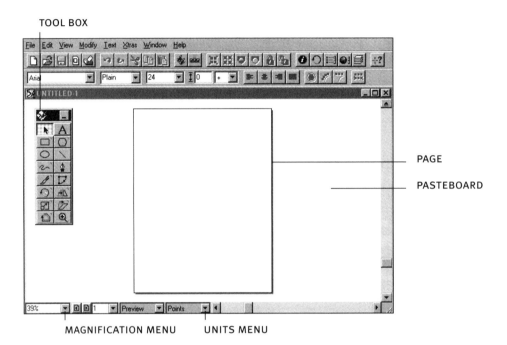

2] Change the unit of measure for this document to Inches using the Units menu at the bottom of the document window.

This menu defines the unit of measurement used throughout the document (with the exception of type size, which is always measured in points). The only visible indication that the units have changed is that the Units menu now displays Inches now instead of Points.

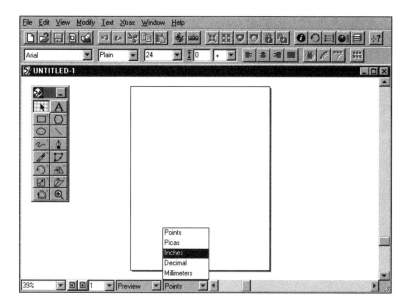

3] Choose Window › Inspectors › Document to display the Document Inspector.

The document inspector contains controls that enable you to change the size, orientation, and number of pages within your document.

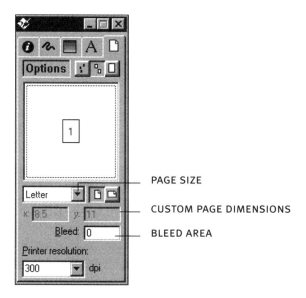

PAGE SIZE

CUSTOM PAGE DIMENSIONS

BLEED AREA

4] Use the Page Size menu in the Document Inspector to change from Letter to Custom.

You will now be able to edit the page dimensions to change the page size to match the size of an Executive page.

You will also need to specify the **bleed** area, the amount of space that elements will print beyond the edges of the layout. On a printing press, layouts that require color extending to the edge of the page must be printed on larger sheets of paper than the document requires, and the color must extend beyond the boundaries of the layout. In this way, when the paper sheets are cut to the correct page size, the color will extend beyond the cut even if the paper shifts a bit on press so the ink is not placed exactly in the same position on each sheet. There will be no strips of paper color showing at the edge of the page where the ink did not reach.

You can set the size of the bleed area in the Document Inspector, which defines the distance around the page that FreeHand will print. The default value is zero, which means nothing beyond the edge of the page will print. Your letterhead includes elements that extend to the edge of the layout, so you need specify a bleed area.

5] Select the value in the *x* field and enter a new width of 7.25. Press the Tab key to highlight the *y* field and enter a height of 10.5. Press the Tab key again to highlight the Bleed field and enter a value of .125 inches. Press Enter on the keyboard to apply these changes.

This will change the size of the page to the size of an Executive page and give the document a one-eighth inch bleed area all around. (One-eighth inch is the standard bleed size used by most printers.) The new page size is now displayed in the document window. The additional dotted line surrounding the page indicates the bleed area.

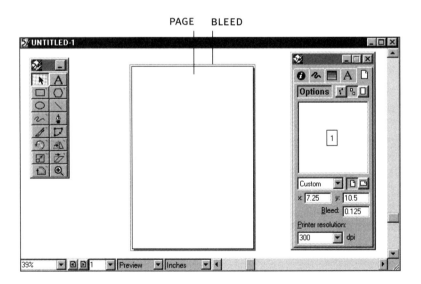

6] Close the Document Inspector. Save your document as *MyWorld* in your MyWork folder on the hard drive.

The page is now ready for you to begin creating the artwork.

tip *Remember to save frequently as you work!*

CREATING AND POSITIONING A RECTANGLE

In the previous lesson, you adjusted the size and position of selected elements directly using the Pointer tool. FreeHand also offers you precise control over the size and position of elements with the Object Inspector. In this task, you will create a rectangle running along the left edge of the page from top to bottom. This will eventually contain the yellow gradient fill that bleeds off the left of the page.

You will start by creating a rectangle somewhere on the page and then adjust the size and position numerically.

1] Select the Rectangle tool and draw a small rectangle of any size anywhere on the page.

When you are finished with the Rectangle tool, the rectangle you drew will be selected. With the rectangle selected, you can enter specific width, height, and position values using the Object Inspector.

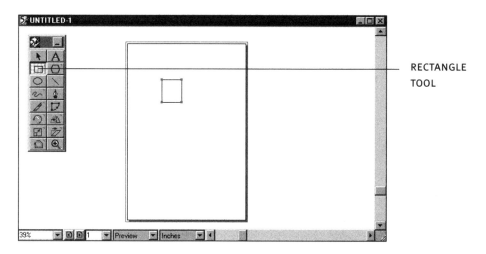

RECTANGLE TOOL

tip *As you work, you may need to open and close panels, depending upon the size of your monitor. If the following instructions call for you to open a panel you already have displayed on your screen, you will not need to issue the command to open it again. You may also wish to use the buttons on the main toolbar to open and close panels instead of choosing commands from the Window menu.*

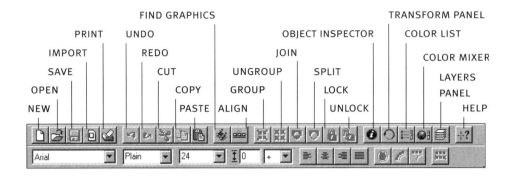

FIND GRAPHICS

PRINT UNDO   OBJECT INSPECTOR TRANSFORM PANEL

IMPORT REDO   JOIN   COLOR LIST

SAVE CUT UNGROUP SPLIT   COLOR MIXER

OPEN   COPY GROUP LOCK   LAYERS

NEW PASTE ALIGN   UNLOCK PANEL

HELP

2] Choose Window › Inspectors › Object to display the Object Inspector.

The Object Inspector indicates that you have a rectangle selected and displays the rectangle's position on the page, width and height, and corner radius. When you select other types of elements, you will see different information presented in the Object Inspector.

The measurements you see in the Object Inspector are in inches since you changed the unit of measure for this document to inches.

These values will change as you move or resize the rectangle.

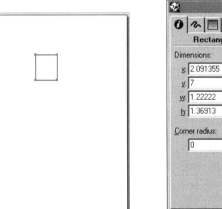

tip *An element must be selected for the Object Inspector to display its information. If nothing is selected, the Object Inspector will not display any values. To select an object, point to a solid part of that object with the Pointer tool and click. For example, this rectangle has a black stroke but no fill. To select this element, you need to click on the black stroke.*

3] Select the Pointer tool from the toolbox. Position the tip of your cursor along a side of the rectangle, hold down the mouse button, and drag the shape to the bottom center of the page.

Notice that the values for *x* and *y* have changed. These indicate the distance from the zero point (which defaults to the lower-left corner of the page) to the lower-left corner of the rectangle. The x value is the distance from the zero point to the left edge of the rectangle, and the y value is the distance from the zero point to the bottom of the rectangle.

Notice that the *w* and *h* values did not change; you changed only the position of the rectangle, not its size.

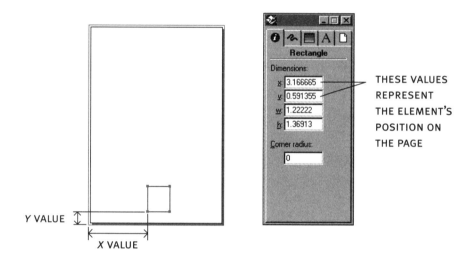

THESE VALUES
REPRESENT
THE ELEMENT'S
POSITION ON
THE PAGE

Y VALUE

X VALUE

4] Watch the *x* and *y* values in the Object Inspector as you choose Edit › Undo to return the rectangle to its previous position.

You can use the Undo and Redo commands when you make a mistake or simply to compare before and after views.

5] Position the Pointer tool on the top-right corner selection box and drag the mouse upward and to the right about an inch to make the rectangle larger.

The width (*w*) and height (*h*) values increase as you make the rectangle larger. The position values did not change since you did not change the position of the bottom left corner of the rectangle (the point on the rectangle from which FreeHand measures).

The corner radius is the same value that you used to create a rectangle with rounded corners for the foot of the robot in the previous lesson. You can leave this at zero for this layout for sharp corners on your rectangle, not rounded.

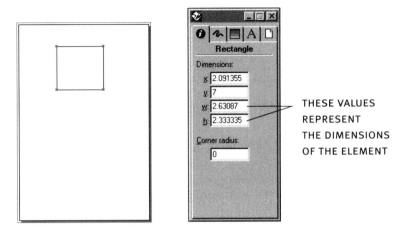

THESE VALUES
REPRESENT
THE DIMENSIONS
OF THE ELEMENT

Now you are ready to move this rectangle to the desired position in the letterhead layout. This box will be filled with the yellow gradient and should extend (bleed) off of the left side, top, and bottom of the page. You will start by precisely positioning the rectangle with the Object Inspector.

6] Select the value for *x* in the Object Inspector. Change this value by typing a negative value, –.125 , and pressing Enter.

Enter a negative value by typing a minus sign before the number. This negative value moves the box beyond the left edge of the page. It now extends off the page and aligns with the bleed area you defined for this document.

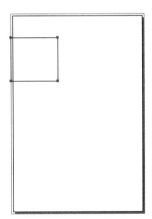

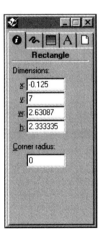

7] Select the *y* value and enter *–.125*. Press the tab key to select the width and enter *1.625*. Press tab again to select the height and enter *10.75*. Press Enter to apply these values.

The rectangle now extends off the top and bottom edges of the page, as well as off the left edge. The rectangle has a width of 1.5 inches plus the left bleed of 0.125 inches and a height of 10.5 inches plus the top bleed of 0.125 inches and the bottom bleed of 0.125 inches.

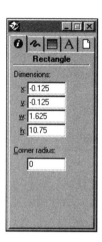

8] Save your work.

CREATING AND ALIGNING ELLIPSES

Although it looks complex, the globe on the letterhead will not be difficult to create. You will start by creating two ellipses and aligning them so that one is centered over the other. To ensure consistent results, you will precisely size each of the ellipses using the Object Inspector.

1] Select the Ellipse tool in the toolbox. Position the cursor anywhere on the page, hold down the mouse button, and drag in a diagonal direction to draw any size ellipse. Use the Object Inspector to change this ellipse into a perfect circle 6 inches across by changing the width value to 6 and the height value to 6. Then press Enter.

Your first ellipse is a perfect circle 6 inches in diameter.

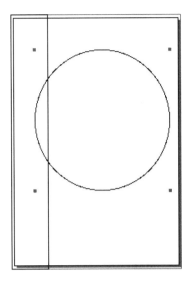
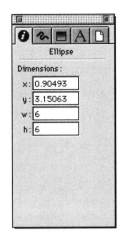

2] Draw a second ellipse with the Ellipse tool anywhere on the page. In the Object Inspector, change the width value to 0.5 and the height value to 6.

These two ellipses are the elements you need to create the globe graphic.

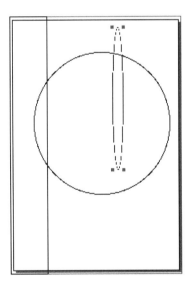
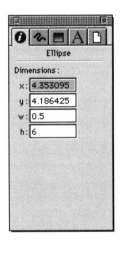

Next you will select both ellipses at once in order to use the Align panel to center one over the other.

3] Change to the Pointer tool by clicking that tool in the toolbox. The narrow ellipse may already be selected. If not, click once on its outline to select it. Hold down the Shift key and click once on the outline of the larger ellipse to add that element to the selection.

Both of the ellipses are selected at the same time. The Shift key enables you to add elements to a selection without deselecting a previous selection.

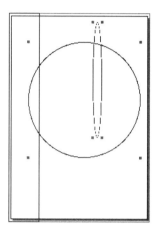

4] Choose Modify › Align to display the Align panel. Click the center of the preview grid to set both the vertical and horizontal alignment to Align center. Click Align or press Enter.

The ellipses are now centered on one another.

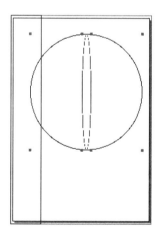
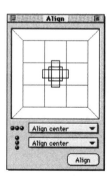

5] Save your work.

Next you will have FreeHand blend these two shapes together.

COMBINING PATHS WITH THE BLEND COMMAND

FreeHand graphics are made up of **paths**. A path is simply a line containing at least two **points**. Paths can be curved or straight, open or closed. (You can fill closed paths; open paths cannot be filled.) An element created with a basic shape tool (a rectangle or ellipse) is actually a grouped path. In this task, you will learn how to create a **blend** between individual paths that creates intermediate steps between the original paths. You will use that feature to automatically create the new paths that will form the latitude and longitude lines of the globe.

The Blend feature in FreeHand combines paths together by creating intermediate shapes—paths that fit between the original paths to create a transition with respect to shape, stroke, and fill. You will now create a blend between the small ellipse and large ellipse.

1] Both ellipses should still be selected. (If they are not selected, click one with the Pointer tool and then hold down the Shift key and click the other one.) Choose Modify › Ungroup to see the points and paths that make up these elements.

You can now see that each of these elements is made up of four points. (The top and bottom points of each path are directly on top of one another.) To create a blend between the two paths, you first will select the top point on each path.

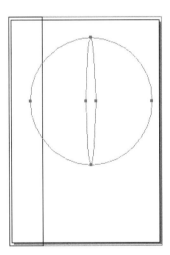

2] Using the Pointer tool, position the cursor above and to the left of the point visible at the top of the paths. (Make sure that you are not pointing to any other object, such as the rectangle!) Hold down the mouse button and drag downward and to the right until the dotted rectangle surrounds that top point. Then release the mouse button.

The dotted rectangle is called the selection marquee. It should surround only the topmost point on each path.

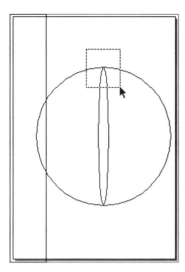

When you release the mouse button, the top point appears as an outlined box, indicating that the point is selected. That point, and the points to its right and left along the path, have sprouted handles. You will learn what those are for in the next lesson.

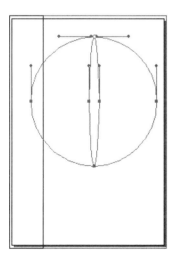

3] Choose Modify › Combine › Blend.

FreeHand creates intermediate paths between the two originals. However, there are many more paths than you want for this graphic.

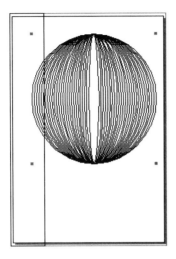

4] Click the Object Inspector button in the main toolbar or choose Window › Inspectors › Object to display the Object Inspector. Change the number of steps in this blend to 5 and press Enter to apply the change.

Blends create a transition between two or more paths with respect to shape, stroke, and fill. The number of steps determines the number of intermediate paths. All of the paths in the blend are also automatically grouped together.

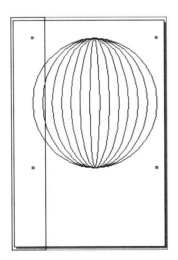

5] Save your work.

PRECISELY ROTATING A COPY

You have created the longitude lines to the globe. Now you need to add the latitude lines. To add these lines and complete the globe, you will make a duplicate of the blend directly on top of the original and precisely rotate it 90 degrees around its center to position it at a right angle to the original.

1] Select the blend and then choose Edit > Clone.

A copy of the object, now selected, is precisely placed on top of the original.

2] Double-click the Rotation tool in the toolbox to display the Transform panel, which contains the rotation controls.

You will use the Transform panel to precisely rotate the clone. (You can also select the Transform panel by choosing Window > Panels > Transform.)

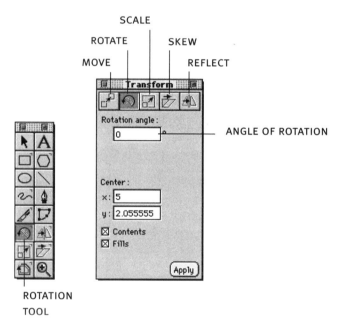

3] Enter *90* as the Rotation Angle and click Apply or press Enter.

By default, the Transform panel rotates the selected element around its center, so this clone is rotated into a horizontal position. (In Lesson 4 you will define a different center of rotation using the Transform panel.) Positive values rotate the selection counterclockwise; negative values rotate the selection clockwise.

Now you need to group the two blends together.

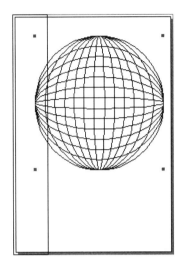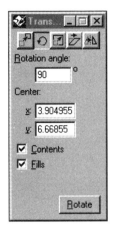

4] Close the Transform panel. Then choose Edit > Select > All.

This selects everything on the page, including the rectangle, which you do not want to group with the globe.

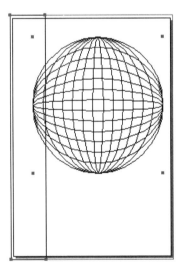

5] Hold down the Shift key and click the edge of the rectangle to deselect that element.

Earlier you held down the Shift key to add elements to a selection. Holding down Shift also deselects selected elements without deselecting any other elements.

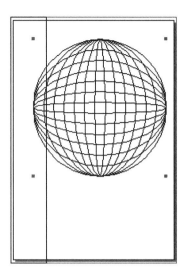

6] Choose Modify › Group to tie the globe components together.

The globe graphic is complete.

7] Use the Pointer tool to move the globe to visually center it on the page.

Position your globe similarly to the one shown here.

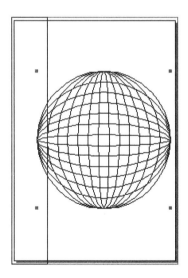

8] Save your work.

IMPORTING AND CREATING COLORS AND TINTS

You now will add two colors and tints of those colors that will be used in your layout to the Color List.

1] Choose Window › Panels › Color List (or click the Color List button on the main toolbar) to display the Color List.

This panel displays the named colors currently available for this document. You need to add two colors to this list.

For projects that will be printed on a printing press, there are several industry-standard color selection systems for which printed swatch books of actual ink colors are available to help you choose colors accurately.

tip *The colors you see on your computer monitor may not accurately represent the actual printing colors. It is a good idea to talk to a printer or look at a swatch book before choosing colors for print projects.*

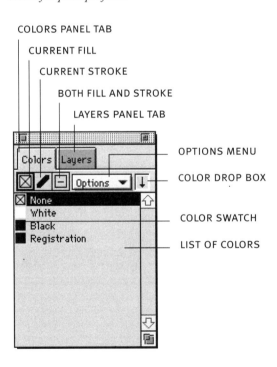

2] Select PANTONE® Coated from the Options menu at the top of the Color List.

This opens a color library containing the colors in the PANTONE Coated color-matching system. These colors are each identified by a unique number, which corresponds with those in the PANTONE Coated printed swatch book, and a color of PANTONE ink.

FreeHand allows you to choose colors from PANTONE Coated and PANTONE Uncoated color libraries from the Color List Options menu. The Uncoated color library shows the colors printed on standard (uncoated) paper. The Coated color library shows the same colors printed on coated paper, which has a thin coating of clay that has been polished to create a very smooth surface. Colors generally appear more brilliant on coated paper because the ink is not absorbed by the paper the way it is by uncoated paper. If you don't know what kind of paper your artwork will be printed on, your printer can advise you. For this lesson, it will not make any difference which of these two systems you choose.

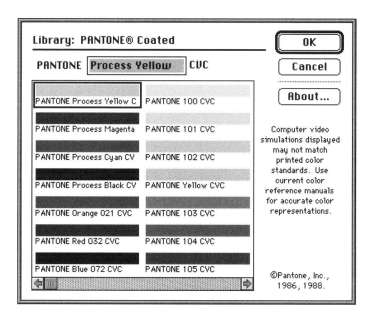

3] Type *135* to select PANTONE 135 and click OK.

The golden color, PANTONE 135 CVC, has been added to the color list.

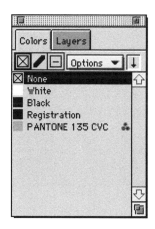

4] Select PANTONE Coated from the Options menu again and add PANTONE 285 to the color list.

The blue color, PANTONE 285 CVC, has been added to the color list. You now have two PANTONE colors in the list.

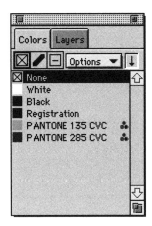

5] Display the Color Mixer by choosing Window › Panels › Color Mixer or by clicking the Color Mixer button on the main toolbar.

In addition to controls for creating new colors, the Color Mixer also provides controls for creating tints of existing colors. You will use this panel to create tints of each of the PANTONE colors.

A tint is a lighter shade of a color expressed as a percentage of that color.

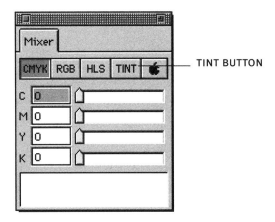

TINT BUTTON

6] Click the Tint button in the Color Mixer to display the Tint controls.

The panel changes to display a range of tints for the base color in 10 percent increments as well as a custom adjustment for creating tints at other values.

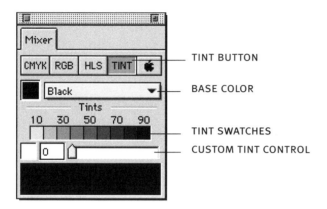

TINT BUTTON

BASE COLOR

TINT SWATCHES

CUSTOM TINT CONTROL

7] Drag the color swatch next to PANTONE 135 in the Color List and drop it on the base color swatch at the top of the Color Mixer tint panel.

Tints for that color now appear in the panel.

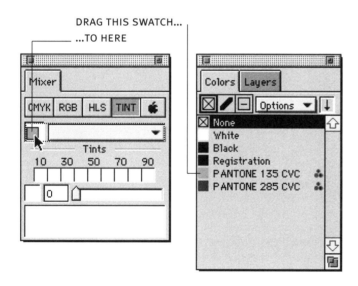

DRAG THIS SWATCH...

...TO HERE

8] Drag the 40 percent tint swatch from the Color Mixer and drop it on an open spot in the Color List.

Don't drop it on another color swatch or you will change that color to this tint.

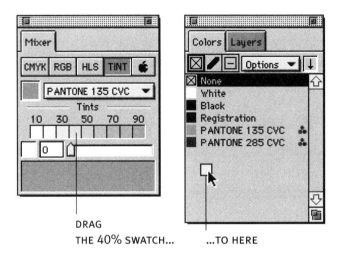

DRAG
THE 40% SWATCH...   ...TO HERE

The tint will be added to the Color List with the name *40% PANTONE 135*.

9] Use the Base color menu at the top of the tint controls to select PANTONE 285. Drag the Custom tint control slider to the right until the value 15 appears in the field just to the left of the slider. Drag the swatch to the left of that field and drop it into the Color List.

The Color List will now have the colors and tints needed for this lesson.

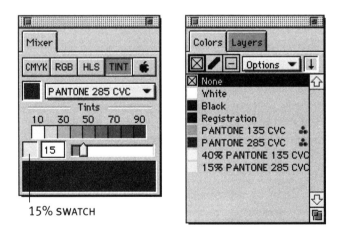

15% SWATCH

10] Close the Color Mixer. Save your work.

You just added the two colors and tints that will be used for the elements of this document.

APPLYING FILLS AND STROKES

Now that the colors you need are in the Color List, you will use the Fill and Stroke Inspectors to apply those colors to the elements on your page.

1] Select the rectangle on the page with the Pointer tool. Display the Fill Inspector by choosing Window › Inspectors › Fill. Using the Fill type menu at the top of the Inspector, choose Gradient as the type of fill for this element.

The rectangle is now filled with a gradient from black to white.

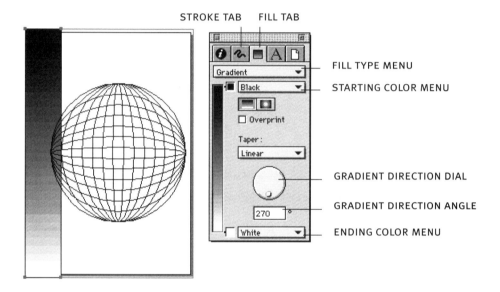

STROKE TAB   FILL TAB

FILL TYPE MENU

STARTING COLOR MENU

GRADIENT DIRECTION DIAL

GRADIENT DIRECTION ANGLE

ENDING COLOR MENU

2] Drag the swatch for 40% PANTONE 135 from the Color List and drop it on the black swatch at the top of the Fill Inspector. Change the gradient direction angle to 0 degrees and press Enter to complete the fill.

The bottom color in the Fill Inspector is White. The direction of the gradient is 0 degrees, which results in a gradient fill that goes from 40% PANTONE 135 on the left to White on the right.

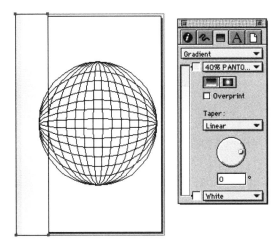

The rectangle would look better if there were no line around it.

3] Click the Stroke tab at the top of the Inspector panel group to display the Stroke Inspector. Change the option for the Stroke type menu to None.

The stroke is removed, and the rectangle is finished.

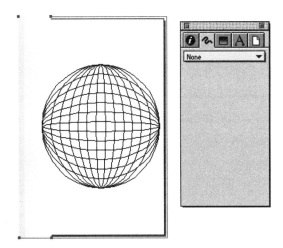

Now change the color and stroke of the globe.

4] Select the grouped globe by clicking it with the Pointer tool. Change the option for the Stroke type menu to Basic. Use the Stroke color menu to select 15% PANTONE 285. Then change the stroke width by selecting 2 pt from the Width menu.

The globe now has a 2-point stroke of 15% PANTONE 285. Because the units for this document are set to inches, the stroke width of 2 points is shown as 0.02778 inches in the Stroke Inspector.

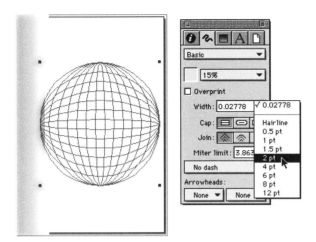

5] Close the Color List and Stroke Inspector for now. Save your work.

CLONING, SCALING, AND POSITIONING

In this task, you will create a second globe on the page that is 40 percent of the original globe's size. Creating this smaller version is easy with the Transform panel. You will then position this smaller globe in the upper-left corner of the layout.

1] Select the globe and choose Edit > Clone.

This creates a duplicate globe directly on top of the original. The duplicate remains selected.

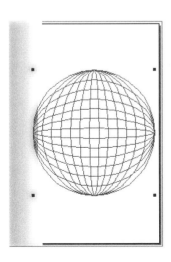

2] Double-click the Scale tool in the toolbox to display the Transform panel.

The Transform panel is displayed with the scale controls.

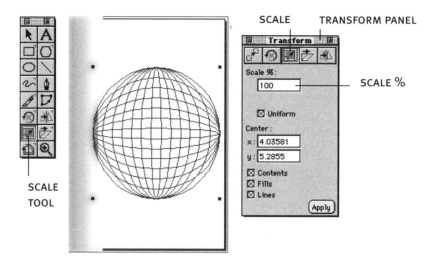

SCALE TRANSFORM PANEL

SCALE %

SCALE TOOL

3] Enter *40* in the Scale % field and click Apply or press Enter.

The copy of the globe is reduced to 40 percent of its original size.

If the Uniform scale box is checked, when you scale an object, it keeps its proportions. If you turn uniform scaling off, you can scale the *x* and *y* values at different percentages, distorting the proportions as you scale the object. In this task, you want uniform scaling turned on.

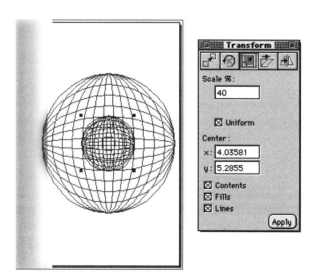

4] Close the Transform panel. Using the Pointer tool, move the smaller globe so that it extends off the top and left edges of the page.

Position the artwork similarly to the example shown here. This artwork extends beyond the bleed area, but FreeHand will print only the portion that appears within the bleed area defined by the dotted line that surrounds the page.

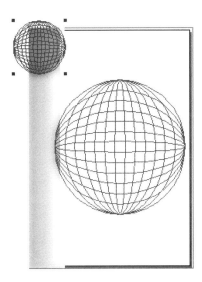

5] Save your work.

Now you are ready to add the company name and address.

ADDING TEXT TO THE LAYOUT

FreeHand has a full array of features for entering, editing, and formatting text. In the next several tasks, you will use these features to position text in your layout and set the font and fill. First, of course, you need to enter the text.

1] Select the Text tool from the toolbox and click once at the top of the page to begin a new text block.

A blinking insertion point will appear on your page where text typed on the keyboard will appear. The arrows that appear above the blinking cursor are used to set custom tabs for the type. These tabs provide formatting controls that are not necessary for this lesson.

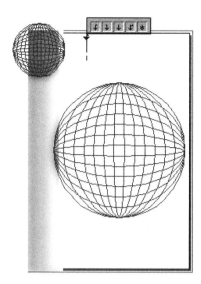

2] Press in the Caps Lock key on your keyboard and enter the company name, *NEW WORLD SHIPPING*.

The text block automatically adjusts to the amount of text you enter. Once you start typing text into the text block, the Text Ruler will also appear. This ruler is needed to set custom tabs.

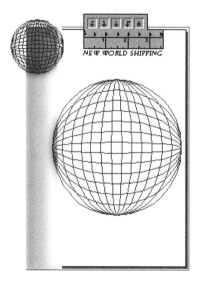

3] Select the Pointer tool and click once on the words you just typed to select the entire block of text.

When the text block is selected with the Pointer tool, you can specify formatting that will apply to all of the text.

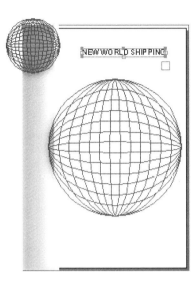

4] Choose View › Magnification › 100% to see the selected text at actual size.

When you change your view using the magnification commands, FreeHand automatically centers the view on an element (or elements) you have selected.

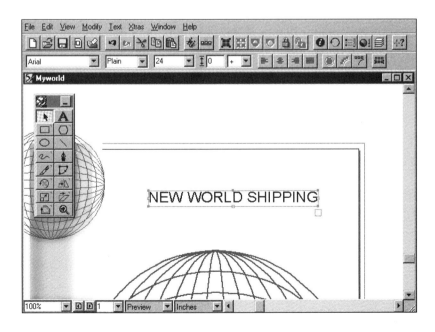

5] Using the controls on the Text toolbar near the top of your screen, change the font to URWGaramondTMed, the style to Italic, and the size to 24 points.

The URWGaramondTMed font is on the FreeHand Graphics Studio software CD-ROM. If you don't have it, you can just use a font you already have installed.

The controls for changing the font, size, and style of the text can also be found in the Text menu and in the Text Inspector.

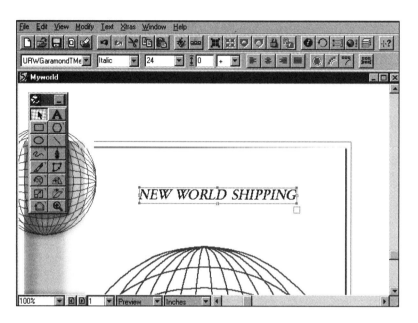

You've entered the basic text. Next you will give it some flair.

6] Save your work.

APPLYING A COLOR FILL TO TEXT

You will now change the black fill of this text to something more subtle, add more text, and position the elements on the layout.

1] Choose Window > Panels > Color List to display the Color List. Change the fill color of the text by dragging the color swatch next to PANTONE 135 in the Color List and drop it directly on the text.

All of the characters should now be filled with yellow. (By default, text has a stroke of None.) When you change the color of text using the drag and drop method, all of the text in the text block will automatically change regardless of what is currently selected or what tool you are using. You will make some additional changes to just a few of these characters next.

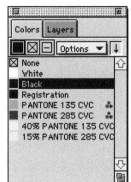

tip   *If the background of the text block changes to the color instead of the characters, you did not drop the swatch directly on a character, but instead dropped it on the text block background. This is easy to correct: Simply choose Edit > Undo to return to the previous state and then drag the swatch onto the text again. Be careful to release the swatch when the tip of the arrow is touching a character of text.*

2] Select the Text tool and click inside the text block to open the block for editing. Highlight the *N* in *NEW* by dragging over it with the Text tool. Change the font to VladimirScrD, the style to Plain, and the size to 48 points using the text toolbar.

This changes only the selected character to the new character formatting.

The VladimirScrD font is on the FreeHand Graphics Studio software CD-ROM. If you don't have it, you can just use a font you already have installed.

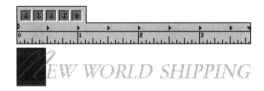

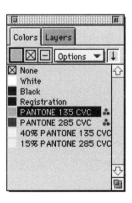

3] Change the fill color of the selected *N* to PANTONE 285 by dragging the color swatch for that color from the Color List and dropping it onto the selected character.

Dropping color on a text selection changes the color of the selected text only.

4] Repeat steps 2 and 3 for the *W* in *WORLD* and the *S* in *SHIPPING*. Then click on the text block with the Pointer tool and close the Color List.

Your artwork should appear similar to the artwork shown here. Now you are ready to move the text block into position.

5] Display the page rulers by choosing View › Page Rulers (Windows Ctrl+Atl+M, Macintosh Command+Option+M). Choose View › Fit To Page to see the entire page in the document window (Windows Ctrl+Shift+W, Macintosh Command+Shift+W).

The rulers will help you position the elements on the page.

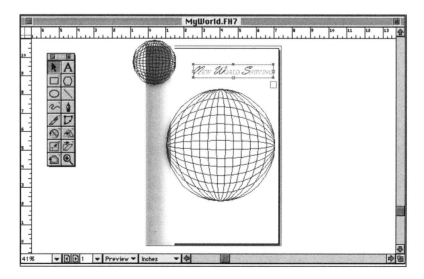

6] Position the Pointer tool on the text, near the middle of the block, and drag the block to visually center the text from left to right on the page approximately one-quarter inch down from the top of the page.

Make sure to move the text block by dragging from the middle of the block. If you were to drag the selection boxes for the text block, you would be resizing, not moving, the block and possibly reformatting the text. As you move, dotted lines in the rulers, corresponding to the edges of the selected objects, will follow the selected element, helping you identify when you are in the correct position. Use this example as a guide to position your text.

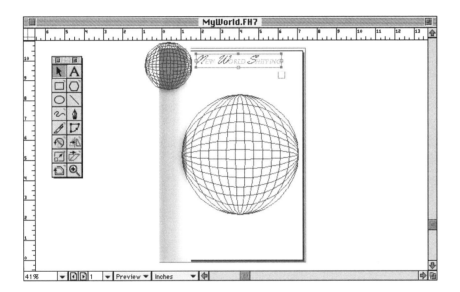

Now add the address line at the bottom of the layout. You'll want this text to be less prominent than the company name.

7] Click the Text tool at the bottom of the page. Change the font to URWGaramondTMed, the style to Plain, and the size to 12 points using the text toolbar controls.

You can change formatting before or after entering the text. In this case, selecting a smaller type size prior to entering the address is advisable so that the text will not come in quite so large. This text block is waiting for the text to be entered.

The URWGaramondTMed font is on the FreeHand Graphics Studio software CD-ROM. If you don't have it, you can just use a font you already have installed.

8] Choose View › Magnification › 100% to see the text you are about to type and enter the following address (make sure the Caps Lock key is off):
1000 Globe Avenue . New York, New York . 11111 . 212-555-2222

Enter a space, a period, and another space between the street, city/state, zip code, and phone number.

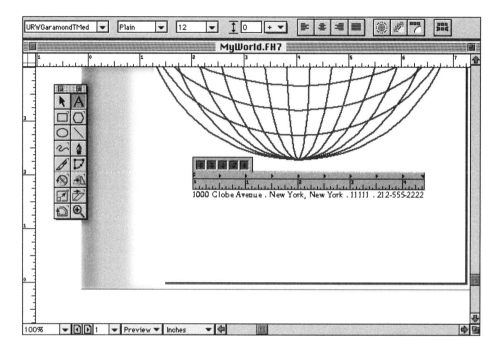

9] Select the text block with the Pointer tool and display the Color List by clicking the Color List button in the toolbar. Change the fill color to PANTONE 285 by dragging the swatch for that color and dropping it on the text on the page. Then close the Color List.

Formatting applied while the text block is selected with the Pointer tool will apply to all characters in the block. Using the Text tool to select text allows you to apply formatting to specific words or characters within the text block.

10] Choose View › Fit To Page to see the entire page. Using the Pointer tool, position the text block so it is visually centered horizontally and approximately one-quarter inch up from the bottom of the page.

Watch the ruler on the left side as you move the text block into position.

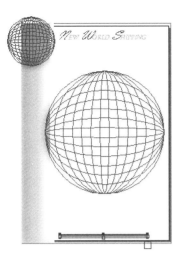

You do not have to rely on visual judgment to position text. FreeHand provides an easier (and more precise) way.

11] Using the Pointer tool, select the text at the top of the page. Hold down the Shift key and click on the large globe and then the text at the bottom of the page to select all three elements. Choose Modify › Align to display the Align panel.
Using this panel, you will align these elements to center them horizontally without changing their vertical positions on the page.

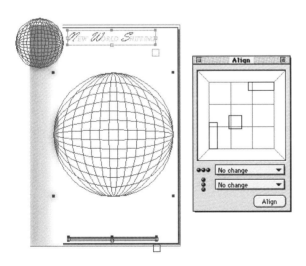

12] In the Horizontal Alignment menu in the Align panel, choose Align center. The Vertical Alignment menu should be set to No change. Click the Apply button.

Your text elements and globe are aligned together.

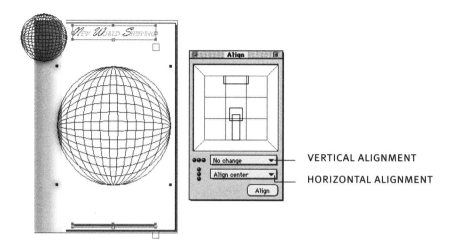

VERTICAL ALIGNMENT

HORIZONTAL ALIGNMENT

13] Save your work.

IMPORTING A FREEHAND GRAPHIC

To add some visual interest to your letterhead, you will add a small airplane graphic to the layout. The graphic has been created for you in a separate FreeHand document. You will need to import it into the document you are creating.

1] Choose File › Import (Windows Ctrl+R, Macintosh Command+R). Select Plane.fh7 from the Media folder within the Lesson02 folder and click the Open button (or press Enter).

Your cursor will change to the import cursor, which represents the top-left corner of the graphic.

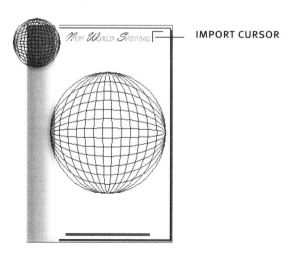

IMPORT CURSOR

2] Position the cursor on the page just to the right of the company name and click the mouse.

The graphic appears on the page in this position.

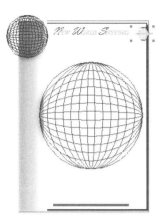

tip *Be careful not to drag the mouse when clicking to position an imported graphic as this will resize the graphic.*

3] Choose View › Magnification › 200%.

This zooms the view in to two times actual size, and the screen is centered on the selected graphic.

To position the graphic element so the lower edge is aligned with the baseline of the company name text, you will use a **ruler guide** to help. Ruler guides are nonprinting lines you can use in your documents to help you position elements accurately. To add a guide with the Page Rulers active, drag from either the horizontal or the vertical Page Ruler.

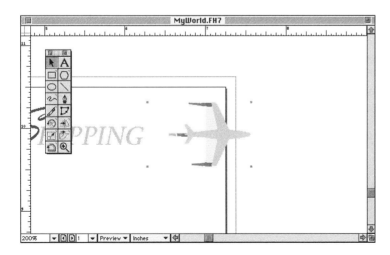

4] Pull a ruler guide onto the page by pointing to the horizontal Page Ruler at the top of the page and dragging the mouse downward. Position this guide at the bottom of the letter *I* in *SHIPPING* and then release the mouse.

If you position a ruler guide in the wrong place, point to the guide and drag it to a new position. (Be careful to point to a spot on the guide away from other elements on the page, so you do not select those elements by mistake.) To remove a guide, drag it off of the page and release the mouse.

This guide is positioned along the **baseline** of the text, the imaginary line on which the characters rest. If this text had uppercase and lowercase characters, the descenders for characters such as *g* and *y* would extend below the baseline.

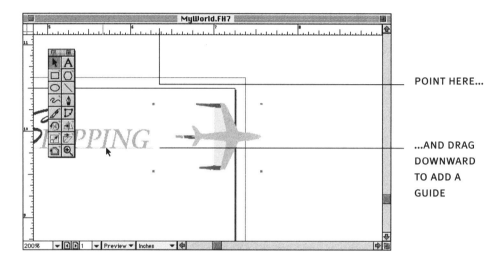

POINT HERE...

...AND DRAG DOWNWARD TO ADD A GUIDE

5] Using the Pointer tool, move the graphic so the bottom of the airplane rests on the ruler guide and the left edge of the graphic is just to the right of the last character, *G*.

Notice that the cursor displays a small alignment icon when the graphic is snapped to the guide.

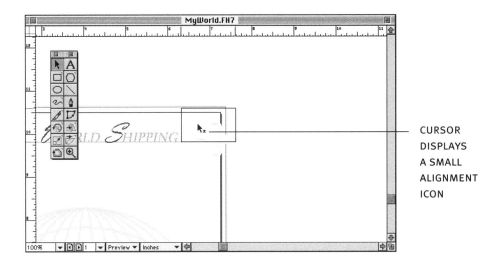

CURSOR
DISPLAYS
A SMALL
ALIGNMENT
ICON

Now you will make the graphic smaller to more closely match the height of the largest text characters. Since the bottom and left edges of the graphic are positioned correctly, you will want to resize the graphic by dragging the selection box at the upper-right corner of the airplane.

6] Pull a new ruler guide down from the top ruler and position it at the top of the *S* in *SHIPPING*. Using the Pointer tool, hold down the Shift key and drag the top-right selection box of the airplane graphic downward and to the left to make the graphic smaller. Release the mouse when the top of the graphic aligns with the top ruler guide.

Use as many ruler guides as you need while working on your projects.

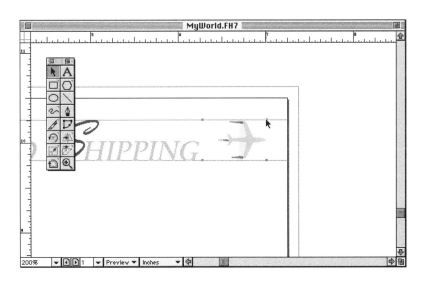

**7] Press the Tab key to deselect all of the elements on the page. Then choose View ›
Fit To Page. Save your work.**

You need to add only one more basic element to make your layout complete.

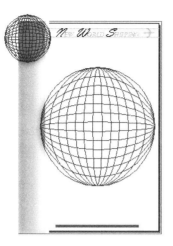

ADDING A DASHED LINE

To make your layout look more dynamic, you will add a dashed line at the top of
the page.

**1] Using the Zoom tool, click on the *N* in *NEW* at the top of the page. Then click on
the *N* a second time to zoom in closer.**

Clicking the Zoom tool will enlarge the view of the page. To zoom out, hold the Alt
key (Windows) or Option key (Macintosh) and click with the Zoom tool.

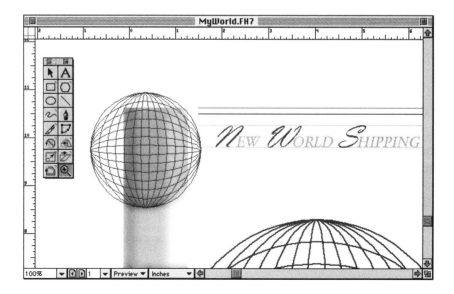

2] Use the Line tool in the toolbox to draw a horizontal line below the company name. Hold down the Shift key to keep the line horizontal and begin on the left side at the left edge of the bleed. Drag to the right until the end of the line is under the *R* in *WORLD*. *Then* release the mouse.

A solid line appears on the page. Holding the Shift key while dragging with the Line tool constrains the line to horizontal, vertical, and 45-degree angles.

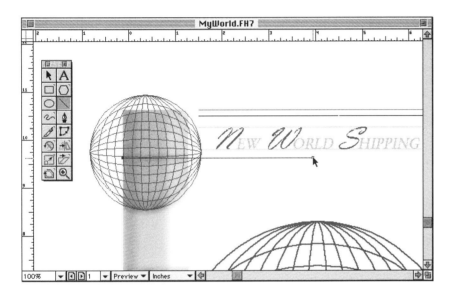

3] Choose Window › Inspector › Stroke to display the Stroke Inspector. Select Basic from the Stroke Type menu and set the color to PANTONE 285 by selecting it from the Stroke Color menu in the upper portion of the Inspector. Change the width to 2 points using the Stroke Width menu.

Since the document's unit of measure is inches, the 2-point stroke width is displayed as 0.02778 inch.

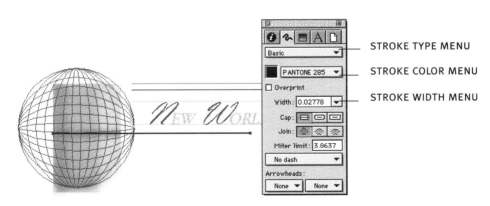

STROKE TYPE MENU

STROKE COLOR MENU

STROKE WIDTH MENU

4] Select the sixth type of dash from the Dash Type menu in the Stroke Inspector.

The line becomes a dashed line.

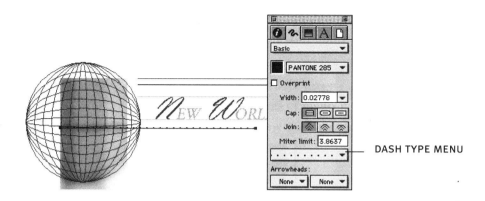

DASH TYPE MENU

5] Press the Tab key to deselect all elements and choose View › Fit To Page. Save your work.

Congratulations—the corporate letterhead is complete!

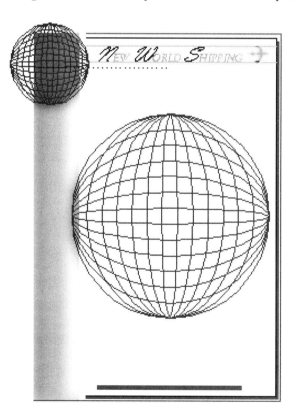

WHAT YOU HAVE LEARNED

In this lesson you have:

Changed the measurement units for the document [*page* **48**]

Used the Page Inspector to set a custom page size and a bleed area [*page* **49**]

Practiced creating, modifying, and combining basic shapes [*page* **51**]

Created shapes with precise dimensions [*page* **54**]

Practiced using the Align panel to position elements relative to one another [*page* **57**]

Created a blend between two shapes [*page* **58**]

Selected multiple items by dragging a selection area with the Pointer tool [*page* **58**]

Used the Transform panel to rotate and scale elements [*page* **61**]

Practiced grouping individual elements together [*page* **63**]

Used PANTONE colors and tints [*page* **64**]

Practiced using the Fill Inspector, Stroke Inspector, Color Mixer, and Color List panels to apply fills, strokes, and colors [*page* **69**]

Entered text and changed the font, size, and other text formatting [*page* **73**]

Imported a graphic from another FreeHand document [*page* **82**]

Used ruler guides to align elements on the page [*page* **84**]

Created a dashed rule [*page* **86**]

paths and points

In this lesson you will complete an advertisement that has already been started for the Greenville Zoo. In the process, you will work directly with the points and paths that make up the graphic elements in FreeHand documents.

As you learned in Lesson 2, graphics in FreeHand consist of paths, which are lines defined by points. The span between two points, either straight or curved, is is called a path segment.

The organic shapes of the animals at the bottom of this advertisement are created by tracing patterns with FreeHand's Bezigon tool and then manipulating the resulting paths. Special text effects like the gradient and striped fills used here can be added by turning text outlines into paths. You will learn those skills in this lesson.

Designed by Julia Sifers of Glasgow & Associates.

As you will see in this lesson, you can manipulate these paths, also known as Bezier curves, to create virtually any shape and to make precise adjustments to those shapes.

In the first part of this lesson, you will experiment with various tracing templates to learn how to create and modify paths and points. Then you will apply these new skills by tracing elements that will complete the zoo advertisement.

If you would like to review the final result of this lesson, open Zoo.fh7 in the Complete folder within the Lesson 3 folder.

WHAT YOU WILL LEARN

In this lesson you will:

Manipulate basic shapes

Create and modify paths to create objects of any shape

Use existing artwork as tracing templates

Copy artwork into different documents

Create gradient-filled text

APPROXIMATE TIME

It usually takes about 1 hour and 30 minutes to complete this lesson.

LESSON FILES

Media Files:

Lesson03\Media\Howl.ft7 (optional)

Starting Files:

Lesson03\Start\Trace1.ft7

Lesson03\Start\ZooStart.ft7

Lesson03\Start\Wolf.ft7

Lesson03\Start\Angelfish.ft7

Completed Project:

Lesson03\Complete\Zoo.fh7

MANIPULATING BASIC SHAPES

In this lesson, you will learn how to create and modify paths using the Bezigon tool to create all kinds of paths, from prickly shapes with pointed corners to smooth, fluid curves. In Lesson 4, you will learn how to create paths using the Pen tool. Both tools can be used to create points and paths, and the choice between the two is a personal one. The Bezigon tool is often easier to learn and has the advantage of creating points that automatically adjust the path as you trace. The Pen tool can be used to create the same paths, but it requires you to make every adjustment manually. If you do not have experience using the Pen tool in earlier versions of FreeHand or in other applications, you may find it easier to learn after you are comfortable with the Bezigon tool.

You will start by creating a basic shape. You will then ungroup the paths in this shape and manipulate them in several ways.

1] Create a new document by choosing File › New (Windows Ctrl+N, Macintosh Command+N).

A new document window containing one page will appear.

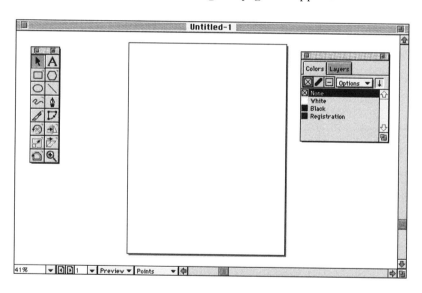

2] Use the Rectangle tool to draw a medium-size rectangle on the page.

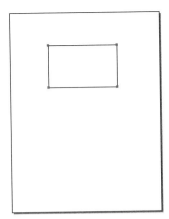

What should you do if the rectangle you create has rounded corners? This could happen if you have Changing Objects Changes Defaults turned on in the Object Editing Preferences dialog box (under File > Preferences). If that happens, choose Edit > Undo and then double-click the Rectangle tool to set the corner radius to zero.

tip *Any time a tool does not behave as you expected and the wrong element is created, remember to use the Undo command by clicking the Undo button on the main toolbar and choosing Edit > Undo, or using the keyboard shortcut (Windows Ctrl+Z, Macintosh Command+Z).*

3] Resize the rectangle by dragging a corner handle with the Pointer tool.
The size of the rectangle changes as you drag the handle with the Pointer tool. The basic shapes you create in FreeHand (rectangles, ellipses, and lines) are actually grouped paths. This means that you cannot manipulate the individual points that create these shapes. These grouped paths, though, will continue to behave as basic shapes until they are ungrouped.

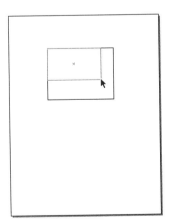

4] With the rectangle still selected, click the Ungroup button on the main toolbar or choose Modify › Ungroup.

Notice that the display will change slightly to show that the path and points are now selected. When a group is selected, the path is not displayed as a selection; only the corner selection handles are displayed as selected. You will soon see how differently the ungrouped selection behaves when you manipulate it.

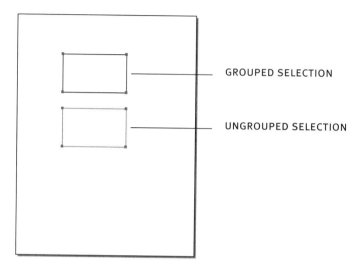

GROUPED SELECTION

UNGROUPED SELECTION

5] With the Pointer tool, drag the right-bottom corner point a short distance to the right.

This time, dragging does not change the size of the rectangle. Instead, it moves that individual point by itself, modifying the path.

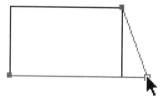

In addition to moving the existing points, you can also add new points to this path. You can add a point to the path with either the Bezigon tool or the Pen tool. For this example, you will select the Bezigon tool and click once along the path to add a point.

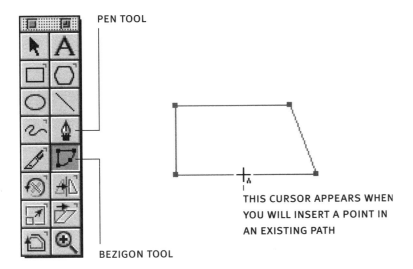

PEN TOOL

THIS CURSOR APPEARS WHEN
YOU WILL INSERT A POINT IN
AN EXISTING PATH

BEZIGON TOOL

6] Select the Bezigon tool in the toolbox, position the cursor in the middle of the bottom segment of the selected path, and then click the mouse to add a new point.

A new point will be added to the path where you clicked.

Now activate the corner points on the path so you can alter the shape of the rectangle.

7] Choose the Pointer tool from the toolbox and click once on a segment of the path.

All of the points on this active path are displayed as solid squares. This indicates that these are **corner points** which are not selected. FreeHand uses three different kind of points: corner points, **curve points**, and **connector points**, which are used at different places on a path and are displayed in different ways on an active path.

To more simply demonstrate the process of creating paths, these lessons work with only corner and curve points. You can create any type of path using only these two types of points.

CLICK PATH SEGMENT

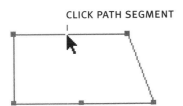

tip   *Corner points are represented by squares and curve points are represented by circles on an active path*

8] Use the Pointer tool to move the new corner point up toward the middle of the shape.

After you move the point and release the mouse, the corner point you moved remains selected and appears as an outlined square.

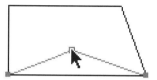

Now you will transform this corner point into a curve point.

9] Display the Object Inspector by choosing Window › Inspectors › Object. Change this selected corner point to a curve point by clicking on the Curve Point button in the Object Inspector.

The point now appears as a circle on the path, but the path did not change—yet.

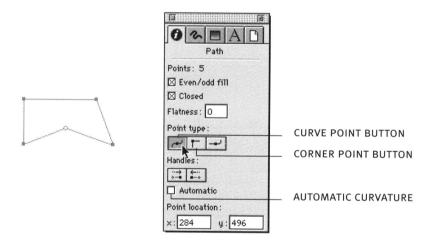

CURVE POINT BUTTON

CORNER POINT BUTTON

AUTOMATIC CURVATURE

10] Click Automatic in the Object Inspector.

The Automatic setting adjusts the path as it passes through this point with respect to the position of the preceding and following points. The path now follows a smooth curve through your curve point, with two **control handles** appearing across the point. Curve points have two control handles that are connected to one another, like a long lever.

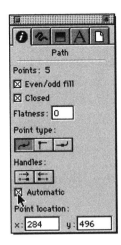

CONTROL HANDLES

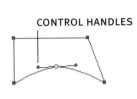

Next you will see how to use these control handles to manipulate the shape of the curve.

11] With the Pointer tool, grab the left control handle and pull down, causing the right control handle to go up.

The distance and direction you move the control handle influences the direction of the path as it passes through the selected point. The distance you pull the control handle from the point determines how far the curve extends in that direction.

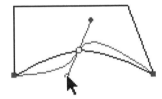

12] To remove the curve point from the path, select the curve point with the Pointer tool and press Delete on the keyboard.

To remove any point from a path, simply select the unwanted point with the Pointer tool and press Delete on the keyboard.

tip *If your entire path was deleted, simply choose Edit > Undo and make sure that an individual point is selected before pressing Delete.*

13] Choose File › Close to close the document without quitting FreeHand. Don't save the changes.

Your work here was just for practice; you don't need to save it. FreeHand may ask if you wish to save changes to Untitled; go ahead and click the Don't Save button.

ON YOUR OWN

You have seen that basic shapes are actually grouped paths, and you can gain precise control over any path by adding, deleting, moving, and modifying points along that path.

Create another new document and experiment further with these techniques. Ungroup a basic shape such as a rectangle, ellipse, or line. Add new points, change points from one type to another, and manipulate the control handles until you understand how the handles act upon the paths.

USING A TRACING TEMPLATE

To simplify the creation of several graphics, you will open an existing template document that contains patterns you will trace with the Bezigon tool. This task is designed to develop your ability to create all types of paths.

1] Choose File › Open, select Trace1.ft7 in the Start folder within the folder for Lesson03, and click the Open button.

A page appears containing tracing patterns that you will use to practice creating different types of paths. Tracing these simple shapes will help you learn how you can create any type of curve or straight line by positioning corner and curve points.

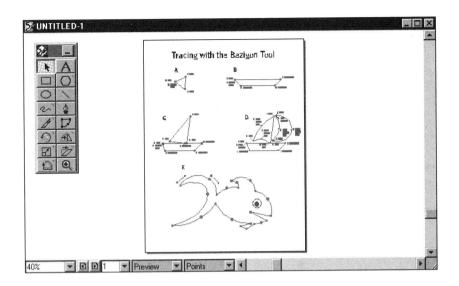

2] Select the Zoom tool in the toolbox. Position your mouse above and to the left of the first pattern, the triangle, at the upper left of the page. Drag downward and to the right until a selection marquee surrounds that pattern. Then release the mouse.

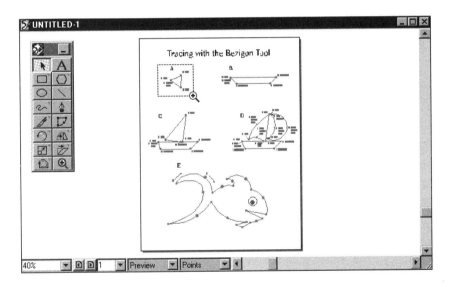

Tracing pattern A is now clearly visible. Next you will trace the triangle pattern by placing corner points with the Bezigon tool.

3] Select the Bezigon tool in the toolbox. Position the cursor on point 1 and click once to create the first corner point. Move the cursor to point 2 and click and then move it to point 3 and click to create the other two corner points. Close the path by clicking once more on the starting point for this path.

You have created a closed path that matches the triangle tracing pattern.

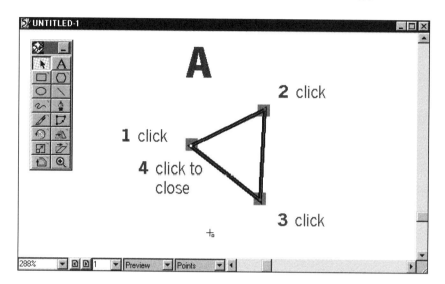

tip *Watch the cursor as you create paths. The crosshair cursor is displayed with an empty square alongside it when you are ready to create a new path. The crosshair appears with a small carat beside it when you can add points to an active path. A solid square appears near the crosshair when the mouse is positioned over the first point in the path, so you know that clicking on that point will close the path.*

4] Save the document as *MyShapes* in your MyWork directory.

Each time you complete something successfully, save it!

5] Scroll to the right to see tracing pattern B.

You may need to zoom out to see the entire shape. This is also a shape you will create using corner points. This path will contain segments that should be horizontal and at 45-degree angles.

Just as the Shift key constrains ellipses and rectangles to create circles and squares, it can also constrain the position of points as you trace. When the next point should be positioned so you have a segment that is horizontal, vertical, or at a 45-degree angle, hold down the Shift key while you click the mouse.

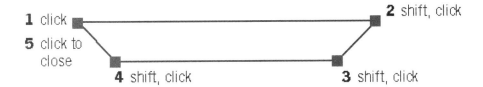

6] Using the Bezigon tool, click corner 1 to begin tracing this shape. To keep the top segment horizontal, hold down the Shift key and click point 2 at the top-right corner. The next segment should be at a 45-degree angle, so hold down Shift and click point 3. Hold down Shift and click point 4, and click again on the starting point to close the shape.

The only segment that Shift will not constrain is the very last one—the one that closes the shape when you click on the starting point—because the last segment must extend from the last point to the first point at whatever angle may be required. If your last segment is not oriented properly, you can use the Pointer tool to reposition one of the points.

tip   *You can use the arrow keys on the keyboard to nudge a selected element or point a small amount in any direction. For example, select a point on the last path—when selected, it should appear as an outlined square. Now instead of using the mouse to move the point, press the right arrow key several times and watch the point move slightly to the right each time. This method works the same way when you select a path, group, or block of type with the Pointer tool. The default movement is 1 point, although this amount, called the Cursor distance, can be customized in the General Editing category of the Preferences dialog box.*

Now try pattern C.

7] Choose View › Fit To Page to see the entire page and zoom in on tracing pattern C, on the left side in the second row. Trace this simple sailboat using the Bezigon tool, beginning at point 1 on the template. Hold down the Shift key when the next point you wish to add should create a segment that is perfectly horizontal, vertical, or at a 45-degree angle.

Follow the steps as shown in the tracing template. If you are not happy with the position of any point as you work, press Delete on the keyboard to delete that point and continue.

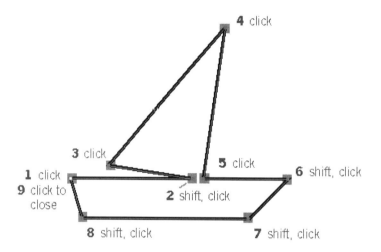

Now you should be ready to create pattern D. This looks complex, but you can see that it's based on the patterns you've already created.

8] Scroll to the right to see tracing pattern D.

This pattern consists of two separate shapes, which you will trace as two paths. Each of these paths consists of both corner and curve points. Corner points should be positioned where the path forms a corner, and curve points should be placed at the outermost part of each curve.

You will first trace the billowing sail on the right. Small squares at the top and bottom tips of the sail indicate that corner points are needed in these positions. The circles positioned at the outermost parts of the curved segments identify the position of the curve points required.

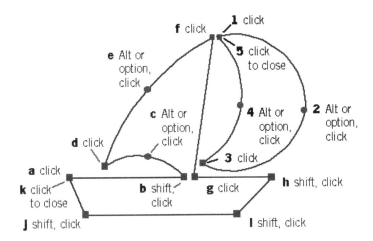

9] Click the Bezigon tool on point 1 to start the path with a corner point at the top of the sail. Add a curve point at position 2 by holding the Alt (Windows) or Option (Macintosh) key and clicking the mouse.

The path does not look like a curve yet, and the curve point you added at point 2 has control handles sticking out the wrong way. Do not stop to make adjustments—continue tracing the path, and the points will *automatically* adjust once the *next* point is added.

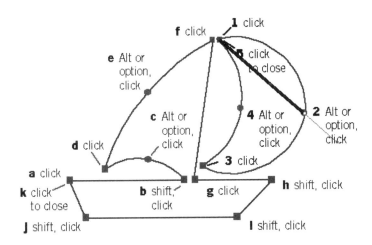

10] Click to add a corner point at the bottom tip of the sail (point 3).

Since this should be a corner point, click without pressing Alt or Option.

The curve point automatically adjusts the control handles to balance the curve between the points on either side.

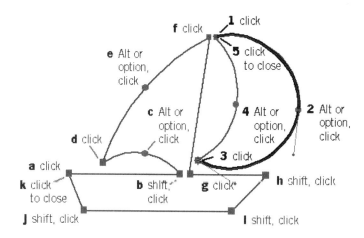

11] Finish the sail by adding a curve point (point 4) and then click the original point again to close the path.

Since the final point should be a corner point, do not hold down the Alt or Option key for the final click. The billowing sail is finished; now you will trace the other parts of this boat.

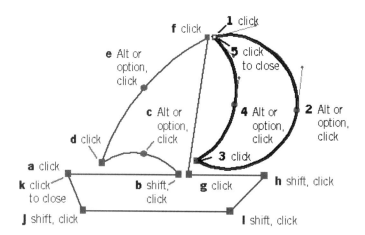

12] Starting at point a, trace the boat pattern using the same techniques as before. Hold down the Shift key to control the direction of segments and the Alt or Option key to add curve points as indicated by the pattern.

Follow the alphabet and read the instructions as you trace. Position corner points where the path should come together to form an angled joint. Place curve points at the outermost spot along a curved part of the path.

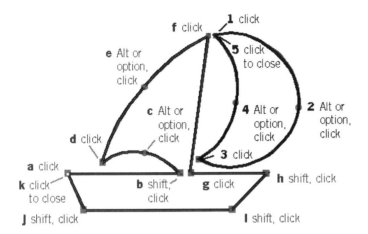

This is such a nice drawing; complete it by adding some color.

13] Click the Pointer tool on an empty part of the page or pasteboard to deselect all elements in the document. Choose Window › Panels › Color Mixer and use the mixer controls to create any color you want, such as a bright green. Drag a swatch from the color well at the bottom of the mixer and drop it inside both of the shapes you created for this boat to fill the shapes.

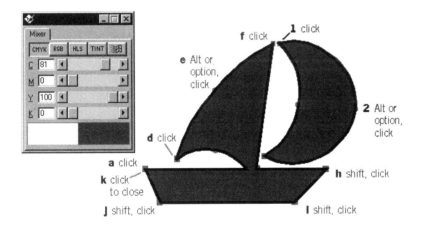

You can also change the stroke to None in the Stroke Inspector, if you like.

14] Save your work.

MANIPULATING CURVES WITH CONTROL HANDLES

Now you are ready to create the fish that appears at the bottom of this template.

1] Scroll down and adjust your view to see the fish (tracing pattern E).

This graphic consists of three elements: two circles (that make up the eye) and a closed path for the body. The tracing path for the body has squares positioned to indicate corner points and circles that indicate where curve points should be located.

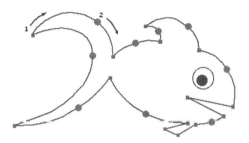

2] Start by adding a corner point at the top left tip of the fish's tail. Then hold Alt or Option and click a curve point at position 2. Continue to trace around the body in a clockwise direction, adding curve and corner points as needed.

It is important to trace around the shape—do not jump across the fish's body.

Don't stop to make adjustments as you trace. Simply put each point in position as you work around the figure. The path may not perfectly match the pattern, but you can easily make adjustments once all of the points are in position and the path has been closed. The graphic below shows the partly traced fish. Notice that you can tell that the curve point at the bottom of the fish was the last point added because this point is selected.

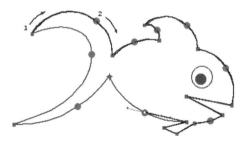

tip *Don't worry if the path does not match the template as you trace. It is easier to create the entire path before stopping to adjust the points or control handles.*

3] After adding all of the points on the fish, close the path by clicking on the starting point.

The path will not follow the template along the inner curve of the tail. You will need to make adjustments to this path with the Pointer tool.

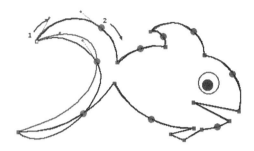

4] Select the last curve point you added, in the center of the tail, with the Pointer tool. Adjust the top control handle for this point to make the control handles vertical.

This adjustment aligns the segment of the path above the curve point much more closely to the tracing pattern. The segment of the path below the curve point still does not look very good.

Every point on a path can have two control handles—even corner points. The handles are visible when the point is selected. When a point is selected, control handles for the preceding and following points, which also control the selected point's path segment, will also appear. Note that the corner point at the bottom tip of the tail has a control handle pointing down and to the right, which is causing the path to dip down.

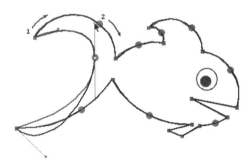

5] Select the corner point at the bottom tip of the tail with the Pointer tool. Point to the control handle that extends downward to the right from this point. Drag this handle up toward the direction you want the path to follow.

The path should now follow the pattern much more closely. You can move the control handle closer to or farther away from the point to adjust the path as needed.

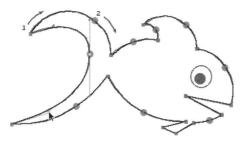

6] Save your work.

The body of the fish is complete.

ADDING FINISHING TOUCHES

You can complete the fish graphic by adding two circles for the eyes, filling the shapes, and grouping the elements together.

1] Use the Ellipse tool to create the larger of the two circles. Then create the smaller circle using the same tool. Fill the larger circle with white and keep the black stroke. Fill the smaller circle with black.

Zoom in closer if you have difficulty filling either shape. If the small circle disappears when you fill the larger one, simply send the larger circle to the back with Modify > Arrange > Send To Back.

> **tip**   *To draw an ellipse from the center out, hold down Alt (Windows) or Option (Macintosh) when drawing with the Ellipse tool. If you would like this shape to be a perfect circle drawn from the center out, hold down the Shift key as well as Alt or Option.*

2] Fill the body with a Gradient fill, using any colors you wish. Set the stroke to None.

If the eye elements are not visible, send the body to the back.

3] Select the small circle, hold down the Shift key and click on the larger circle and on the body of the fish, and group the elements together.

It is often helpful to group elements together when a graphic is complete. This will make it easier to move, resize, or duplicate the entire graphic.

4] Save your work.

CREATING THE ELEMENTS FOR THE ZOO AD

Now that you have explored how to add and adjust points and paths, you will begin to create the elements you will add to the Greenville Zoo ad. You will be putting all your tracing skills learned thus far to use here.

1] Close your MyShapes document and open Wolf.ft7 from the Start folder within the folder for Lesson03. Adjust your view as needed so you can clearly see the tracing pattern.

This document contains a tracing pattern for a wolf.

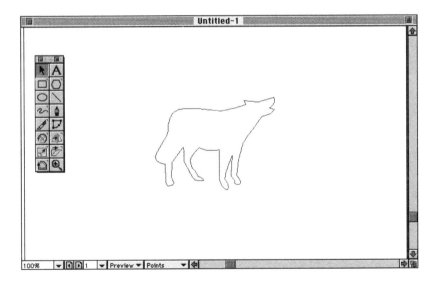

2] Save the document as *MyWolf* in your MyWork folder.

Save frequently while you work.

3] Trace the wolf using the Bezigon tool. Start by putting a corner point at the tip of the nose. Work your way around the shape, adding curve points at the outermost spot along curved sections and corner points where appropriate. Make sure to close this shape by clicking on the first point again after tracing the entire path.

Use this illustration as necessary to identify the types and locations of the points you use to create this shape.

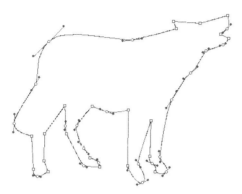

tip   *If you make a mistake as you trace the shape, press Delete on the keyboard. Use the Alt or Option key when placing curve points. Don't worry if the path does not match the template as you trace; you can adjust points and control handles with the Pointer tool after completing your path.*

4] Save your work.

In the next few tasks, you will mix a color and fill the path. Then you will copy the wolf and paste it into an unfinished ad layout document.

You can see a completed version of this wolf by opening Howl.fh7 in the Media folder within the folder for Lesson 3.

APPLYING COLOR

This task explores the process of creating new colors, adding them to the Color List, and applying these colors to elements on the page—in this case, to the wolf drawing.

1] Make sure that nothing is selected by clicking the Pointer tool on an empty part of the page or pasteboard. Choose Window › Panel › Color List to display the Color List and display the Color Mixer by choosing Window › Panel › Color Mixer.

The Color List displays the named colors currently available for this document. The Color Mixer provides controls to create new colors and tints to apply to elements and add to the Color List.

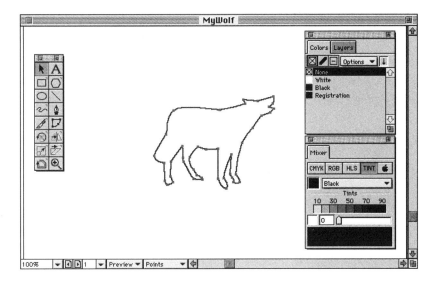

2] Select CMYK at the top of the Color Mixer to use the process ink colors.

The panel changes to display four sliders, one for each of the process ink colors: cyan (C), magenta (M), yellow (Y), and black (K). Tints of these four ink colors can be used in printing to create a broad range of colors. Now you will create a new color by mixing these four primary colors.

3] Using the CMYK controls in the Color Mixer, create a color with 27 percent cyan, 56 percent magenta, 4 percent yellow, and 13 percent black by dragging the sliders or entering values in the Color Mixer fields.

As you enter information, a new purple color is displayed in the color well at the bottom of the Color Mixer panel. This is the color that results from combining these four inks in these percantages.

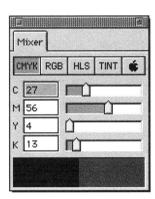

4] Drag the color from the color well at the bottom of the Color Mixer and drop it on an empty spot in the Color List.

Your new color will automatically be named and added to the list.

5] Close the Color Mixer. Rename the new color by double-clicking the assigned name (27c56m4y13k) in the Color List, entering *Wolf,* and then pressing Enter.
Double-clicking a color name selects the name so you can enter text to replace the current name. Note that when you are changing the name of a color, any element that is currently selected when you double-click on the color name would then have that color applied to it.

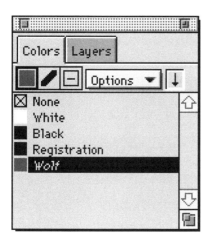

6] Drag the color swatch for your new color and drop it inside of the wolf path on your page. Then drag the swatch for None and drop it on the path to set the stroke around the wolf to None.

The wolf is now ready to use in the Zoo layout.

7] Save your work.

PRACTICING TRACING TECHNIQUES

Another tracing pattern is provided to help you practice your tracing skills.

1] Open Angelfish.ft7, which is located in the Start folder within the folder for Lesson03.

2] Trace the angelfish using the Bezigon tool.

Begin your tracing at a corner point for easier tracing. The tip of a fin would be a good starting point. If you make a mistake, press Delete on the keyboard. Use the Alt or Option key when placing curve points.

Don't worry if the path does not match the template as you trace. Adjust points or control handles after completing your path. Use the illustration for assistance in the placement of points.

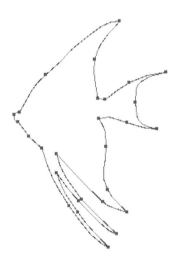

3] Fill the fish as desired and save the document as *MyFish* in your MyWork folder. Close this document when you are finished working on the fish.

ADDING A TRACED ELEMENT TO ANOTHER DOCUMENT

You need to place the wolf you created into the zoo ad. You will do this by simple copying and pasting.

1] In your MyWolf document, select the wolf with the Pointer tool. Copy this element to the clipboard by choosing Edit > Copy.

Next you will open the ad layout and paste a copy of the wolf into that document.

2] Open Zoo1.ft7, located in the Start folder within the folder for Lesson03.

Zoo1.ft7 has many of the elements of this layout already completed and in position on the page. You will add your wolf and some text to the layout.

Notice that several colors are already defined in the Color List.

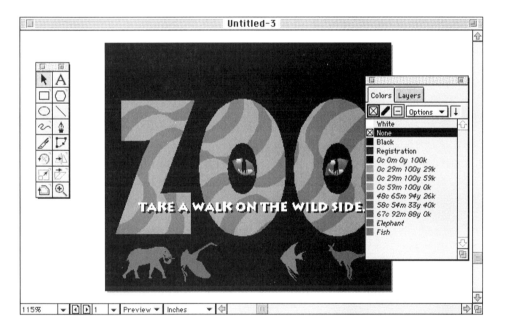

3] Save the document as *MyZoo* in the MyWork folder.

Now paste the wolf into the zoo add.

4] Choose Edit › Paste.

The wolf is pasted into this document (because it was the last thing you copied to the clipboard). The Wolf color has also been added to the Color List.

However, your wolf is a bit large for this layout, don't you think?

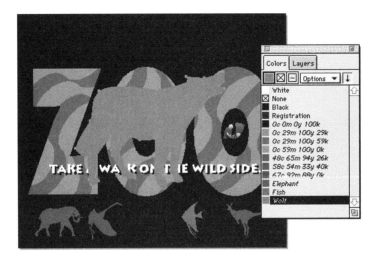

SCALING AND ALIGNING ELEMENTS

You will now reduce the size of the wolf and align it to fit evenly between the illustrations of other wildlife at the bottom of the page.

1] Display the Transform Panel by choosing Window › Panels › Transform. Select the Scale tool in the Transform panel. Enter a scaling percentage of *25,* make sure Uniform is checked, and click Apply (or press Enter).

This will scale your artwork to match the size of the other creatures at the bottom of this ad.

SCALE PERCENTAGE

UNIFORM SCALING

tip   *For further information on other scale options, consult Macromedia's Using FreeHand manual.*

2] Using the Pointer tool, point to the middle of the wolf and move it to the open spot between the bird and fish figures. Close the Transform panel.

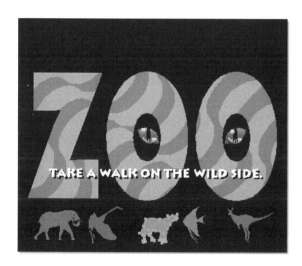

You can use FreeHand's align features to precisely distribute these figures across the bottom of the page. To distribute these objects, all five wildlife figures need to be selected.

3] Since the wolf is still selected, hold down the Shift key while you click on the elephant, bird, fish, and kangaroo. Display the Align Panel by choosing Window › Panel › Align. Set the vertical alignment to Align center and the horizontal alignment to Distribute widths. Click Align or press Enter.

This will evenly space the objects across the bottom of the ad as well as align the centers of the objects vertically.

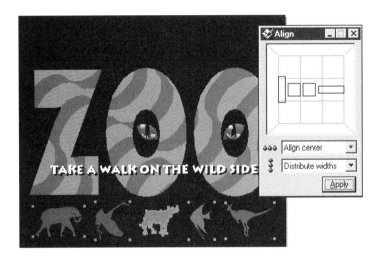

4] Save your work.

ADDING GRADIENT FILLED TEXT

You will now add the name *GREENVILLE* to the top of the ad and apply a gradient fill inside of this text.

1] Scroll up so that you see part of the pasteboard above this ad. With the Text tool, click once on the pasteboard to start a new text block.

You will move this text onto the ad once the effect has been created. Right now, though, the text will be easier to see and work with on the pasteboard.

2] Press in the Caps Lock key on your keyboard and enter the name *GREENVILLE*.

tip *Your text may not look just like this because the default font may be different on your machine.*

Now you will change the font and size of this text.

3] Select the text using the Pointer tool. Using the controls on the text toolbar near the top of your screen, change the font to URWGaramondTMed and the size to 56 points.

Selecting a text block with the Pointer tool lets you change all the characters within that block.

tip   *The fonts specified in these lessons are on the FreeHand Graphics Studio software CD-ROM. If you do not install these specific fonts, simply choose other fonts available on your system and adjust type size and formatting as needed to make your projects similar in appearance to the lesson files.*

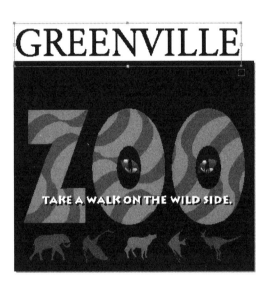

You want to fill this text in with a gradient fill, but FreeHand allows only basic fills in text. In the next step, you will convert this text to paths, just like the paths you created with the Bezigon tool. Once the characters are paths, you will be able to fill them with a gradient.

4] With the text block still selected, choose Text › Convert to Paths.

When you convert text to paths, each letter is converted to a path consisting of corner and curve points. You do not see the points at this time because all of the character paths are grouped together. This will now allow you to place a gradient fill inside of the word.

tip   *Once text has been converted to paths, you can no longer change its text characteristics such as font or point size.*

5] With the text group selected, change the fill type in the Fill Inspector to Gradient. Select Wolf in the color menu at the top of the Inspector and White in the color menu at the bottom. Set the direction of the gradient to 270 degrees.

The text now is filled with a gradient that ranges from the Wolf color at the top to White at the bottom. If the text had not been converted to paths and was selected with the Pointer tool, the text block would now be filled with a gradient, not the text.

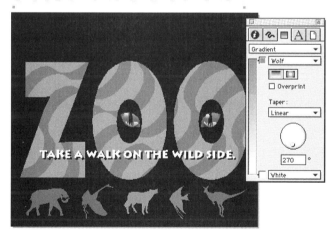

6] Using the Pointer tool, move the text onto the top of the ad so that it is positioned above the word *ZOO*. If you cannot see the entire page, choose View › Fit To Page.

7] Using the Pointer tool, hold down the Shift key and click on the black rectangle behind all of the artwork on the page to select it along with the name. Display the Align panel by choosing Window › Panel › Align. Set the vertical alignment to No change and the horizontal alignment to Align center. Click Align or press Enter.

This will center the type on the page.

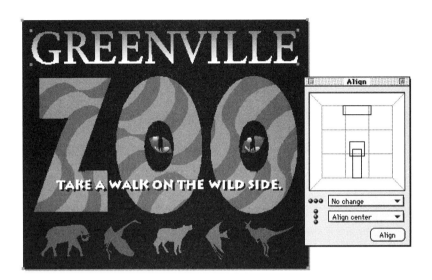

8] Save your work.

Congratulations! The advertisement is now complete.

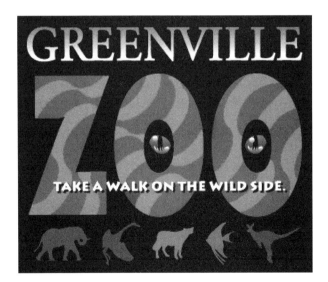

WHAT YOU HAVE LEARNED

In this lesson you have:

Ungrouped basic shapes and edited the resulting paths [*page* **94**]

Created and modified points on Bezier curves [*page* **95**]

Used templates as patterns to trace [*page* **98**]

Created and named colors for process color printing [*page* **110**]

Combined artwork from different documents with Copy and Paste [*page* **115**]

Practiced scaling and aligning artwork for a layout [*page* **116**]

Converted text to paths to apply a gradient fill [*page* **118**]

and styles

using layers

LESSON 4

Layers and styles are among FreeHand's most powerful features for organizing and simplifying your documents and making it easier to apply and modify the look of an element. Layers are transparent planes or overlays that help organize objects and control how they stack upon each other in an illustration. A style is a set of graphic attributes such as color, fill, and stroke or a set of text attributes such as font, style, space before and after, indents and tabs, and alignment.

Creating a complex illustration, like this picture of a country sunset, is made easier by FreeHand's ability to combine and manipulate different layers, as you will learn to do in this lesson.

Designed by Julia Sifers of Glasgow & Associates.

You will apply these features to the creation of a stylized drawing of sunbeams radiating above a hillside. As you work, you will use the Pen tool, perform and duplicate transformations, work with layers and styles, apply path operations, and use the powerful Paste Inside command. You will also export your artwork so it can be imported into other applications.

If you would like to review the final result of this lesson, open Sunbeams.fh7 in the Complete folder within the Lesson04 folder.

WHAT YOU WILL LEARN

In this lesson you will:

Import tracing patterns to help you accurately create paths and elements

Organize a document into layers

Create paths with the Pen tool

Create and duplicate transformations

Create an object style so you can easily apply and modify visual characteristics

Trim unwanted portions from graphics

Export artwork for use in other applications

APPROXIMATE TIME

It usually takes about 2 hours to complete this lesson.

LESSON FILES

Media Files:

Lesson04\Media\Pattern1.tif

Lesson04\Media\Pattern2.tif

Lesson04\Media\Pattern3.tif

Lesson04\Media\Frame.fh7

Starting Files:

None

Completed Project:

Lesson04\Complete\Sunbeams.fh7

Lesson04\Complete\Sunbeams.eps

CREATING A NEW CUSTOM-SIZE DOCUMENT

You will begin working on the artwork for this lesson in a new document.

1] Create a new document by choosing File > New (Windows Ctrl+N, Macintosh Command+N).

A blank page appears, which you will now adjust to the page size needed for this illustration.

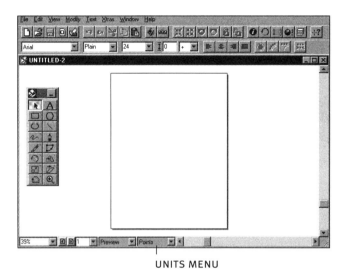

UNITS MENU

2] Change the unit of measure to Inches using the Units menu at the bottom of the screen. Choose Window > Inspectors > Document to display the Document Inspector.

The Document Inspector shows the current page dimensions and orientation.

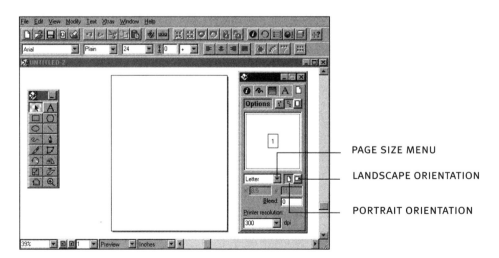

PAGE SIZE MENU

LANDSCAPE ORIENTATION

PORTRAIT ORIENTATION

3] In the Document Inspector, change the Page Size menu from Letter to Custom, enter the dimensions 6.125 by 4.875 inches, and click the icon for Landscape orientation.

Landscape orientation displays the page so that the height is the smaller dimension and the length is the larger dimension.

Your page is now the correct size, but it appears small in the document window.

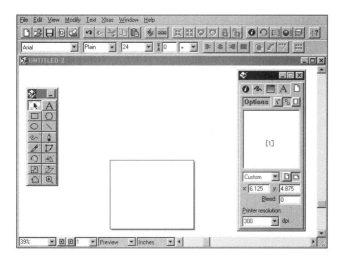

4] Close the Document Inspector and choose View › Fit To Page (Windows Ctrl+Shift+ W, Macintosh Command+Shift+W) to make the document larger in the window.

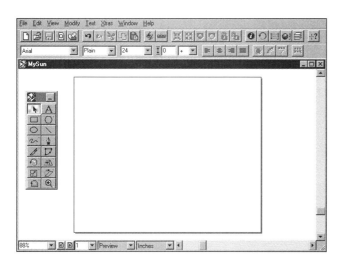

5] Save the document as *MySun* in your MyWork folder.

The page is now ready for you to begin creating the illustration.

IMPORTING A TRACING PATTERN AND MOVING IT
TO A BACKGROUND LAYER

As you learned in the last lesson, a good way to accurately create paths and elements is to trace an existing image of the desired layout or artwork. For example, you can use a scanned image of a pencil sketch or other printed source as a pattern for tracing in FreeHand.

In the last lesson, you opened a template containing a tracing pattern. Here you will import an image called Pattern1.tif to use as a tracing pattern in the drawing you will be creating. This pattern will become the basis for the sunbeams.

You will want this pattern in the background, so you can trace over it, but you will not want it to print. You will accomplish this by using layers. By placing elements on layers, you can control the visibility and printing of individual elements.

1] Choose File > Import (Windows Ctrl+R, Macintosh Command+R). Select Pattern1.tif from the Media folder within the Lesson04 folder and click Open (or press Enter). Align the cursor with the top-left corner of the page and click the mouse to position the artwork accurately on the page.

The artwork—a rectangle enclosing a circle with one ray—appears, but it does not look very clean at this time.

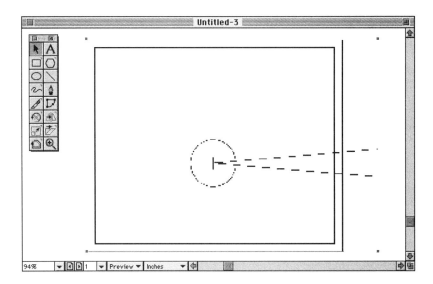

2] Choose File > Preferences to display the Preferences dialog box. From the left column, select Redraw. In the right column, select High-resolution image display to turn on this option. Then click OK.

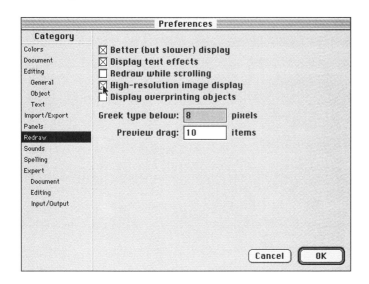

In a moment, the image on the page looks much cleaner. This tracing pattern is a small file, so it should not cause your system to noticeably slow down. However, if you import very large image files for other projects, be aware that your system may slow down significantly when using the high-resolution option. You can turn off this preference setting if large images ever do cause a problem.

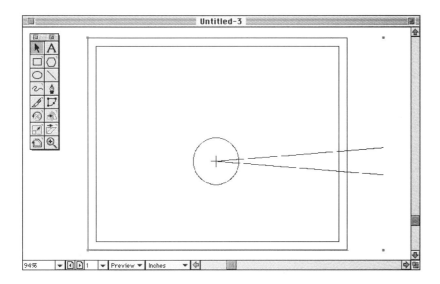

Now place this pattern on a layer so you can move it into the background.

3] Choose Window › Panels › Layers to display the Layers panel.

Three layers initially appear in the Layers panel: Foreground, Guides, and Background. These are preset layers in every FreeHand document. Notice that the Background layer appears below a separator line in the panel.

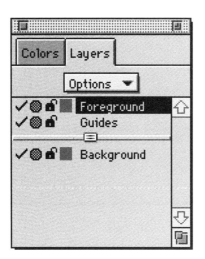

You can add additional layers in any FreeHand document, and you can use these layers to organize elements and control the visibility and printing of the elements on each particular layer. You can move graphic elements from one layer to another, with the exception of the Guides layer, which holds all of the guides you use for aligning elements in your document. As you learned when you used guides in Lesson 1, the Guides layer does not print. Any other layer that appears above the separator line in the panel is a printing layer and is considered a foreground layer. Any layer appearing below the separator line is a nonprinting background layer.

In this first use of layers, you will move the pattern image into the background so it will be visible to trace over, but will not print.

4] With the image still selected, click on the name Background in the Layers panel.

The lines in the image will dim, indicating that this artwork is now on a nonprinting background layer.

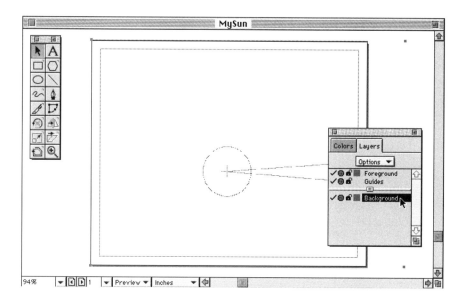

5] Lock the Background layer by clicking once on the Lock icon next to the layer name in the panel.

This will prevent accidental changes to the layer as you work. It also prevents you from accidentally adding the next elements you create to the Background layer. Notice that the Foreground layer is selected in the panel. This indicates the current active layer, where the next elements will be added.

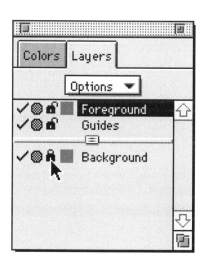

6] Save your work.

Creating the elements of the sky will be much easier now that the tracing pattern is in place.

7] Create a new layer by choosing New from the Options menu in the Layer panel. Double-click the name of the new layer, Layer-1, and enter *Sky* as the new name for this layer. Press Enter to complete the name change.

You can see that the Sky layer is a foreground (printing) layer because it appears above the separator line in the Layers panel. This new layer is now the active layer, so the artwork you create next will be added to this layer.

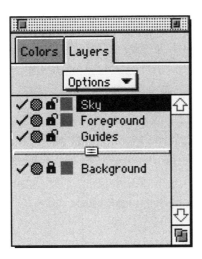

8] Using the Rectangle tool, create a rectangle that matches the size and position of the large rectangle visible in the background.

This rectangle will define the edges of your picture and will appear behind all of the other artwork.

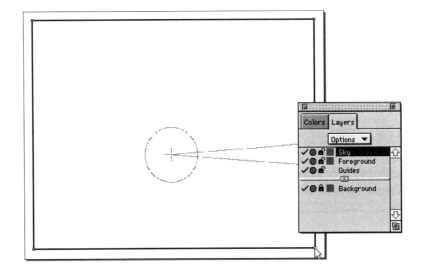

9] Save your work.

You will assign a gradient fill to this element, but first you need to import the colors you will use for this illustration.

DEFINING PROCESS COLORS

When defining colors in FreeHand, you must determine whether to create **spot colors** or process colors. Spot colors match the color of the specific ink that will be used on a printing press to print that color in a FreeHand illustration. For example, to use green and red in your document, you could use a green ink and a red ink. In that case, you would define the red and green colors in your document as spot colors, as you did for the letterhead elements in Lesson 2.

Alternately, you could define every color you use as a process color, a combination of cyan, magenta, yellow, and black inks, as you did for the wolf in Lesson 3. The majority of full-color printed pieces you see use process color printing, and process color is always used to reproduce photographic art realistically.

Why choose one rather than the other? If you have fewer than four colors in your document, printing with spot color can be cheaper, since it uses fewer inks. You can also match colors precisely with spot color, and choose from a wider variety of colors than CMYK colors can reproduce. On the other hand, if your artwork contains many colors, it is much cheaper to use process color, which can create almost any color you need using the same four ink colors. (The exceptions are some very bright colors and specialty inks, such as flourescents and metallics, which CMYK cannot reproduce.)

FreeHand includes libraries of spot and process colors for use in your artwork, including PANTONE for spot color (which you used in Lesson 2), PANTONE for process color, Trumatch, Focaltone, Toyo, and Munsell. You will be importing colors from the PANTONE Matching System for process colors in this lesson.

1] Choose Window › Panels › Colors to display the Color List. Choose PANTONE Process from the Options menu in the Color List.

This displays the colors available in the PANTONE Process color library. You will select several colors from this library to import into your document.

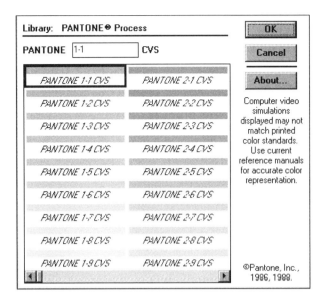

2] Click the color named 1-5. Then scroll to the right. Hold down the Control (Windows) or Command (Macintosh) key and click 18-7 to add it to the selection. Continue to hold down Shift while adding 161-6, 221-5, and 289-1 to the selection. Then click OK.

This imports all five of these colors into the Color List panel.

3] Display the Fill Inspector by choosing Window › Inspectors › Fill. Select the rectangle on your page with the Pointer tool (if it is not already selected). Change the fill to Gradient, with PANTONE 221-5 (light blue) at the top and PANTONE 1-5 (yellow) at the bottom.

The entire rectangle should be filled with a gradient from blue at the top to yellow at the bottom. Because the filled rectangle is on the top-most layer, no other elements are now visible.

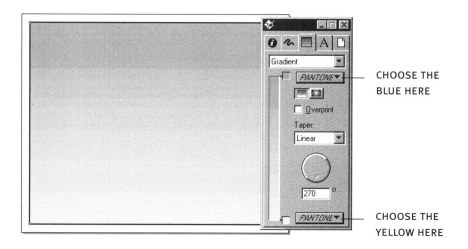

CHOOSE THE
BLUE HERE

CHOOSE THE
YELLOW HERE

4] Display the Stroke Inspector by clicking the Stroke tab at the top of the Inspector panel group. Change the stroke to None in the Stroke Type menu.

Another way to display the Stroke Inspector is to choose Window > Inspector > Stroke.

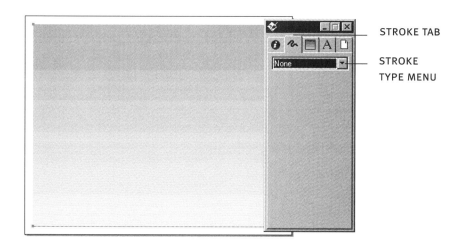

STROKE TAB

STROKE
TYPE MENU

5] Press the Tab key to deselect all elements. Hide the Inspector and display the Layers panel.

6] Now create a new layer by choosing New from the Options menu in the Layers panel. Double-click the default name, enter the new name *Sun,* and press Enter.

On this layer, you will trace the sun and sunbeams. However, the sky is blocking your view of the tracing pattern. To solve that problem, you will temporarily hide the artwork on the Sky layer while creating new elements in the Sun layer.

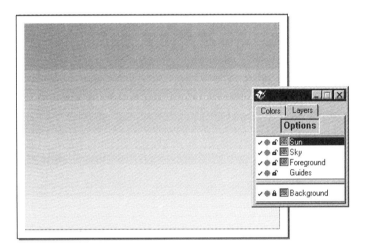

7] Hide the Sky layer by clicking the check mark to the left of the name *Sky* in the Layers panel to remove it. Then save the document.

You can use the check mark to display or hide the contents of any layer whenever it is helpful to do so. The Sun layer should be the active layer at this time, as indicated by the layer name Sun reversed out of a black bar in the Layers panel.

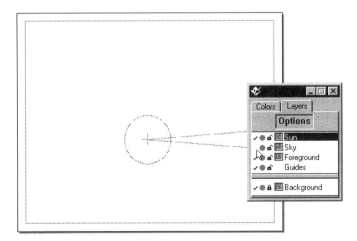

CREATING AN ELEMENT WITH THE PEN TOOL

The Pen tool offers another way to create paths and points and is an alternative to the Bezigon tool you used in the previous lesson. With the Pen tool, you click and release the mouse to add a corner point and drag the mouse to define the control handles of a curve point.

In this task, you will trace the sunbeam displayed in the background by creating corner points with the Pen tool. Then you will make a copy of that element and rotate it around the center of the sun and duplicate the transformation to create a sky full of sunbeams radiating out from the sun.

1] Select the Pen tool by clicking it once in the toolbox.

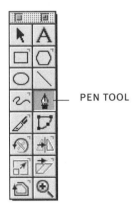

PEN TOOL

2] Position the Pen tool cursor at the center of the sun and click the mouse once. Move to the top-right corner and click, and move to the bottom-right corner and click again. Now close the path by clicking once on the starting point.

Only closed paths can be filled, so it is important to close this path by clicking on the starting point. You have created an empty triangular shape, which you will now fill.

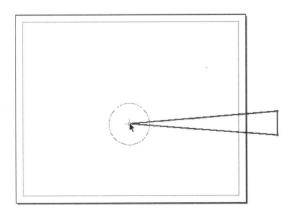

137

3] Display the Fill Inspector by choosing Window › Inspectors › Fill. Change the type of fill to Gradient and use the menus to change the top color to PANTONE 161-6 and the bottom color to PANTONE 1-5. Change the angle to 180 degrees.

You could also drag swatches of these colors from the Color List and drop them on the top and bottom swatches on the gradient in the Fill Inspector. The angle of 180 degrees makes the gradient go from the top color on the right to the bottom color on the left.

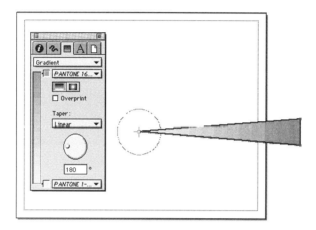

4] Click the Stroke tab in the Inspector panel group to display the Stroke Inspector. Change the type of stroke to None.

The first sunbeam is complete.

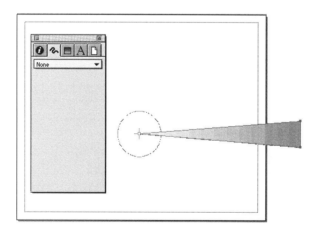

5] Press the Tab key to deselect the artwork. Then save your work.

Now you will create additional copies of this sunbeam rotating around the center of the sun.

ROTATING A COPY AND DUPLICATING THE TRANSFORMATION

You have used the Rotation tool to manually rotate elements into position. In this task, you will use the Transform panel to precisely control both the amount and the center of rotation.

Important: Follow these steps in this exact sequence; missing a step or clicking on something else can disrupt the sequence and alter your results.

1] Select the sunbeam with the Pointer tool. Double-click the Rotation tool in the toolbox to display the Transform panel showing the rotation controls.

This panel allows you to enter specific information for transforming elements. The transformations include moving, rotating, scaling, skewing, and reflecting elements.

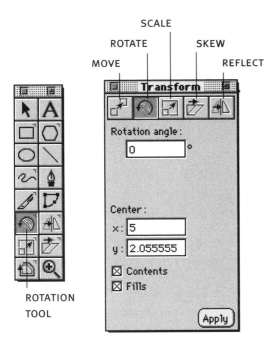

2] With the original sunbeam selected, choose Edit › Clone (Windows Ctrl+Shift+C, Macintosh Command+=).

The Clone command creates a duplicate of the selected item directly on top of the existing item, so no change is visible on the screen.

3] Click the Rotation tool once and release it at the center of the circle (on the left tip of the sunbeam) to specify the center of rotation.

This spot will now be the point the sunbeam will rotate around.

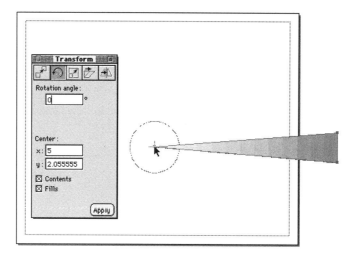

4] Enter a rotation angle of 20 degrees in the Transform panel and click Apply (or press Enter).

The cloned sunbeam now appears in position, rotated 20 degrees counterclockwise from the original.

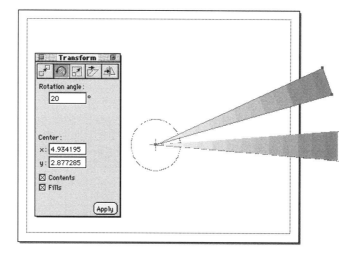

5] Choose Edit › Duplicate (Windows Ctrl+D, Macintosh Command+D).

This duplicates the cloning and transformation (rotation) of the sunbeam to create a third sunbeam.

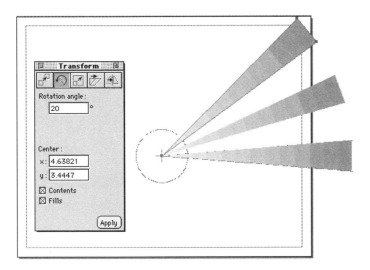

6] Repeat step 5 seven more times to complete the sunbeams.

There should now be nine sunbeams, evenly spaced, radiating out from the center of the circle (which will become the sun in your illustration).

If you have trouble, you probably got some steps out of order. Try deleting all the sunbeams except the first and starting again with step 2.

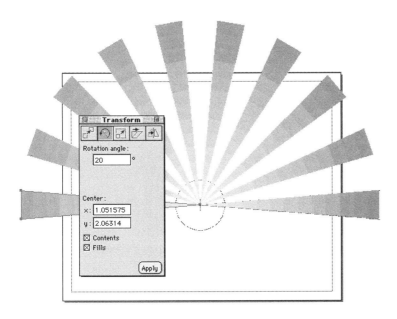

7] Close the Transform panel and save your work.

The sky is almost complete.

COMBINING ELEMENTS WITH PASTE INSIDE

Now that the sunbeams are complete, you will add the sun and use the Paste Inside feature to create **clipping paths** to limit the visible portion of the sunbeams to the area within the sky rectangle. To create a clipping path, you paste artwork inside a closed path using the Paste Inside command. Only the part of the artwork located inside the closed path will appear; the part of the artwork that extends outside of the clipping path will not display or print.

1] Select the Ellipse tool from the toolbox. While holding down Shift to create a perfect circle and Alt (Windows) or Option (Macintosh) to draw the circle from the center, position the cursor on the center of the circle in the tracing pattern and drag downward and to the right. Release the mouse when your circle is the same size as the circle in the tracing pattern.

To ensure that the new ellipse you create remains a perfect circle, always release the mouse before you release the Shift and Alt or Option keys.

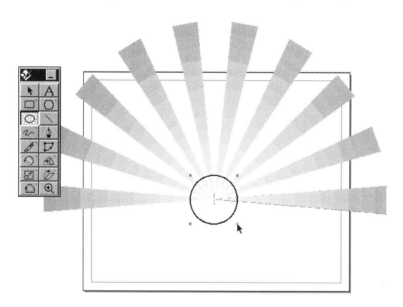

2] Fill the sun with PANTONE 1-5 and set the stroke to None. Choose Edit › Select › All to select all of the sunbeams and the sun (Windows Ctrl+A, Macintosh Command+A). Choose Modify › Group to group these elements together (Windows Ctrl+G, Macintosh Command+G).

Grouping these elements will make it easier to select all of the elements at once to work with them later.

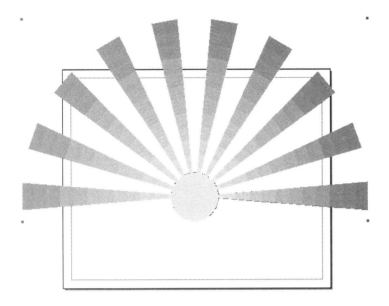

3] Display the Layers panel and click the space to the left of the Sky layer in the column where a check mark appears for the other layers.

The Sky layer should now be visible (indicated by the check mark) and should appear behind the sunbeams, since the Sky layer is below the Sun layer in the Layers panel.

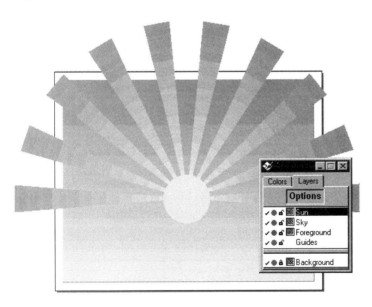

4] With the sunbeam group still selected, click the Sky layer in the Layers panel to move the sunbeam artwork to the Sky layer.

Clicking on a layer name in the Layers panel moves the selected elements to that layer.

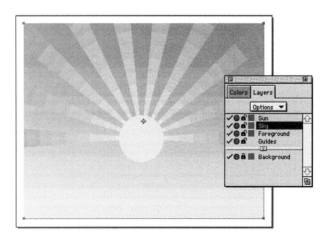

tip *You can check to see which layer any element is on by selecting the element. The layer containing the selected element will be selected in the Layers panel. If you have artwork selected on several layers at once, no layer name will be selected in the Layers panel.*

Next you will use the sky rectangle to mask the unwanted portions of the sunbeams using FreeHand's Paste Inside command.

5] With the sunbeam group selected, choose Edit › Cut. Then click on the sky rectangle and choose Edit › Paste Inside.

The sunbeam artwork was in the desired position over the sky when you cut the artwork. The cut operation removed the artwork from the page. After you select the sky rectangle and choose Paste Inside, only the portion of the sunbeam artwork that appears within the edges of the sky rectangle appears on the page. This makes the sky a clipping path that hides the portions of the sunbeams that extend beyond the rectangle.

tip *The Paste Inside feature can save a great deal of time. Instead of having to trace each sunbeam individually and try to match the edges of the sky rectangle for each one, one sunbeam was created that extended well beyond the edge of the rectangle. All of the other sunbeams were cloned and rotated from that first one—each one extending beyond the edge of the rectangle. Paste Inside clips all the elements to the correct border in one step, saving you time in creating the elements and ensuring that the edges of all elements are perfectly aligned.*

6] Save your work.
Now that the sky is complete, you will begin working on the hills.

CREATING OTHER LAYERS
You will use a different tracing pattern to create the next elements.

1] Press the Tab key to make sure that no elements are selected. Hide the Sky layer by clicking the checkmark to the left of the layer name in the Layers panel. Rename the Sun layer by double-clicking the name, typing *Pattern 2,* and pressing Enter.
An advantage of using layers is you can hide layers that are not currently being used. Remember that clicking a layer name when elements are selected moves those elements to that layer. Pressing the Tab key deselects all elements, so no elements will change layers when you rename this layer.

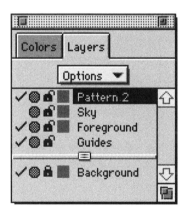

2] Create a new layer by choosing New from the Options menu in the Layers panel. Double-click the default name of the new layer, type *Hills,* and press Enter.

This will be a layer where you will create the hills artwork.

3] Drag the Pattern 2 layer down below the Background layer in the Layers panel.

Moving this layer below the separator line in the Layers panel makes Pattern 2 a background layer. Any artwork you put on this layer will be visible as a tracing pattern but will not print.

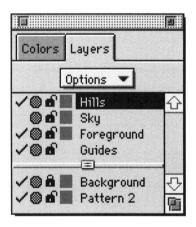

4] Hide the artwork in the Background layer by clicking the check mark to the left of that layer name in the Layers panel.

Since Background is above Pattern 2 in the Layers panel, the artwork on the Background layer will cover up artwork you will put on Pattern 2 in the next step. Hiding the Background layer will allow you to see the Pattern 2 layer.

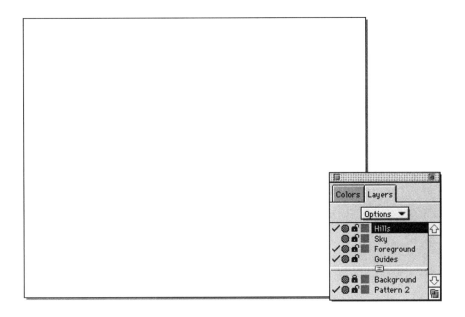

5] Choose File › Import, select Pattern2.tif from the Media folder within the Lesson04 folder, and click Open (or press Enter). Align the cursor with the top-left corner of the page and click the mouse to position the artwork accurately on the page.

This image extends below the bottom edge of the page.

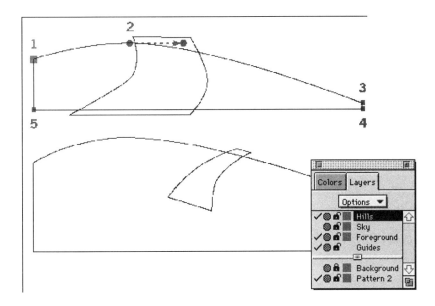

6] With this image selected, click once on the Pattern 2 layer in the Layers panel to send the artwork to that layer. Click the Lock icon to the left of the Pattern 2 layer to lock the layer and prevent accidental changes.

The Hills layer should be the active layer, ready for you to begin tracing the shapes.

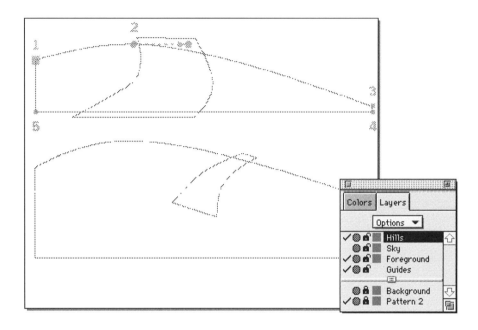

7] Save your work. You can hide the Layers panel if you wish.

CREATING CURVED PATHS WITH THE PEN TOOL

You need to create three hills for this illustration, each with its own road. You will use the Pen tool to create these features.

1] Using the Pen tool, click once on the top-left corner of the top pattern (point 1) to start the path.

This first pattern has the point positions identified. You will create this path by adding the points in order, from 1 to 5, and then clicking again on point 1 to close the path. Clicking on point 1 adds a corner point in this position.

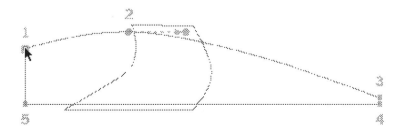

2] Position the cursor on point 2 at the top of the curve. Drag to the right to pull out the control handles until the first segment of the path matches the pattern (which will occur when the cursor is positioned over the red dot in the pattern). Then release the mouse button.

When you drag with the Pen tool, you create a curve point.

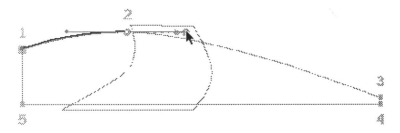

3] Click once on point 3 to add a corner point.

The top right segment may not match the pattern exactly, but don't stop to make adjustments until you have completed and closed the path. It will be much easier to make the adjustments after all of the points have been created.

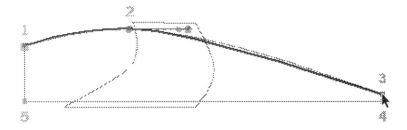

4] Hold down the Shift key and click point 4 and then point 5. Then click on the original point (point 1) to close the path.

Holding down the Shift key when adding additional points ensures that the segment being added will be vertical, horizontal, or at a 45-degree angle to the previous point.

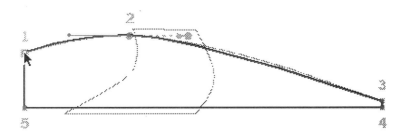

5] Using the Pointer tool, click on the curve point (2) to display the control handles. Drag the right handle out farther to the right until the curve matches the pattern. Save your work.

Try to drag directly to the right to avoid changing the segment to the left of the curve point, which already matches the pattern.

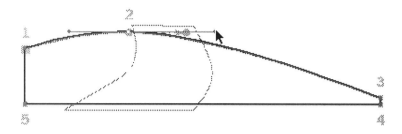

note *If the pattern for the road is not visible, it's probably because your hill shape has a fill. If so, change the fill to None in the Fill Inspector.*

6] Press the Tab key to deselect the hill path. Trace the road that overlaps this hill shape by clicking the Pen tool at the upper-right corner of the road pattern to create a corner point.

The road will extend beyond the edges of the hill; you will trim off the excess later.

7] Add a curve point at the outermost part of the curve on the right side by holding the mouse and dragging downward to pull out control handles. Release the mouse and then trace around the rest of the pattern, adding corner and curve points as needed. The last step is to click on the original point to close the path.

tip *Always work around a path, and trace the entire path before making adjustments with the Pointer tool.*

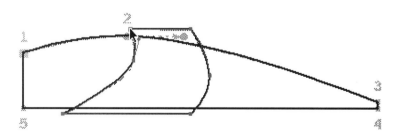

8] Display the Color List by choosing Window > Panels > Color List. Drag the swatch next to PANTONE 18-7 and drop it inside the road you just created. Drag the swatch next to None and drop it on the edge of the path to change the stroke to None.

You can also make these changes using the Fill and Stroke Inspectors.

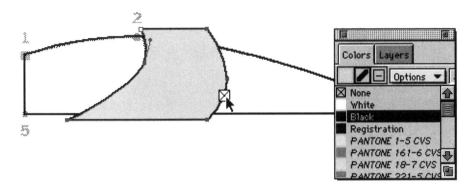

9] Press the Tab key to deselect the road. Fill the hill with PANTONE 289-1 and set the stroke to None.

Drag color swatches from the Color List or use the Fill and Stroke Inspectors to make these changes.

10] Save your work.

Next you will define object styles for these two elements.

CREATING OBJECT STYLES

You can record the visual characteristics of an element as an **object style** to make it easier to apply the same characteristics to other elements in the future. In addition, when you change a style definition, all of the elements that have been assigned that style will automatically be updated to reflect the changes.

You will create two styles for filling the hills and roads in your illustration.

1] Display the Styles panel by choosing Window › Panels › Styles.

FreeHand offers two types of styles: Object and Paragraph. Object styles, which you are using in this task, record the stroke and fill characteristics of a selected element. **Paragraph styles** record character and paragraph formatting for text. Two default styles—a Normal style for objects and a Normal style for text—are already created.

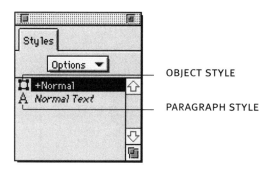

OBJECT STYLE

PARAGRAPH STYLE

2] Select the hill element with the Pointer tool. Choose New from the Options menu in the Styles panel to define a new style based on the fill and stroke of the selected element.

A new object style appears in the Styles panel, named Style-1. The artwork does not visibly change, but it is now connected to this style.

3] Double-click the name Style-1, enter *Hill,* and press Enter to change the name of this style.

The Hill style is defined as a basic PANTONE 289-1 fill with no stroke—the current style of the selected object.

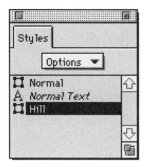

4] Select the road element with the Pointer tool and create another new style by choosing New from the Options menu in the Styles panel. Double-click the default new style name and change it to *Road*.

The Road style is defined as a basic PANTONE 18-7 fill with no stroke.

5] Save your work.

Next you will trim off the excess portion of the road to match the edges of the hill.

COMBINING ELEMENTS WITH PATH OPERATIONS

In an earlier task, you used the Paste Inside feature to make the sunbeams visible only within the sky rectangle. In this task, you will use the Intersect command to trim off the excess portions of the road to match the edges of the hill.

Although Paste Inside will work here as well, the Intersect command creates less complex artwork when you are dealing with an individual element that you will not need to move later. Paste Inside is useful when there are multiple elements, or when you may wish to move the artwork in the future. No matter how you arrange the elements later, the clipping path will always define the visible edges of the artwork. Intersect and the other path operations permanently clip off unwanted portions of selected elements, simplifying the document. However, your work will be much more difficult if you ever need to move these elements.

If you have multiple elements or may need to move elements later, it is usually best to use Paste Inside. Otherwise, Intersect, Union, and the other path operations can make it easy to create complex and accurate paths.

1] Select the hill with the Pointer tool and choose Edit › Clone to make a duplicate of the hill in the same position, on top of the existing artwork. The clone of the hill is already selected, so now add the road to the selection by holding down the Shift key and clicking on the edge of the road that is visible.

Do not use the Select All command, since that would select both copies of the hill.

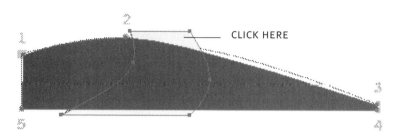

2] Choose Modify › Combine › Intersect.

The two individual shapes are replaced by the shape defined by the intersection, or overlap, of the two selected shapes—the trimmed road. You cloned the hill before creating the intersection, so the trimmed road now sits in front of the original hill.

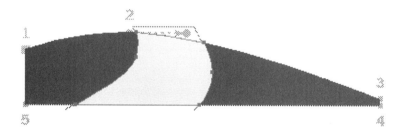

3] The trimmed road is already selected. Add the hill to the selection by Shift-clicking on it with the Pointer tool. Then group the hill and road together by choosing Modify › Group.

Grouping the elements will prevent you from accidentally moving either the road or the hill without the other.

4] Save your work.

CREATING THE OTHER ELEMENTS

Now you will trace the other two hills and roads.

1] Press the Tab key to make sure that no elements are selected. Click Normal in the Style panel so that the next items you create will have a black stroke and no fill.

The active style when no elements are selected determines the style that is assigned to the next elements automatically. Using Normal while tracing the shapes will make it easier to see the patterns, since Normal specifies a black stroke and no fill.

2] Use the Pen tool to trace the next hill pattern in the same manner as the first, clicking to position corner points and dragging to pull out control handles for curve points.

Remember to trace around the entire shape and to click on the starting point to close the path.

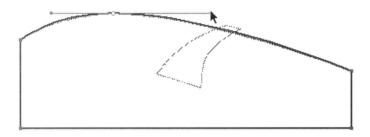

tip *To trace the remaining elements, you can use either the Pen or Bezigon tool, as you prefer.*

3] Trace the road for this second hill.

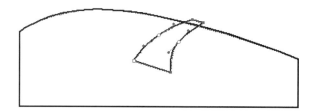

4] Apply the Road style to this element by clicking Road in the Styles panel. Select the hill element and apply the Hill style.

You can also apply a style by dragging the icon to the left of the style name in the Styles panel and dropping it on the desired object.

Next you will trim off the excess portion of the road with the Intersect command.

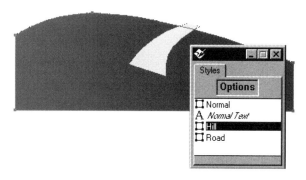

5] With the hill path selected, choose Edit > Clone. Hold down the Shift key and click on a visible portion of the road to select it along with the clone of the hill. Choose Modify > Combine > Intersect.

The road is trimmed to match the edges of the hill.

tip   *Zoom in closer if you have difficulty selecting the road and the hill at the same time.*

6] Select the hill and road and choose Modify › Group.

The second hill is now complete—only one more hill to go!

7] Repeat steps 1 through 5 for the third hill pattern and its road.

This third pattern is visible below the page, so you may need to scroll down to see it clearly.

8] Save your work.

ALIGNING ELEMENTS

The three groups that make up the hillsides in this illustration need to be aligned to one another so the road appears to be continuous. To align the three individual hill groups, you will select them together and use the Align panel.

1] Choose Edit › Select › All In Document to select all three hill groups.

Note that the Select All command selects only the items on the page, not those on the pasteboard. Select All in Document selects all of the elements in the document, on pages and pasteboard, in any unlocked and visible layers.

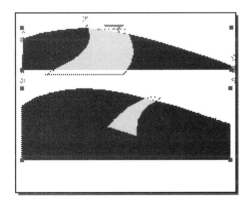

2] Choose Window › Panels › Align to display the Align panel. Click the bottom-middle square on the Align panel grid to set the panel to center the groups horizontally and align the bottom edges.

You can set the alignment settings by clicking the grid or by choosing from either menu at the bottom of the Align panel.

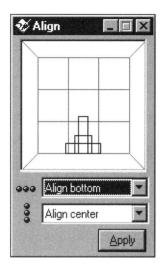

3] Click Apply.

All three hills are now aligned to one another, but they are stacked up in the wrong order. The road should be visible going over all of the hills.

4] Press the Tab key to deselect all elements. Click on the visible road with the Pointer tool to select the hill in front and choose Modify › Arrange › Send To Back.

The most distant road segment is now on the bottom and the middle segment is in front of the others, hiding the closest segment.

5] Press the Tab key to deselect all elements and click on the middle (larger) road with the Pointer tool. This element must be moved only one item back, rather than all the way to the back, so choose Modify › Arrange › Move Backward.

Send To Back and Bring To Front move selected items to the very back or front within its current layer. Move Backward and Move Forward move selected elements one item backward or forward. If more than one element is on top of the element you want to move forward, you select this command again until the element is placed correctly.

Now group the hills in their correct positions.

6] Choose Edit › Select › All In Document to select all three hill groups and choose Modify › Group. Save your work

The hills are ready to be positioned on the page.

POSITIONING ARTWORK AND EDITING STYLES

Now turn on the Sky layer so you can see how the Hill layer looks with it and make any modifications to the styles.

1] In the Layers panel, hide the Pattern 2 layer and show the Sky layer by turning their check marks off and on, respectively. Use the Pointer tool to move the hills into position so that the bottom and sides of the hills slightly overlap the edges of the sky rectangle.

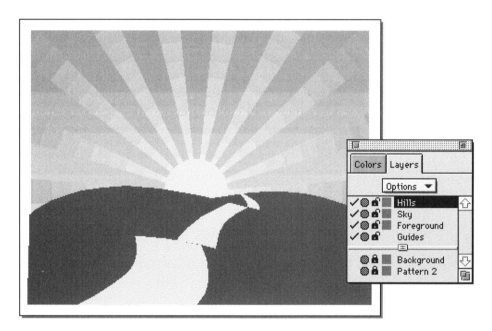

You will use the Paste Inside feature to trim these hills the same way you did with the sunbeams earlier. Before you do this, though, you will change the style definitions to change the appearance of the hills.

2] Display the Color Mixer (Window › Panels › Color Mixer) and click the Tint button at the top. Also display the Color List (Window › Panels › Color List). In the Color Mixer, select PANTONE 289-1 as the base color in the menu at the top. Drag the 40 percent swatch from the tint display and drop it on the Color drop box (the downward arrow at the top right of the Color List).

This will add 40 percent PANTONE 289-1 to the Color List as soon as you release the color swatch on the Color drop box.

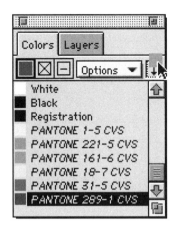 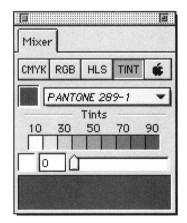

3] Display the Styles panel (Window › Panels › Styles) and press the Tab key to make sure that no elements are selected in your document. Click the Hill style once in the panel and choose Edit from the Options menu in the Styles panel.

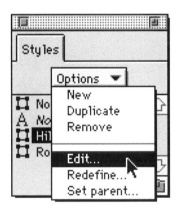

This displays the Edit Style dialog box, where you can change the characteristics of elements that have this style assigned.

4] Change the fill to Gradient, with PANTONE 289-1 at the top and the 40 percent tint of that color at the bottom, and change the angle to 90 degrees.

The fill settings appear on the left side of the dialog box. You can change the angle by entering a new value into the field just above the bottom color in the gradient strip or by rotating the angle dial just above the angle field.

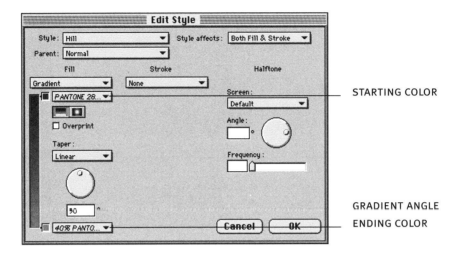

STARTING COLOR

GRADIENT ANGLE
ENDING COLOR

5] Click OK to apply the changes and return to the artwork.
Changing the style definition automatically changes the style of all elements that have this style applied.

6] Edit the Road style by selecting that style in the Styles panel and choosing Edit from the Styles Options menu in the panel. Change the fill to Gradient, with PANTONE 18-7 at the top and PANTONE 31-5 at the bottom, with an angle of 270 degrees.
In both the hill and road elements, the gradients will flow from a lighter color on the top to a darker color at the bottom.

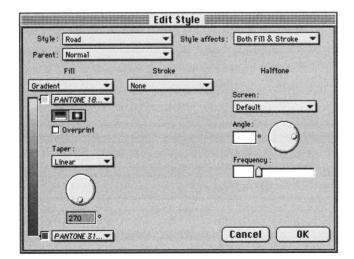

7] Click OK to see the results. Then save your work.

The hills and roads are now filled with gradient fills. Notice how the gradients give the impression of sunlight highlights on the hilltops.

tip *This is a simple demonstration of the power that object styles can offer. Imagine that you had created a state map and made all interstate highways 2 points wide and blue by defining and applying a style. If your client then decides that these highways should all be 4 points wide and red, you can simply edit the style definition to update every highway on the map.*

ADDING ELEMENTS TO THE CLIPPING PATH

You will hide the parts of the hills that extend beyond the edges of the sky rectangle by adding the hill group to the clipping path you created earlier.

1] The hills are in the correct position, so select the hill group and choose Edit > Cut.

The hills disappear from the page.

2] Select the sky rectangle and choose Edit > Paste Inside.

The hills are added to the sunbeam artwork inside the sky rectangle, and the edges of the artwork are defined by the rectangle.

The hills have been removed from the Hills layer and pasted into the Sky layer. Notice how the edges of the hills now perfectly match the edges of the sky graphic.

3] Save your work.

SCALING AND REFLECTING ARTWORK

You still need to create the trees in the illustration. The artwork for the four trees is identical, so you can create one tree and then scale and reflect copies into position.

1] Hide the Sky layer. Use the Layers panel Options menu to create a new layer and change the name of that layer to *Trees*. Rename the Hills layer *Pattern 3*. Move the Pattern 3 layer below the separator line to make it a background layer.
Remember that the check mark next to a layer name allows you to control the visibility of the individual layers. Also remember that you rename layers by double-clicking the layer name and entering a new one.

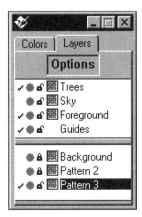

Now open the tracing pattern for the trees.

2] Choose File › Import, select Pattern3.tif from the Media folder within the Lesson04 folder, and click Open. Position your cursor at the top-left corner of the page and click the mouse.

The image of four trees appears on the Pattern 3 layer, because it is the active layer.

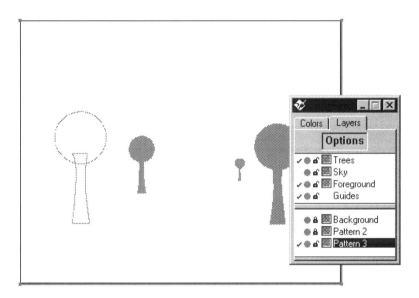

tip *If the image does not appear on the Pattern 3 layer, move it to that layer by clicking that layer in the Layers panel when the image is selected.*

3] Press the Tab key to deselect the image. Lock the Pattern 3 layer and click the Trees layer to make it the active layer. Save your work.

You are now ready to begin creating a tree.

4] Zoom in to see the tree pattern on the left clearly. Trace the tree trunk using the Pen or Bezigon tool.

Make sure to close the path so it can be filled in later.

5] Import one additional color from the PANTONE process color library by choosing PANTONE Process from the Options menu at the top of the Color List. Enter 31-5 in the dialog box to select the desired color and click OK. Now fill the tree trunk path with this color and change the stroke to None.

The next element to trace is a circle. You can make it easier to create a circle that will accurately match the pattern by using nonprinting ruler guides.

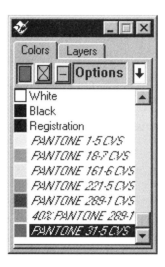

6] Choose View › Page Rulers to display the rulers at the top and left edges of the document window (Windows Ctrl+Alt+M, Macintosh Command+Option+M). Position your cursor on the numbers in the top ruler and drag a nonprinting ruler guide down to the top of the circle pattern. Drag a ruler guide from the left ruler and position it at the left edge of the circle pattern.

These guides will make it easier to trace the circle pattern.

7] Select the Ellipse tool and position the cursor at the intersection of the two ruler guides. Hold down the Shift key to create a perfect circle and drag downward and to the right until the circle you are drawing matches the pattern

Use ruler guides any time you need assistance in positioning or aligning elements

8] Using the Fill Inspector, change the type of fill to Gradient. Click the Radial Fill button and change the top color to PANTONE 18-7. Change the bottom color to 40% PANTONE 289-1. Then drag the PANTONE 289-1 color swatch from the Color List and drop it along the Color Ramp to add a third color to the gradient. Then move the center point up and to the left by dragging the knob in the Fill Inspector.

The Color Ramp can be used to create a gradient fill combining up to 32 colors. Your Fill Inspector settings should look similar to the ones shown here.

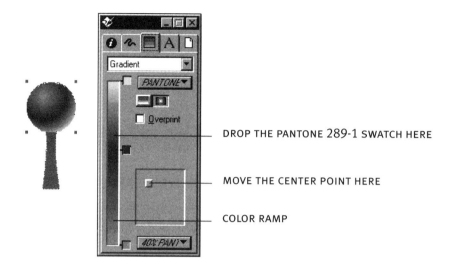

DROP THE PANTONE 289-1 SWATCH HERE

MOVE THE CENTER POINT HERE

COLOR RAMP

9] Change the stroke around the circle to None. Then select both the circle and the trunk and group them together to complete the tree. Save your work.
The first tree is finished.

10] Choose Edit > Duplicate to create another copy of the tree. Move this tree just to the right of the second tree pattern from the left, so its trunk bottom aligns with the trunk bottom of the pattern tree.
This second tree is much too large.

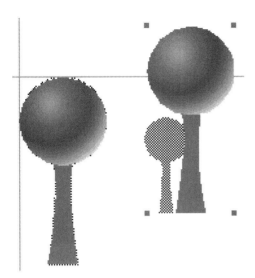

11] **Hold down the Shift key and use the Pointer tool to drag the upper-right selection handle downward and to the left until the height of the tree matches the pattern. Then move the tree to position it to match the pattern.**

tip *Holding the Shift key prevents the object proportions from changing.*

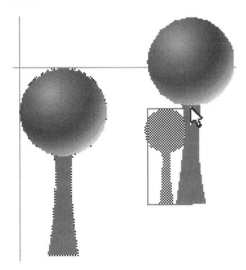

Two trees have been created, and there are only two more trees to go. However, you want the sides of the trees with the lighted lower edge to face the sun, so the trees on the right must be reflections of the trees on the left.

12] Select both trees and choose Edit › Clone. Using the Reflection tool, position your cursor in the center of the page, between the center two trees. Hold down the Shift key and drag the mouse downward to reflect the trees around a vertical axis. Press the Tab key to deselect the new trees.

The two trees on the right now have the "lighted" lower edge on the left, facing the sun. The line that appears when you reflect an object is the reflection axis. By holding down the Shift key, you constrain the reflection axis to vertical, horizontal, or a 45-degree angle.

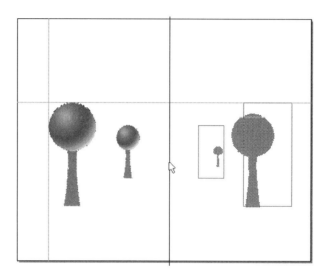

13] Resize and position the two trees on the right to match the pattern.

Remember to hold down the Shift key while resizing so you do not accidentally distort the trees.

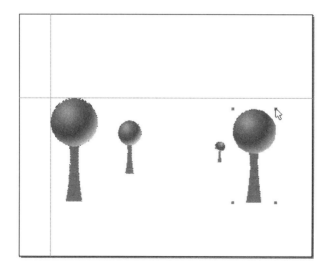

14] Show the Sky layer to see your trees in position on the rest of the artwork you have created. Save your work.

If you do not see the trees in front of your sky and hills, make sure that your layers are in the right order.

Your work in this lesson is almost complete.

IMPORTING A PICTURE FRAME

Layers make it easy to add optional elements to your documents, allowing you to show or hide the artwork as needed. Organize your documents into layers when this will make it easier to select, modify, or view the elements.

In this task, you will import a frame to surround your illustration. By placing this frame on a layer by itself, you will be able to easily view and print the artwork with or without the picture frame.

1] Create a new layer and rename it *Frame*.

The Frame layer will now be the active layer, where the artwork you are about to import will appear.

2] Import Frame.fh7 from the Media folder within the Lesson04 folder. Position your cursor at the top-left corner of the page and click.

This picture frame graphic was created to fit this page; by positioning the import cursor at the top-left corner of the page, the artwork will be imported in the correct position on the page. Reposition the frame if necessary so it fits on the page.

3] Save your work.

USING OTHER LAYER PANEL CONTROLS

The Layers panel provides two more controls that may be useful to you in the future: You can change the colors of the selection boxes that appear on different layers so you can more easily identify the layer you are using, and you can use the Keyline view to see your artwork without fills or strokes.

Experiment with changing the color of selection boxes.

1] Select one of the trees on your page.
Notice that the selection boxes appear in a light blue—the same blue that appears next to the name of the Trees layer where that artwork is located. You can change these colors so selection items indicate the layer on which artwork is located by the colors of the selection boxes.

2] Display the Color Mixer and create a bright red or magenta color. Drag the new color from the color well in the Mixer and drop it on the color swatch next to the Trees layer.

The selected tree should now have selection boxes displayed in this new color, which also appears next to Trees in the Layers panel. Items on the trees layer now display green selection boxes when selected.

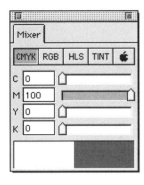 

Now experiment with using the Keyline view.

3] Click the small gray circle next to Trees in the Layers panel.

This changes the display of this layer from Preview to Keyline. Preview shows the printing image, whereas Keyline shows the paths without the fills and strokes. This view can be useful when you need to see the position of elements on another layer, but do not want that other layer to obstruct a background image. Clicking the circle again turns the Preview for this layer back on.

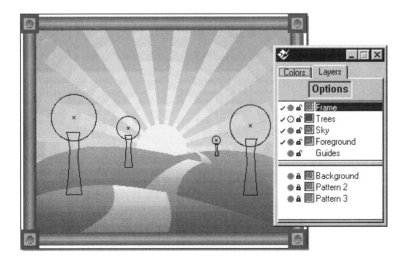

4] You do not need to save these changes, so choose File › Revert.

The Revert command restores the document to the last saved version. This command is useful only if you save frequently as you work.

EXPORTING THE FINISHED ILLUSTRATION

There will be times when artwork you have constructed in FreeHand needs to be used in other applications. You can easily export your work.

1] Choose File > Export. Select the EPS format for your computer platform from the Format menu. Choose your MyWork folder as the location in which to save this file and click the Export button.

The Encapsulated PostScript, or EPS, format provides the most reliable way to transfer FreeHand artwork to other page layout applications such as QuarkXPress and Adobe PageMaker. EPS graphics maintain the high quality and resolution independence that you count on with FreeHand.

Macromedia Director users have several bitmap formats to choose from in the Export format menu, and Photoshop users can export files in the Photoshop EPS format. Transferring artwork from FreeHand to the other FreeHand Graphics Studio applications is as simple as dragging and dropping, as you will learn in Lessons 9 through 11 in this course. Lesson 12 will explore the options you have if you wish to export your artwork for use on the World Wide Web.

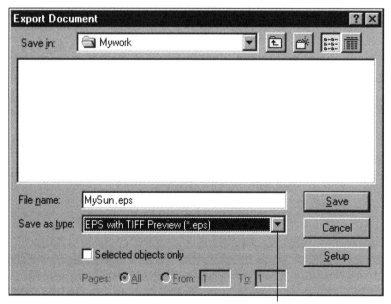

EXPORT FORMAT MENU

WHAT YOU HAVE LEARNED

In this lesson you have:

Imported tracing patterns into nonprinting background layers [*page* **128**]

Locked tracing pattern layers so they cannot be accidentally changed [*page* **131**]

Created and named multiple foreground and background layers to organize elements [*page* **132**]

Learned when to use spot color and when to use process color [*page* **133**]

Practiced importing colors into the Color List [*page* **134**]

Created paths with the Pen tool [*page* **137**]

Rotated elements around a point and duplicated that transformation [*page* **139**]

Created clipping paths with the Paste Inside command and trimmed artwork using the Intersect command [*page* **142**]

Activated and repositioned layers to organize your document [*page* **145**]

Defined and modified object styles [*page* **151**]

Scaled objects proportionately using the Shift key [*page* **169**]

Practiced reflecting objects around a central axis [*page* **170**]

Color-coded layers so that an object selection box shows which layer the object is on [*page* **172**]

Used the keyline view [*page* **173**]

Exported your illustration as an EPS file [*page* **174**]

page documents

In addition to creating a wide variety of graphics and illustrations, you can use FreeHand to design and construct multiple-page documents by adding pages to your documents and flowing text from one page to the next. In fact, FreeHand allows you to create several different-size pages within the same document. For example, you could add a business card and envelope as additional custom-size pages in the letterhead document you completed in Lesson 2.

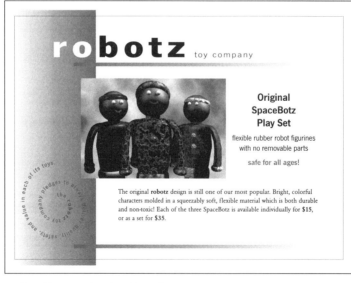

r **obotz** toy company

Original SpaceBotz Play Set

flexible rubber robot figurines with no removable parts

safe for all ages!

The original **robotz** design is still one of our most popular. Bright, colorful characters molded in a squeezably soft, flexible material which is both durable and non-toxic! Each of the three SpaceBotz is available individually for **$15**, or as a set for **$35**.

This three-page catalog was created entirely in FreeHand, using the program's page layout tools, which combine the text-handling features you find in page layout programs with the graphics management features you expect from a professional level drawing program.

LESSON 5

Designed by Tom Faist of Datrix Media Group.

In this lesson, you will construct a three-page mini-catalog that will incorporate illustrations created and rendered in Extreme 3D.

If you would like to review the final result of this lesson, open Robotz.fh7 in the Complete folder within the Lesson05 folder.

WHAT YOU WILL LEARN

In this lesson you will:

Attach text to a path

Add pages to a document

Import text into a layout

Flow text from one page to another

Format text using styles

Wrap text around graphics

Copy colors from imported images to use elsewhere in a document

Print your document

APPROXIMATE TIME

It usually takes about 2 hours to complete this lesson.

LESSON FILES

Media Files:

Lesson05\Media\Robotz1.tif

Lesson05\Media\Robotz2.tif

Lesson05\Media\Robotz3.tif

Lesson05\Media\Robotz.rtf

Starting Files:

Lesson05\Media\Robotz.ft7 (optional)

Completed Project:

Lesson05\Media\Robotz.fh7

SPECIFYING A CUSTOM PAGE SIZE

The catalog you will be creating requires a custom page size, plus a specific amount of bleed area around the page. In addition, you will enter the printer resolution of the output device that will be used to print this document. This allows FreeHand to optimize the resolution of gradient fills for the best printed results.

1] Close any open FreeHand document windows and then Choose File › New to create a new document.

A page appears within a new document window. You will change the page size and document settings to match the layout.

2] Choose Window › Inspectors › Document to display the Document Inspector. Change the Page Size menu option to Custom and enter *7i* as the value for x and *5i* as the value for y. Then press Enter and click the Landscape orientation button.

Currently the measurement units for your document are set to points, so the values in these fields are displayed that way. To enter a value with a different unit of measure than that in which the value is displayed (for instance, to enter 7 inches in a field that displays values in points), simply add the unit to the measurement. For example, FreeHand understands that *7i* indicates 7 inches instead of 7 points.

When you press Enter, the values you entered will be converted to the current measurement unit. Thus, your 7-inch by 5-inch page will appear as a 504-point by 360-point page in the Document Inspector.

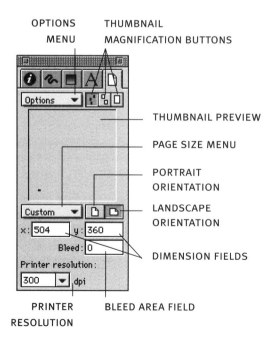

OPTIONS MENU
THUMBNAIL MAGNIFICATION BUTTONS
THUMBNAIL PREVIEW
PAGE SIZE MENU
PORTRAIT ORIENTATION
LANDSCAPE ORIENTATION
DIMENSION FIELDS
PRINTER RESOLUTION
BLEED AREA FIELD

3] Choose View > Fit To Page. Enter a value of 0P9 as the bleed size (0 picas and 9 points) in the Document Inspector.

Identifying a bleed size defines how much beyond the edge of the page FreeHand will print when this document is output. This is important when preparing artwork for a printing press. The measurement of 9 points is equal to the standard one-eighth inch bleed you specified earlier.

4] In the Document Inspector, set the printer resolution to 600.

Setting the printer resolution to match the characteristics of the printer or output device that this project will be printed on allows FreeHand to optimize color transitions—graduated fills and blends in the document—so you will get the best possible results. Set this value to the resolution of your final output device. For example, as you are creating a document, you may print it on a 300-dot-per-inch (dpi) printer, and then you may send it to a service bureau for final output at 1270 dpi. Since the final output is what you are concerned with, you would enter 1270 as the printer resolution in FreeHand for that document.

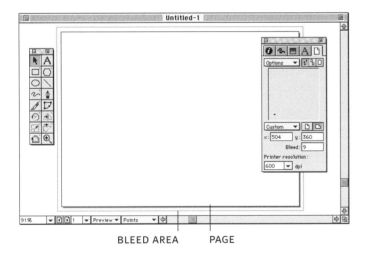

BLEED AREA   PAGE

5] Close the Document Inspector and choose View > Magnification > 100%.

Working at actual size makes it easier to precisely adjust the size and position of elements.

6] Save the document as *MyToys* in your MyWork folder.

Instead of adding the two additional pages at this time, you first will first set up one page with all of the elements and guides you want to appear on every page. Then you will duplicate that page, which duplicates the elements as well, so you don't have to copy, paste, and reposition items manually.

CREATING GUIDES FOR A CONSISTENT LAYOUT

To position elements on your pages consistently, you will set up several nonprinting guides on the page.

1] Show the rulers by choosing View > Page Rulers, and show the Info Bar by choosing View > Info Bar.

The rulers must be visible for you to add ruler guides to the page. The info bar will help you position them accurately.

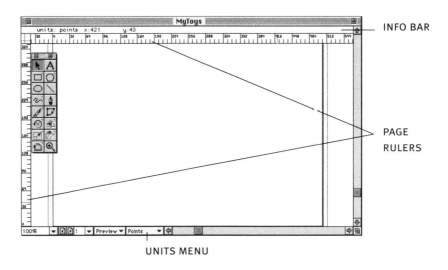

INFO BAR

PAGE RULERS

UNITS MENU

2] Change the unit of measure for this document to Picas using the Units menu at the bottom of the document window.

Picas and points are units of measure widely used in the graphic arts field. You already have been using points to specify type sizes and stroke widths. There are 12 points per pica, and 6 picas per inch. Each inch, therefore, is equivalent to 72 points. With this system, you can avoid having to deal with the fractional or decimal values required when working with inches.

3] Drag a ruler guide out from the center of the vertical ruler on the left side of the document window. Watch the info bar at the top of the window and position this guide when the x value is 7P8 (7 picas, 8 points).

This nonprinting guide is 7 picas and 8 points out from the left edge of the page.

INFO BAR X VALUE

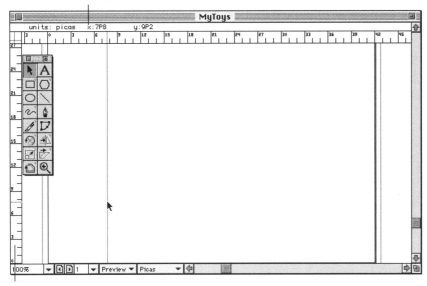

DRAG FROM HERE

tip *Make sure to drag ruler guides out from the center of the rulers. If you drag from the top-left corner of the rulers, where the vertical and horizontal rulers intersect, you will reposition the zero point on the page. If the zero point is repositioned, all of the values for the horizontal (x) and vertical (y) positions will be now measured from that new point. If this ever happens by mistake, double-click the point where the rulers intersect to reset the zero point to the lower-left corner of the page. All measurements in these lessons assume that the zero point is in this default position—the lower-left corner of the page.*

4] Drag a new vertical guide out to 10P6. Now drag a ruler guide from the horizontal ruler across the top of the window down to 25P.

You can pull ruler guides from the vertical or horizontal ruler as needed.

In addition to the ruler guides, any element on the page can be converted into a guide. Next you will create a rectangle to indicate the position of the text block that you will create on this page, and then convert that rectangle into a guide.

5] Create a rectangle anywhere on the page using the Rectangle tool. Then choose Window › Inspectors › Object to display the Object Inspector. For the x dimension in the Inspector, enter *13P4*. Press the Tab key to select the y value and enter *2P8*. Press Tab again to select the width value and enter *25P5*. Then press Tab and enter *18P0* into the height field, and press Enter.

This rectangle is now the precise size and in the correct location required for this layout.

tip *Entering specific values in the Inspectors helps you position elements with precision.*

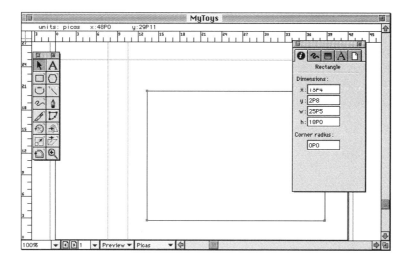

6] Click the Layers button on the main toolbar to display the Layers panel, or choose Window › Panels › Layers. With the rectangle selected on the page, click once on the name of the Guides layer to convert the selection into a guide.

If you move elements to the Guides layer, they automatically become nonprinting guides, just like the ruler guides you created earlier.

You have used foreground and background layers in previous lessons. The Guides layer is special—even though it appears above the divider in the Layers panel, elements on the Guides layer do not print. You can move this layer above or below other layers, depending on how you want the guides to appear. You can also hide and lock the Guides layer the same way you can other layers.

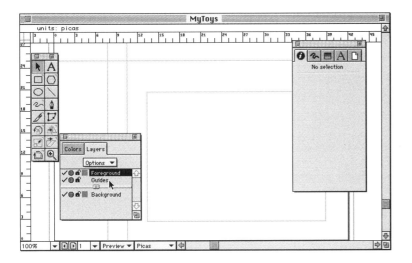

7] Create another rectangle that has a width of 18P6 and a height of 12P4. Position it so that *x* is 8P7 and *y* is 10P0. Then convert this rectangle into a guide.

All of the guides are now in place.

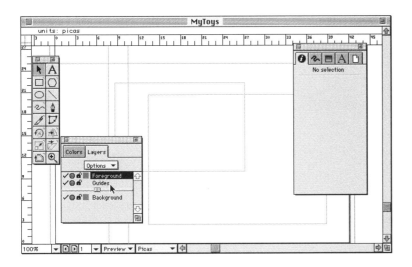

8] Hide the page rulers and info bar and save the document.

You are now ready to begin assembling elements on the page.

USING THE EDIT GUIDES COMMAND

Another way to set up and manipulate guides is to use FreeHand's Edit Guides controls. In the Guides dialog box you can create new guides in precise positions, adjust the positions of existing guides, evenly distribute guides across a page, and release guides. Try it!

1] Create a new document. Choose View › Guides › Edit.

The Guides dialog box appears, displaying a list of the guides on the designated page. No guides have been created for this new document, so the list is empty.

CURRENT PAGE

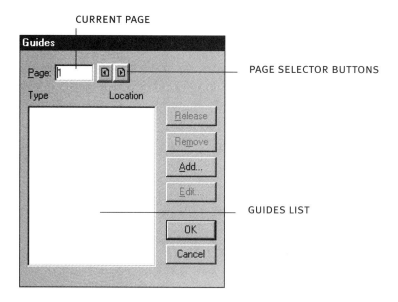

PAGE SELECTOR BUTTONS

GUIDES LIST

2] Click the Add button. Click Vertical, enter *6* into the Count field, *.5i* in the First Position field, and *8i* in the Last Position field.

The First and Last position values allow you to enter a distance in from the edge of the page where you want the first and last guides to be placed. As in all FreeHand entry fields, if you want to enter an inch value in a field that currently displays points or picas, simply add the unit after the value, such as *.5i*.

These settings will create six vertical ruler guides that are evenly spaced across the page, starting and ending 0.5 inch in from the left and right edges of the page.

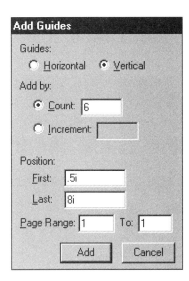

3] Press Enter or click Add to return to the Guides dialog box.

All of your new guides now appear in the Guides list, which displays the type and location of each guide.

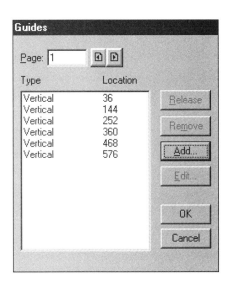

4] Click OK in the Guides dialog box to apply these changes and view your document.

FreeHand has added the six guides to the page, positioned precisely as you indicated in the dialog boxes.

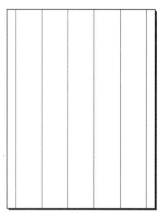

5] Return to the Guides dialog box and experiment with the other options—deleting, editing, and releasing guides.

The Edit button allows you to numerically reposition guides individually.

The Release button actually releases a guide from the Guides layer and changes it into a printing path on the active layer in your document. Ruler guides created by dragging out from the rulers become lines when released.

Delete will do exactly as you would expect, removing the selected guide completely from the document.

If you add a path to the Guides layer, the Guides dialog will display the path as one of the guides in the list, and can be modified in the same ways as any other guides.

6] Close this document and return to the MyToys document window.

You do not need to save changes in the Untitled document.

IMPORTING PANTONE PROCESS COLORS

In the previous lesson, you learned that documents that use many colors, and especially those that include photographic artwork, are usually printed with process colors. The Robotz catalog fits this description, so you will specify process colors for this document. In this task, you will import a set of process colors from a color library for accurate results.

In the first step you will create the rectangle at the left side of the page. Then you will fill the rectangle with a PANTONE color.

tip *Since most computer monitors cannot represent color exactly as it will be printed, it's best to choose your colors from a swatch book—a printed book that shows how colors from the PANTONE or other color libraries will look when printed on coated or uncoated papers. (You can purchase these swatch books from a graphic arts supplier.) Then, when you have chosen the colors you want, you can specify them in FreeHand.*

1] Draw a rectangle that begins at the upper-left corner of the bleed area (off of the page) and extends over to the second vertical ruler guide and down to the bottom of the bleed area below the page.

This rectangle should extend off of the top, left side, and bottom of the page. Your rectangle should be similar to the selected one shown here extending off of the left edge of the page.

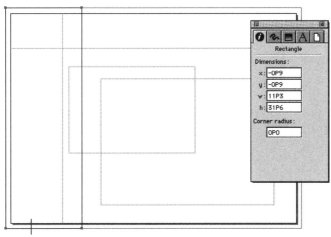

CREATE THIS RECTANGLE

tip *When setting up a bleed, you must do two things. First you need to specify the desired bleed size in the Document Inspector. (Your commercial printer can tell you the size of bleed you need.) Then make sure all elements you create that should run off the edge of the page also extend out to or beyond the edge of the bleed.*

2] Display the Color List by clicking the Color List button on the toolbar. Choose PANTONE Process from the Options menu at the top of the panel.

The PANTONE Process color library dialog box appears, from which you will select two colors to be imported.

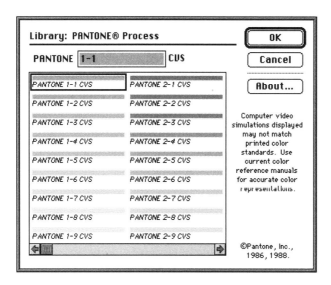

3] In the field at the top, enter *140–5*. Hold down the Ctrl key (Windows) or Command key (Macintosh) and click 140-6 (the color directly below the original selection). Click OK to import both colors.

The two new colors now appear at the bottom of the Color List.

4] Select the rectangle on your page with the Pointer tool. Click the Stroke tab in the Inspector panel and set the stroke to None. Click the Fill tab and change the fill to a gradient that goes from white on the left to PANTONE 140–6 on the right.

Notice how the color bleeds off the edge of the page.

STROKE   FILL

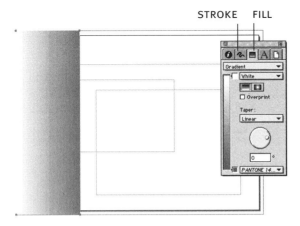

5] Save the document.

CREATING TEXT AND GRAPHIC ELEMENTS

Now you will add the other text and graphic elements that should appear on each page of the catalog.

1] Using the Text tool, click at the top of the page and enter *robotz toy company* (all lowercase). Select all of the text by dragging across the type with the Text tool, and use the controls in the text toolbar to change the text to 12-point News Gothic T Light.
You could also select the text with the Pointer tool to change all of the text in the text block.

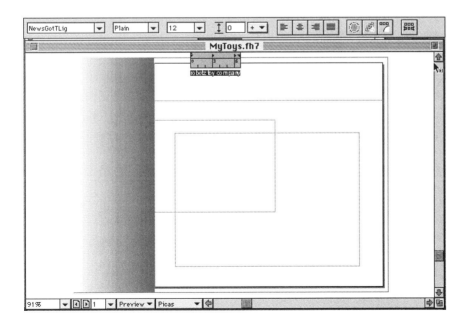

2] Now select the word *robotz* by itself and change it to 48-point News Gothic T Bold.
To change some of the text within a text block, you must use the Text tool to select
the desired characters.

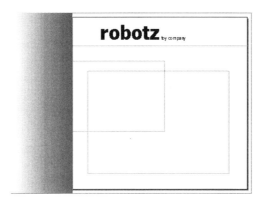

**3] Click on the text with the Pointer tool to select the text block. Position the tip of
the Pointer tool cursor precisely on the bottom edge of the first character in the text.
Hold the mouse button down and drag the cursor toward the ruler guide that runs
across the top of the page. Release the mouse when FreeHand snaps your cursor
and the baseline of the text to the ruler guide.**

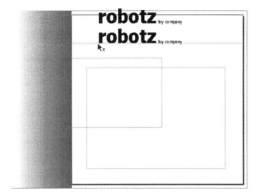

This demonstrates FreeHand's Snap to Guides feature. When an object you are
moving or creating comes within a few pixels of a guide, FreeHand snaps the object
to the guide. You can snap the edges of objects to guides, or you can position your
cursor at a significant location on the object (as you did here in pointing to the
bottom of the text), and FreeHand will snap the object into position when the
cursor nears the guide.

4] Display the Text Inspector by clicking the Text tab at the top of the Inspector panel. Click the Spacing button and change the Horizontal Scale value to 130 percent.

Horizontal Scale adjusts the width of the characters without changing the height. Entering a value greater than 100 percent (the original font width) expands the characters. Entering a value less than 100 percent compresses the characters.

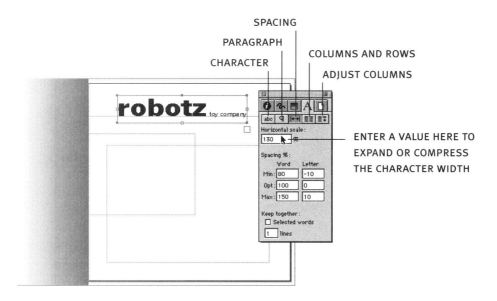

5] Click the Character button in the Text Inspector and change Range Kerning to 12 percent.

Kerning changes the spacing between individual characters, without changing the shapes of the letters. Entering a positive value increases the letterspacing; entering a negative value reduces the spacing between characters. Entering zero for range kerning restores the original letterspacing defined by the font.

Notice that no font or size is identified in the Inspector. When the Text Inspector (and text toolbar) do not display a font or size for a selected block of text, the text block contains more than one font or size.

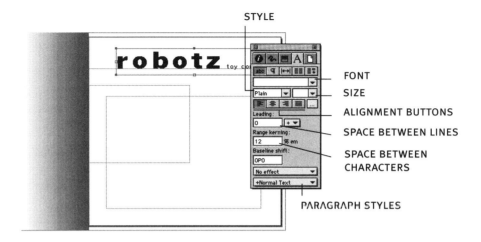

6] To slide the text left or right without moving it up or down off of the ruler guide, start to move the text block with the Pointer tool. Then hold down the Shift key as you continue to move left or right, and position the text so that the first two letters are over the filled rectangle on the left.

Holding down the Shift key constrains the movement to horizontal, vertical, or 45-degree angles, determined by the direction your mouse travels the farthest.

7] Change those first two letters to white by selecting them with the Text tool and then dragging the white color swatch from the Color List onto the selected characters. Save your document.

Always select text with the Text tool when you want to change some of the characters in the text block without changing others.

The text is now complete.

8] Save your work.

Now you will add a rectangle below the text. To view the ruler guides that you placed on the left part of the page, you will first change the view so you can see the artwork without the fills and strokes.

9] Use the View menu at the bottom of the document window to change the view from Preview to Keyline (Windows Ctrl+K, Macintosh Command+K). Draw a wide, short rectangle just beneath the text that begins at the left ruler guide at the far left and extends almost to the right edge of the page.

Keyline displays the elements without fills and strokes, which allows you to see through the rectangle to find the ruler guide.

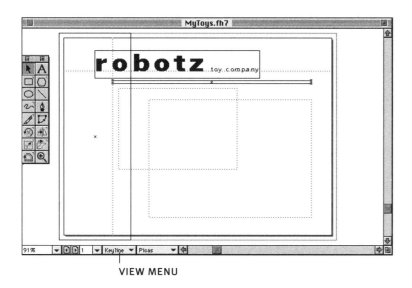

VIEW MENU

10] Fill this rectangle with a gradient that goes from PANTONE 140–6 on the left to white on the right and set the stroke to None. Change the view from Keyline back to Preview so you can see the filled artwork.

Keyline view provides an excellent way to see through elements while you work. Don't forget to turn Preview back on when you want to see the fills and strokes.

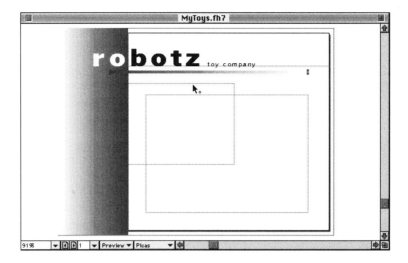

Next you will create a duplicate of this element and position it at the bottom of the page.

11] Choose Edit › Clone to create a copy of this rectangle directly on top of the original. Begin to move this copy downward with the Pointer tool and hold down the Shift key after you have started to move the object. Position the rectangle just above the bottom of the page.

Again holding the Shift key constrains the movement of the element.

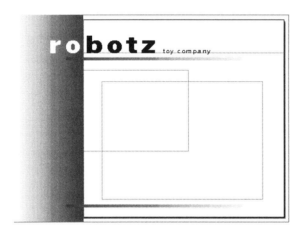

12] Save the document.

Now there is just one more element to add before you duplicate the page.

ATTACHING TEXT TO PATHS

In this task you will attach text to a spiral path, so it follows the path as it circles outward from the center. Text in FreeHand can be attached to open or closed paths.

1] Choose Window › Xtras › Xtra Tools to display the Xtra Tools panel.

This panel contains additional drawing, manipulation, and special effect tools. Xtras are plug-in software extensions that enhance FreeHand's capabilities. Each Xtra adds a specific feature or group of features; Xtras providing additional tools are located in the Xtra Tools panel.

A wide variety of Xtras are included with FreeHand and are installed when you install the program.

2] Double-click on the Spiral tool to set preferences for this tool before you use it to create a path. Click the Loose Spiral button to select the spiral type, specify 3 rotations, click the Clockwise Direction button, and click OK.

Remember that all tools displaying a small mark at the upper-right corner have preferences you can set by double-clicking the tool.

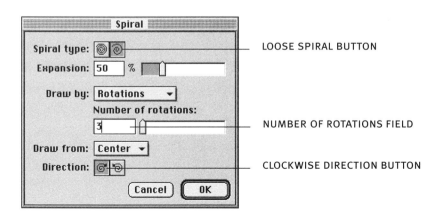

3] Position the cursor, hold the mouse button down and drag upward to draw this spiral.

Release the mouse when the size and orientation is similar to the example shown here.

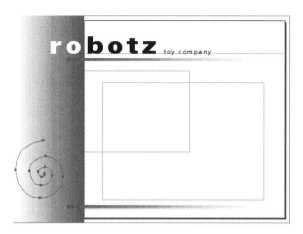

4] Choose Text › Attach to Path to enter text along this path. Change the type size to 9 points and the font to News Gothic T Medium.

A blinking insertion point appears near the center of the spiral.

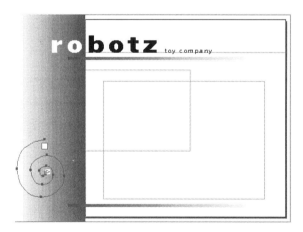

5] Enter *the robotz toy company pledges to always deliver quality, safety, and value in each of its toys.* **Select the word** *robotz* **by itself with the text tool and change it to News Gothic T Bold.**

The words wrap around the spiral as you enter the text directly onto the path.

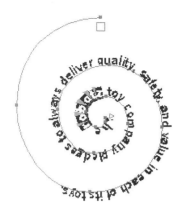

6] Select the text on the spiral with the Pointer tool and drag the small triangle at the center of the spiral to reposition the start of the text out from the center to make the text easier to read. Enter 12 in the Range Kerning field in the Text Inspector to extend the text to fill the spiral.

Make sure that the text all fits on the spiral. If the Link box at the outside end of the spiral is filled with a black dot, there is an overflow—some of the text does not fit and is not displayed. If a black dot appears, reduce the Range Kerning or Horizontal Scale values as needed so the entire sentence appears. Remember, range kerning increases or decreases the space between letters, horizontal scaling changes the width of the letters themselves.

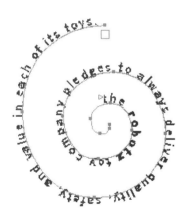

7] Display the Color List and click the Fill Selector at the top of the panel. Select PANTONE 140–5 to change the fill of the text characters.

Alternatively, you can drag the swatch for PANTONE 140–5 and drop it on the spiral text, but you may want to zoom in to see the text more clearly before attempting to drop a color on it.

Remember, if something goes wrong—for instance, if the spiral fills in with color instead of the text—you can just choose Edit > Undo (Windows Ctrl+Z, Macintosh Command+Z).

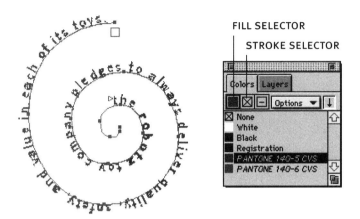

FILL SELECTOR

STROKE SELECTOR

8] Use the Pointer tool to move the spiral into position on the lower portion of the rectangle. Save the document.

tip *Change to the Keyline view to make sure that the entire spiral text element is positioned on the page. Then return to Preview to continue.*

The common elements for all pages are now in place.

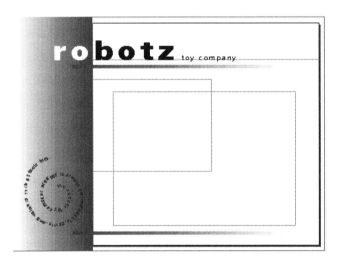

DUPLICATING PAGES IN A DOCUMENT

The basic design you just created will serve as a master for all the pages of the catalog. You will now create two additional pages that look just like the one you have been working on.

1] Display the Document Inspector and choose Duplicate from the Options menu at the top of the panel. This creates a second page just like the first.

The Document Inspector now displays two numbered icons, or **thumbnails,** that represent document pages on the pasteboard.

FreeHand supports multiple-page documents—it even allows you to add pages with different dimensions and orientations as needed for your specific projects. In this case, you want the three pages identical to the one you just created.

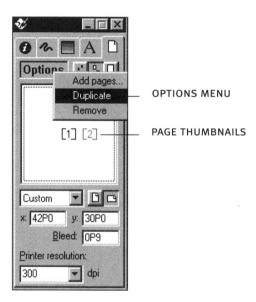

OPTIONS MENU

PAGE THUMBNAILS

2] Repeat the Duplicate command to create a third page. Save the document.

The Document Inspector now displays three numbered page thumbnails on the pasteboard.

3] Click the right Thumbnail Magnification button to see one page displayed in the page thumbnail preview in the Document Inspector. Then click the middle Thumbnail Magnification button to see several page thumbnails in the preview (which displays all three of the pages in this document).

The left Thumbnail Magnification button will display tiny thumbnails showing where the pages are positioned on the pasteboard.

This display shows you how the pages are arranged on the pasteboard. If the new pages appear to the right of page 1 in the Inspector, that is where they are located in the document window.

THUMBNAIL MAGNIFICATION BUTTONS

4] Double-click the thumbnail for page 2 in the Document Inspector.

The Inspector indicates the active page with a black outline and page number. The number of the current page is also displayed at the bottom of the window in the Page Selector field.

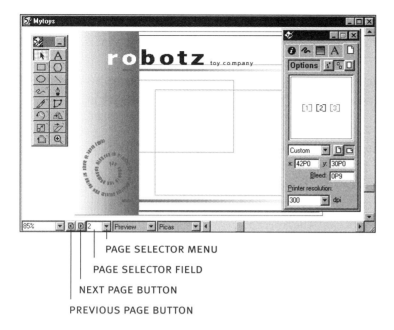

PAGE SELECTOR MENU

PAGE SELECTOR FIELD

NEXT PAGE BUTTON

PREVIOUS PAGE BUTTON

5] Change to page 1 by selecting it from the Page Selector menu at the bottom of the Document window.

You can also change pages by clicking the Previous Page and Next Page buttons. As you can see, you can change pages in several different ways.

6] Save your work.

Make sure that the Page Selector field and Document Inspector thumbnails indicate that you are on page 1 before you continue.

IMPORTING TEXT AND LINKING TEXT BLOCKS

The text for this project has already been entered into a word processor and saved as a Rich Text Format (RTF) file. FreeHand can import RTF files, which retain text formatting characteristics, and ASCII text files, which do not retain any formatting.

In this task, you will import the text into your layout. Then the text will be continued on the other pages by linking text blocks together, allowing the text to flow from one text block to another.

The text will be flowed into text blocks that will duplicate the size and position of the large rectangular guide you positioned on the page earlier.

1] Choose File › Import, locate Robotz.rtf in the Media folder within the folder for Lesson 5, and click Open. Position the import cursor at the upper-left corner of the large rectangular guide, drag down to the bottom-right corner of this rectangle and release the mouse button.

Formatted text flows into this text block. RTF files contain both text and formatting.

The text will not look like the finished layout yet—some of the text is not formatted properly, and this page contains more text than you need for page 1.

Notice that there is a black dot in the Link box, the small square near the bottom corner of the text block. This indicates an overflow—there is more text than will fit within the current text box.

Before you can flow the remaining text onto the other pages, you must first create a text block for the text to flow into on each of those pages.

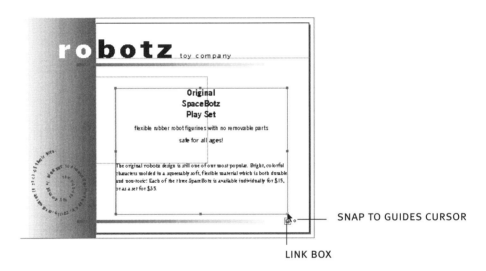

SNAP TO GUIDES CURSOR

LINK BOX

2] Change to page 2. Use the Text tool to create a text block the same size and position as the large rectangular guide. Then change to page 3 and create a new text block in the same position on this page. Save your work.

Now each page has a text container, so you are ready to link the text blocks together.

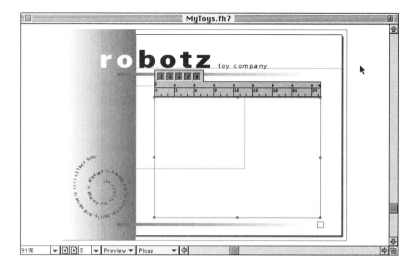

3] Choose View › Fit All. Close any panels that interfere with your view of the pages (except the toolbox).

This reduces the view so you can see all of the pages within your document. This will help in the next step, where you will link text from page 1 to the text blocks on the other two pages.

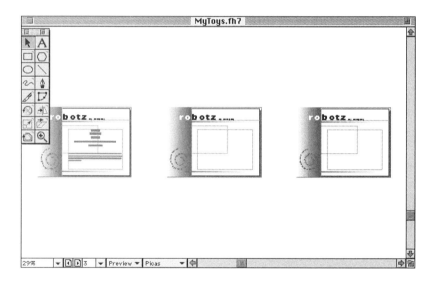

4] Select the text block on page 1 with the Pointer tool to see the Link box with its black dot indicating an overflow. Point to the Link box and drag a link line to the inside of the empty text block on page 2.

The text will flow into the text block on page 2, and the Link box for this text block will also indicate an overflow.

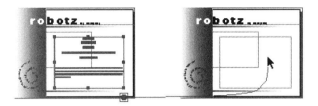

5] Repeat this process for page 3 by dragging a link line from the Link box on page 2 into the empty text block on page 3.

The text is now linked across all three pages. All of the text fits.

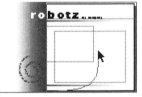

6] Select the text block on page 1 and choose View › Magnification › 100%.

FreeHand centers the selected elements on screen when you change magnification, so you now see the text block on page 1.

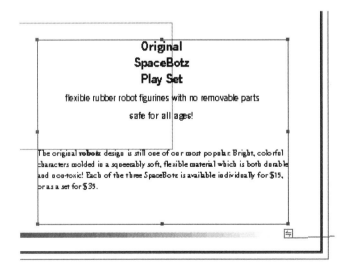

7] Save your work.

WORKING WITH PARAGRAPH STYLES

In the previous lesson, you used object styles to apply preset fill and stroke attributes to multiple objects. Paragraph styles can provide similar benefits for text.

1] Choose Window > Panels > Styles to display the Styles panel. Select the title at the beginning of the text ("Original SpaceBotz Play Set") with the Text tool. This was imported as 16-point News Gothic T Demi. To create a style based on the selected text, choose New from the Options menu at the top of the Styles panel.
A new paragraph style named Style-1 appears in the panel. Paragraph styles can record text formatting information, including font, size, alignment, color, and leading, that you can apply to paragraphs elsewhere in the document.

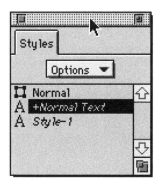

2] Double-click Style-1 and enter a new name, *Title*.
The style has automatically picked up the formatting of the selected text, and that text now is linked to this style.

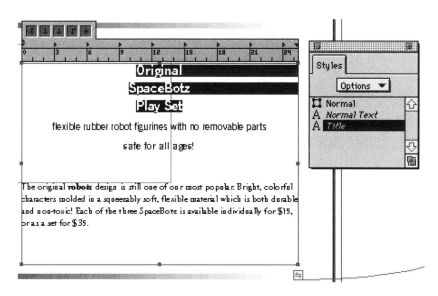

**3] Using the Text tool, double-click on the word *flexible* in the second paragraph
to select that word. Create another new style and name it *Subhead 1*.**

Styles apply to entire paragraphs. By selecting a portion of a paragraph when creating
a style, you have recorded the characteristics of that text and assigned that new style
to the entire paragraph to which the selected text belongs.

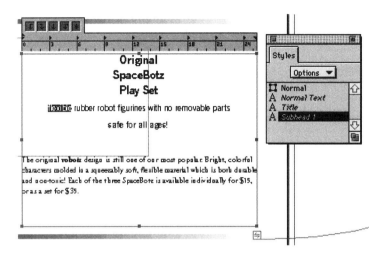

**4] Use the Text tool to select all of the text in the third paragraph (*Safe for all
ages!*). Change the color of this text to PANTONE 140-6. Then create a new style
and name it *Subhead 2*.**

Paragraph styles record the color of the text also.

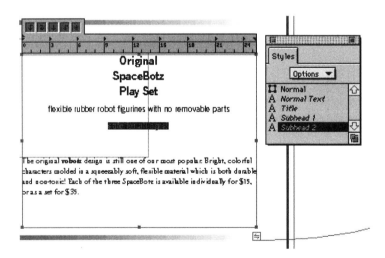

The last remaining new style you need is for the description. However, suppose you select the word *original* in the first line of the description paragraph. This text is 10 point URW Garamond Regular—but the word *robotz* and the two prices in this description are the Demi version of the same font. Styles apply to entire paragraphs, so you will make a style for the Regular text and then manually apply the Demi weight of the font to those select words within the paragraph that require it.

5] Select the word *original,* create a new style, and name it *Body.*

When you create a new style, it sets the characteristics of the style to those of the first character selected. Assigning this new style to the paragraph eliminated the bolder words from the paragraph.

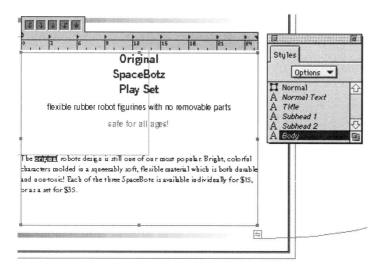

6] Select the word *robotz* and change it to URW Garamond Demi. Repeat this process for the two prices.

Local formatting of individual characters within a paragraph must be performed manually, one selection at a time—there is no way to select separate portions of the text at the same time. When local formatting has been applied to selected text, the Styles panel displays a plus sign next to the style name, to indicate that this text no longer exactly matches the style characteristics.

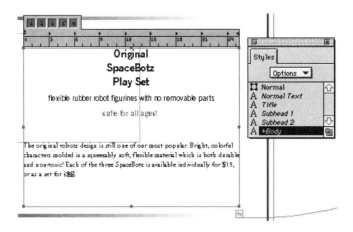

7] Save your work.

The four styles you need are now defined, so now you can apply them throughout the remaining text.

8] Go to page 2 and select any characters in the name of the next product ("Master TerraBotz Action Figures"). Click Title once in the Styles panel to apply the Title formatting.

The font, size, and alignment applied to the paragraph containing the selected text match those defined for the Title paragraph style.

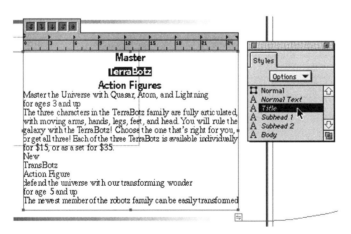

Styles apply to entire paragraphs, even though you may have selected only one word within the paragraph.

9] Select one word of the next paragraph and apply the Subhead 1 style. Select the third paragraph and apply the Subhead 2 style. Then select a word in the description paragraph and apply the Body style.

As you work through the rest of the document applying styles, don't worry about text that appears on the wrong pages. When the graphics are added, the text will flow differently.

10] Apply local formatting by changing the word *robotz* and the prices to URW Garamond Demi wherever they appear in the description.

The TerraBotz description has two prices that should be set to URW Garamond Demi.

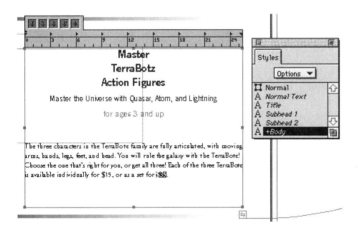

11] Select a word in the name of the last product ("TransBotz") and apply the Title style. Repeat steps 9 and 10 to format the remaining text.

The TransBotz description has *robotz* in the first and fourth lines and a price at the end which should be changed to URW Garamond Demi.

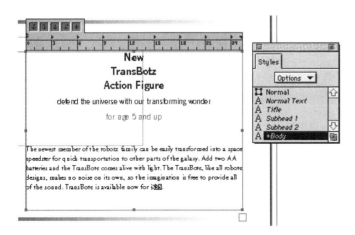

12] Select the Pointer tool and click an empty part of the pasteboard to deselect all elements. Return to view page 1 and save your work.

The text is completely formatted, but it will not fit the pages properly until you add the graphics.

tip *You have used the Tab key to deselect elements as you work. Be careful not to press the Tab key when text blocks are being edited, or FreeHand will enter a Tab character in the text instead of deselecting the element.*

IMPORTING IMAGES

The images you will import into this document were modeled and rendered in Extreme 3D and composited with background images in xRes. This is an example of how the FreeHand Graphics Studio applications can be used together on your projects.

1] Change to the Keyline view.

This allows you to see the small rectangular guide on the page, where the image should be positioned.

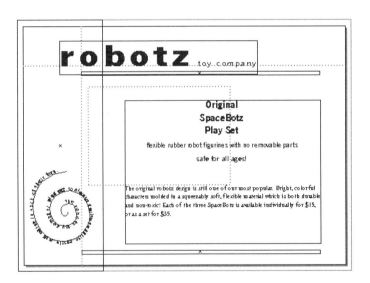

2] Choose File > Import, locate Robotz1.tif in the Media folder within the Lesson05 folder, and click Open. Position the import cursor at the upper-left corner of the small rectangular guide and click once to put the graphic onto the page.

The graphic is displayed in the Keyline view as a rectangle with an X inside it. You have to change to Preview to see the image itself.

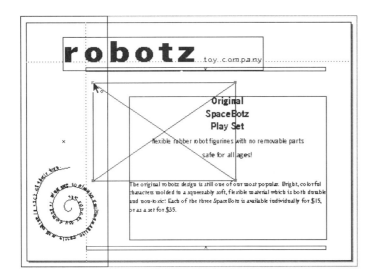

tip   *When importing graphics, always just click to put the image on the page, rather than dragging the import cursor as you do to define a text area when importing text. Clicking once will put the image on the page with its original size and proportions. If you drag the cursor, you will distort the graphic to fit between the points on the page where you start and stop dragging.*

3] Change to Preview so you can see the image as it appears on the page.

The image appears on the page, overlapping the text.

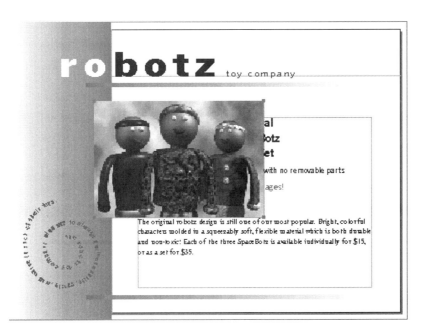

4] Switch to page 2 and repeat steps 1 to 3 to import the Robotz2.tif image.

5] Repeat steps 1 through 3 to position the Robotz3.tif image on page 3.

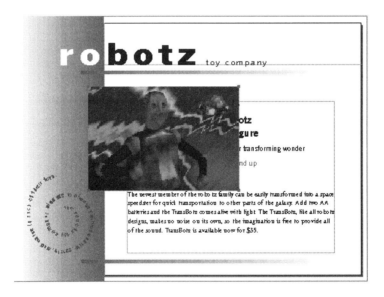

All three images are in the correct position on their respective pages. However, the images overlap the text on all three pages, and the text does not fit on the correct pages throughout the document. You will fix this in the next task.

6] Return to page 1 and save your work.

WRAPPING TEXT AROUND GRAPHICS

FreeHand can easily run text around graphics. You will use this capability to fit the images into the layout without overlapping the text.

1] Select the image on page 1 and choose Text › Run Around Selection. Assign a text wrap to the selected image by clicking the button at the top right of the dialog box. Specify a space of 6 points along the right and bottom edges of the image.

Since your document is set to measure in Picas, you must enter *0P6* in order to specify 6 points. If you just enter *6* with no units, FreeHand will set the **standoff**, or space between the text and the graphic, to 6 picas (6 picas equals 1 inch).

The left and top standoff values can remain at zero, since text will not be touching the image along those edges in this layout.

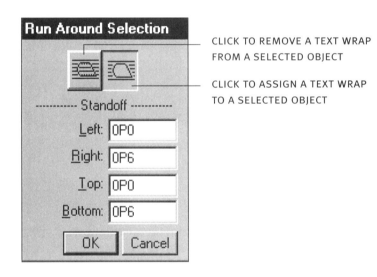

CLICK TO REMOVE A TEXT WRAP
FROM A SELECTED OBJECT

CLICK TO ASSIGN A TEXT WRAP
TO A SELECTED OBJECT

2] Click OK in the Run Around Selection dialog box (or press Enter).

The text now flows around the graphic, with a small space between the graphic and the text along the image's right and bottom edges.

If your text stays about an inch away from the right and bottom edges of the graphic, go back to the Run Around Selection dialog and enter *0P6* (that is, 6 points instead of 6 picas).

If the text does not wrap around the image at all, choose Modify > Arrange > Bring To Front—graphics must be in front of text for this feature to work.

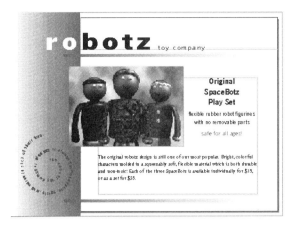

The text should wrap around the image and the entire description should fit on this page. (The descriptions on each page end with the words *for $35.*)

No text below this paragraph should appear on page 1. If text does appear below this point, you will need to adjust the size of this text block. (If the text fits properly on this page, skip to step 4.)

3] If the name of the next toy appears at the bottom of page 1, use the Pointer tool to drag the bottom-corner handle of the text block up slightly so the next toy's name no longer fits in this block.

You must drag a *corner* handle to make this adjustment. Dragging the bottom-middle handle of the text block adjusts the leading for the text block, but will not change the amount of text that the block contains.

When you make this text block shorter, the text that no longer appears in this block is automatically pushed to the top of the text block on the next page, where it belongs. Once the text on this page fits as it should, you are ready to go to the next page.

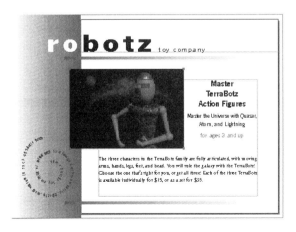

4] Repeat Steps 1 through 3 for pages 2 and 3.

The text should now flow around the graphics on each page as desired.

5] Return to page 1 and save your work.

There is one last task remaining before you complete your work on this layout.

ADDING COLORS FROM BITMAP IMAGES TO THE COLOR LIST

Another exciting Xtra tool allows you to copy a color from any element in the document, including colors within a bitmap image. You can then use that color elsewhere within your document.

1] Display the Xtra Tools panel by choosing Window › Xtras › Xtra Tools. Select the Eyedropper tool. Then display the Color List.

You will pick up a color from the robot illustration on this page and use that color for the name of this toy. This will tie the text and illustration together nicely.

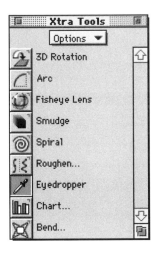

2] Position the tool over a bright blue color in the image and drag the color swatch into the Color List.

Your color is added to the list, so you can use it for other elements in your document. It is defined in this list by its CMYK values since the image is a CMYK tiff file.

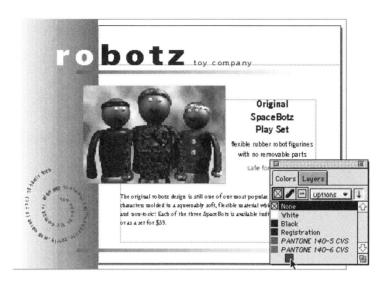

3] With the Text tool, select the name of the toy on page 1, "SpaceBotz." Drag the color swatch for your new color from the Color List and drop it on the selected text. Switch back to the Pointer tool to see the results.

That individual word now appears in the color that you picked up from the image.

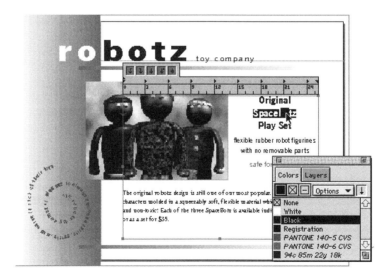

4] Go to page 2 and add a bright red color from the page 2 image to the Color List. Apply that color to the name on this page, "TerraBotz." Repeat this process for page 3, applying a color of your choice from the image on page 3 to the name "TransBotz."

The three new colors are displayed in the Color List.

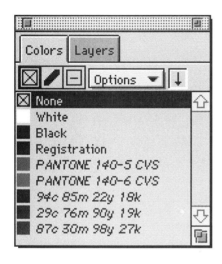

5] Change back to page 1 and save your work.

The layout is now complete.

PRINTING YOUR DOCUMENT

Now it is time to output your work. FreeHand is designed to take full advantage of PostScript printers and high-resolution output devices, which are the standard for desktop publishing and the graphic arts community. However, FreeHand can print to other types of printers as well. If you are printing to a non-PostScript printer, the options displayed in the Print dialog box will vary depending upon the type of printer selected.

If your system is configured to print to a PostScript printer or a high-resolution output device, FreeHand offers several special capabilities when it comes time to print. The steps in this task illustrate the options available for PostScript printers.

1] Choose File › Print to display the Print dialog box.

If your system is not configured to print to a PostScript output device, the dialog box will be different than the example shown here.

A variety of controls enables you to set the most common printing options within this dialog box. The Print setting menu provides quick access to preset or custom print setup configurations.

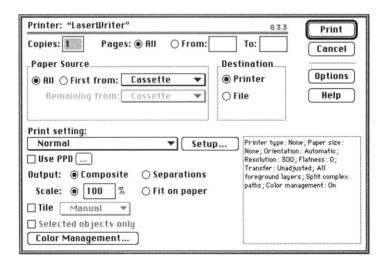

2] Click the Setup button to display the Print Setup dialog box.

Print Setup enables you to customize settings for this print job or specify print settings you can use on future print jobs. The preview on the left shows how the document will print on the page with the current settings. At the right, three tabbed panels allow control over printing separations, imaging options, and paper size and orientation. At the top left, the current Print Setting file is displayed.

You can save your print settings in a settings file that then becomes available from a menu in the Print dialog box. You record custom settings by clicking the Save Settings button at the top left of the Print Setup dialog box.

The Print Setup dialog box has three tabbed sections. The first one you see, Separations, controls how your printer will print the colors in your document—as a **composite** print, with all the colors printing on the same page, or as **separations**, with each color printing on a different sheet. (This is the setting used by printers to create separate printing plates for each color.) A commercial printer can advise you how to use the other settings in this dialog box when you need output for a printing press.

tip *Print settings can also be shared easily with other users. Each of the settings files are saved in a folder called PrintSet installed with FreeHand. Simply copy the specific settings files into the PrintSet folder on another workstation to make them available on that system.*

SAVE SETTINGS BUTTON

CONTROLS SETTINGS FOR COLOR OUTPUT

CONTROLS FOR PAPER SIZE AND ORIENTATION

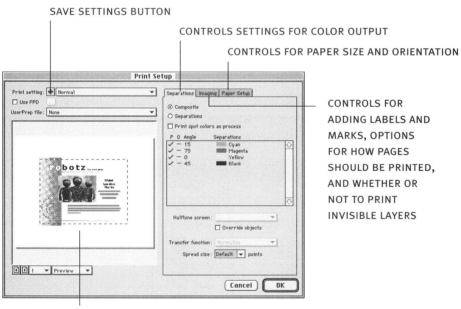

CONTROLS FOR ADDING LABELS AND MARKS, OPTIONS FOR HOW PAGES SHOULD BE PRINTED, AND WHETHER OR NOT TO PRINT INVISIBLE LAYERS

PREVIEW OF THE DOCUMENT PRINTED WITH CURRENT SETTINGS

3] Click the Imaging tab on the right and turn on Crop Marks.
Crop marks indicate the edges of your page. (They will only print if your document's page size is smaller than the paper size, as it is here.)

Imaging also contains an option that allows you to choose whether to print invisible (hidden) layers or not. There are no hidden layers in this document, so it does not make any difference in this case.

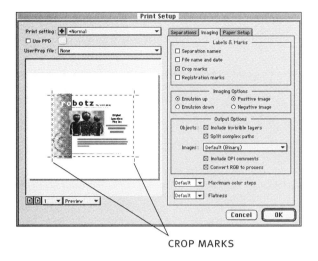

CROP MARKS

4] Select Paper Setup.

FreeHand can automatically determine the orientation of the paper in many situations. This option enables FreeHand to determine the optimum orientation depending upon the size of the pages in your document, the output device, and the paper size identified.

To select from among other paper sizes that your specific printer may offer, click the Use PPD button at the upper left and select the PostScript Printer Description file for your printer. These PPDs contain optimized print settings for specific PostScript printers. You will achieve the best printing results when you use PPD information, and FreeHand will be able to support the full range of features and paper sizes your printer offers.

CHECK THIS BOX AND CHOOSE A PRINTER DESCRIPTION FILE FOR YOUR
PRINTER TO ACCESS ANY SPECIAL OPTIONS YOUR PRINTER OFFERS

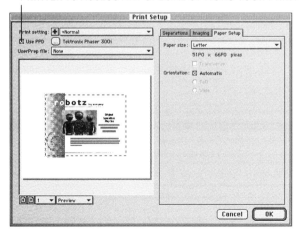

5] Click OK to return to the print dialog box. If you want to print at this time, click the Print button. If not, click Cancel.

Remember that this is a multiple-page document, so you have the choice of printing the entire document or just specific pages.

6] Save your work.

You have now completed the three-page catalog.

WHAT YOU HAVE LEARNED

In this lesson you have:

Specified document measurements in alternate units [*page* **178**]

Set printer resolution for gradient fills [*page* **179**]

Created custom, nonprinting guides for a document layout [*page* **180**]

Practiced importing PANTONE process colors [*page* **187**]

Used Snap to Guides to exactly position elements [*page* **190**]

Used FreeHand's kerning and scaling controls to manipulate text [*page* **191**]

Attached and repositioned text on a path [*page* **195**]

Duplicated pages in a document [*page* **199**]

Imported RTF text into your layout [*page* **201**]

Linked text from one text block to another [*page* **203**]

Formatted text with paragraph styles [*page* **205**]

Used the View menu to see the document in Keyline view [*page* **210**]

Practiced importing bitmap images [*page* **210**]

Assigned the Run Around feature to graphics [*page* **213**]

Copied colors from imported images with the Eyedropper tool [*page* **215**]

Made adjustments to the Printer Setup settings for PostScript printing [*page* **218**]

techniques

advanced FreeHand

FreeHand provides many advanced features that enable you to produce rich illustrations such as the artwork for Lighthouse Publishing that you will create in this lesson. In creating this drawing, you will import files, including a 3D image, from different sources and work with graphics on multiple foreground layers. You will use one of FreeHand's special effects—transparency—and blend multiple shapes.

To create the logo for Lighthouse Publishing, you will trace a graphic you import from another program and add a three-dimensional graphic. You will also use transparency effects, multiple layers, and blends to achieve the final result.

Designed by Julia Sifers of Glasgow & Associates and Craig Faist and Tom Faist of Datrix Media Group.

LESSON 6

WHAT YOU WILL LEARN

In this lesson you will:

Import graphics created in other programs

Trace an imported graphic

Work with multiple foreground layers

Use a transparency effect

Create blends between multiple shapes

APPROXIMATE TIME

It usually takes about 2 hours to complete this lesson.

LESSON FILES

Media Files:

Lesson06\Media\Sky.jpg

Lesson06\Media\Beacon1.fh7

Starting Files:

Lesson06\Start\Water.ft7

Lesson06\Start\Ground.ft7

Completed Project:

Lesson06\Complete\Beacon2.fh7

CREATING A NEW CUSTOM-SIZE DOCUMENT

You will begin working on the artwork for the lighthouse illustration in a new document. You'll need to create a special page size for this project.

1] Create a new document by choosing File > New (Windows Ctrl+N, Macintosh Command+N).

A blank page appears, which you will now adjust so that the page size matches the size you need for this illustration.

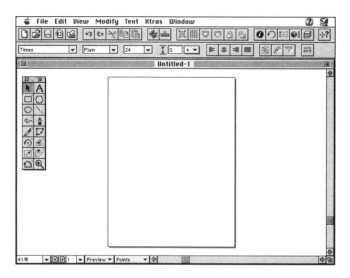

2] Change the unit of measure to Inches using the Units menu at the bottom of the screen. Choose Window > Inspectors > Document to display the Document Inspector.

The Document Inspector shows the current page dimensions and orientation.

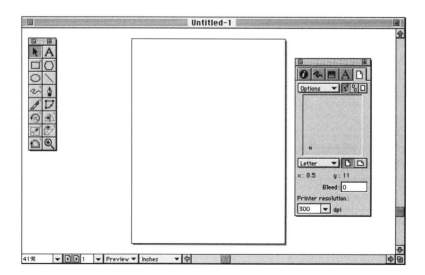

3] In the Document Inspector, change the page size from Letter to Custom, enter the dimensions 7.25 by 6 inches, and click the Landscape orientation icon.

Your page is now the correct size, but it appears small in the document window.

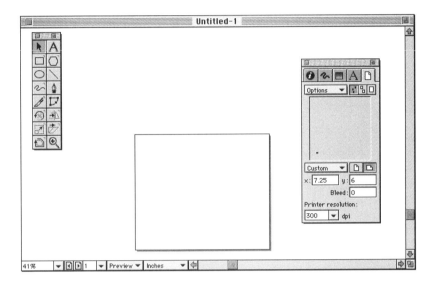

4] Close the Document Inspector and choose View › Fit to Page (Windows Ctrl+Shift+W, Macintosh Command+Shift+W). Save the document as *MyBeacon* in your MyWork folder.

The page is now ready for you to begin the illustration.

IMPORTING AND TRACING AN IMAGE

In this section you will import a JPEG image of the sky created in Adobe Photoshop as a tracing pattern. JPEG (one of the many graphic formats FreeHand can import) is a file format for compressing bitmap images so they take up less room on the disk while retaining nearly the same image quality as an uncompressed file.

You have already learned to trace patterns manually with the Bezigon and Pen tools. Here, you will use the Trace tool to do it automatically.

1] Choose File › Import (Windows Ctrl+R, Macintosh Command+R). Select Sky.jpg from the Media folder within the folder for Lesson 6 and click Open (or press Enter). Position the cursor on the page and click the mouse.

The sky image appears on the page. You will position it next.

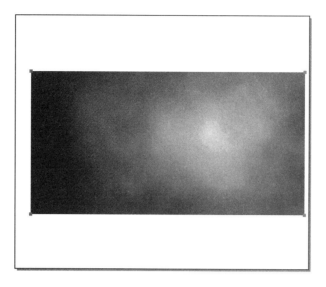

2] To position the sky image accurately, display the Object Inspector. Enter an *x* dimension of *0.25* inch and a *y* dimension of *2.35* inches.

This will position the artwork so there is a 0.25-inch border on the left and right sides of this image. The *x* and *y* coordinates define the position of the lower left corner of the selected object.

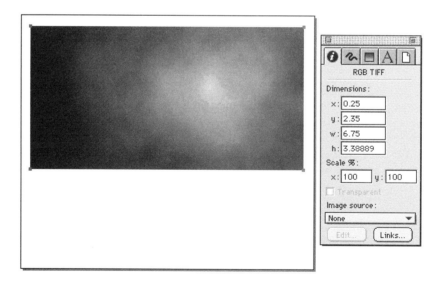

3] Deselect the sky image by either using the Tab key on the keyboard or clicking with the Pointer tool in any empty area of the page.

You must not have anything selected when you create a new layer in the next step, or you may accidentally move the selected artwork to the new layer.

4] Create a new layer by choosing New from the Options menu in the Layers panel. Double-click the name for the new layer, Layer-1, and enter *Sky* as the new name for this layer. Press Enter to complete the name change.

The Sky layer is a foreground (printing) layer since it appears above the separator line in the Layers panel. This new layer is now the active layer, so the artwork you will create next will be added to this layer.

5] Select the Trace tool in the toolbox. To change the settings for this tool, double-click the Trace tool. Verify that the Trace tool has the settings pictured here. (These are the default settings for the tool.)

The default settings for the Trace tool provide good results when tracing bitmap and vector graphics. You will apply the Trace tool to the sky image to create editable shapes that look like that image.

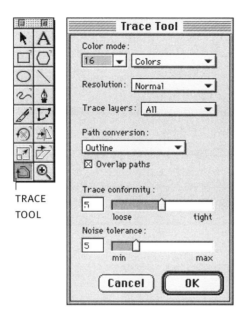

TRACE
TOOL

tip *For information on options for this tool, consult the Using FreeHand manual that is included with FreeHand Graphics Studio software.*

6] Use the Trace tool crosshair cursor to drag a selection area around the sky image.

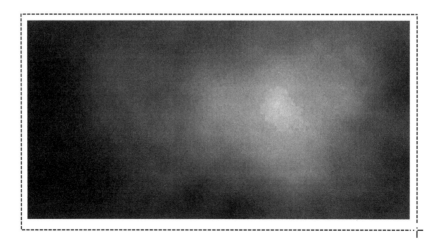

The part of the image you select—in this case, the entire image—will be traced when you release the mouse. (It may take a few moments for the tracing process to be completed.) The result is a series of paths that traced the shapes in the image, dividing it into 16 colors (as specified by the Color Mode setting in the tool preferences dialog box). These new paths appear on the Sky layer since it was the active layer when you used this tool.

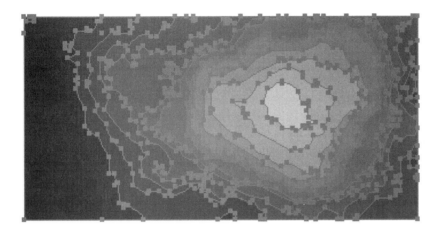

tip *Using multiple layers is helpful when using the Trace tool. Place the image to be traced on a layer by itself and then activate a different layer when using the Trace tool. This will place the results of the Trace tool on a separate layer. By doing this, you can now easily access both the original image and the editable shapes. (To delete the original image, you simply delete the layer the original image is on.)*

7] With the results of the Trace tool still selected, choose Modify › Group.
This makes all the resulting shapes into one single grouped element. You can now more easily use the sky image shapes in your drawing.

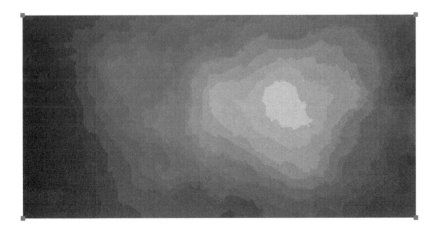

8] Deselect the grouped element by pressing the Tab key. To remove the original sky image, activate the Foreground layer in the Layers panel and choose Remove from the Options menu in the Layers panel.

This will remove the original sky image and the layer named Foreground from the illustration since they are no longer needed.

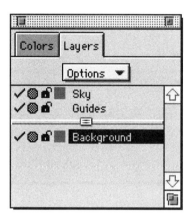

9] Save your work.

ADDING A 3D IMAGE AND A TRANSPARENCY EFFECT

Now you will import another image: a lighthouse that was created in Extreme 3D. You will then add the beam of light and create a transparency effect using the beam and text.

1] Create a new layer by choosing New from the Options menu in the Layers panel. Double-click the name for the new layer, Layer-1, and enter *Lighthouse* as the new name for this layer. Press Enter to complete the name change.

This will create the layer that will contain the imported lighthouse graphic.

2] To import the lighthouse graphic, choose File › Import. Select Beacon1.fh7 from the Media folder within the folder for Lesson 6 and click Open (or press Enter). Position the cursor anywhere on the page and click the mouse.

The three-dimensional lighthouse graphic you just imported was created in Extreme 3D and pasted inside a path in FreeHand to remove the background. The path and image were then grouped together and were imported as a group into your document. This will be a printing element in your illustration.

3] To position the lighthouse image accurately, display the Object Inspector. Set the *x* dimension to 5 inches and the *y* dimension to 1.1 inches.

The placement of the lighthouse is important because the beam of light that will be created depends on the position of this graphic.

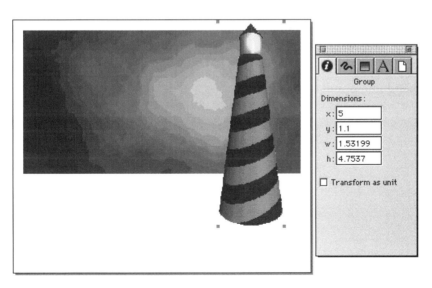

4] Using the Bezigon or Pen tool, draw the beam of light. All points used will be corner points. Make sure that the resulting closed path goes into the lighthouse light and continues off the page at the left.

The actual placement of points is not critical; the picture shows the approximate placement.

The width of the resulting beam of light can vary; its dimensions are not critical. What is important is that this be a closed shape and that it is well into the lighthouse and continues off of the page; otherwise, the transparency effect you will be creating will not work. Currently, this beam is on the Lighthouse layer, but you will move it. First, though, you will sets its fill and stroke.

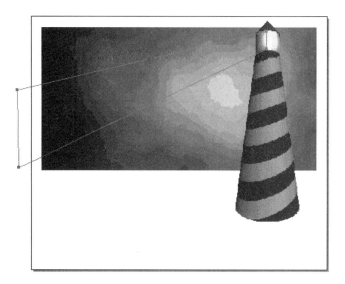

5] With the beam of light still selected, change the fill to white and the stroke to None.

These are the settings required to duplicate the effect used in the original Lighthouse Publishing logo. Use the Color List panel to change the fill and stroke. To display the Color List, choose Window > Panels > Color List.

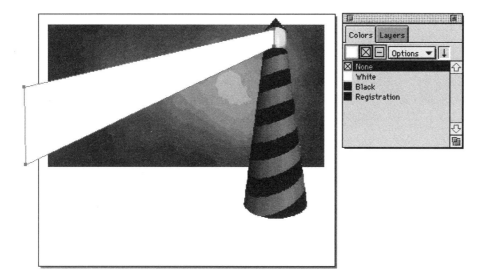

6] With the beam of light still selected, click on the name Sky in the Layers panel.

This will move the beam of light from the Lighthouse layer to the Sky layer.

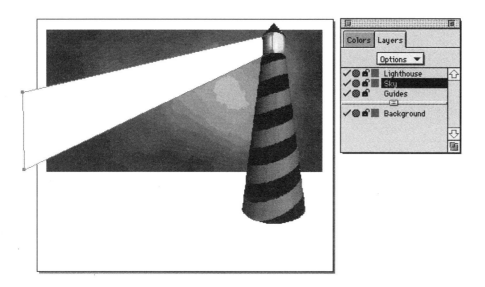

7] Using the Text tool, type *Lighthouse Publishing*. Press Return after the word *Lighthouse*. Still using the Text tool, select all of the text. Using the controls on the text toolbar near the top of your screen, change the font to URWGaramondTMed, with a size of 76 points, a fixed leading of 66 points, and center alignment.

This places the type on the Sky layer. Exact positioning of this text will be done later. The Sky layer now consists of the grouped Sky elements, the beam of light, and the text.

8] Using the Color Mixer panel, click the CMYK button and create a color that is 100 percent yellow and 0 percent cyan, magenta, and black. Add this color to the Color List panel. With the text still selected with the Text tool, change the fill color to 100 percent yellow.

On the screen, the text appears to be blue and not yellow. Why? This is because you have the text highlighted with the Text tool. Once you deselect the text, it will become yellow as the Color List indicates.

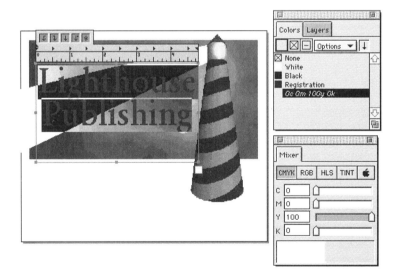

9] Using the Pointer tool, position the text so it is roughly centered between the left edge of the sky and the lighthouse.

Exact positioning is not critical, but use the graphic here for an idea of what you're aiming for.

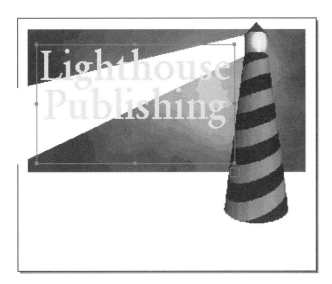

10] With the text still selected, choose Text > Convert To Paths.

The text is now a grouped element that is no longer editable as text.

11] With the text group selected, choose Modify › Arrange › Move Backward.

Choosing Move Backward moves the text so it is in front of the sky but behind the beam of light. If you chose Send to Back, then the type would be incorrectly behind both the sky and the beam of light.

12] Using the Pointer tool, select the beam, the text, and the sky.

To select multiple objects, hold down Shift and click with the Pointer tool.

Now you will create the transparency effect.

13] Choose Xtras > Path Operations > Transparency. Type *25* in the Transparency dialog box and click OK.

The resulting selection is the new paths that were created from the Transparency path operation.

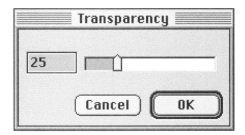

Using Path Operations on existing paths creates new paths. Applying the Transparency path operation creates a new path (or paths) filled with colors that combine those in the original paths, which gives the appearance that the overlapping areas are transparent. Entering a value that is less than 50 in the Transparency dialog box makes the topmost path (in this case, the light) appear more opaque. Values that are greater than 50 make the topmost path appear more transparent. To make the light beam still easily visible, a value of 25 was used.

14] With the Pointer tool, select the original white beam of light. Then press the Delete key.

The original beam of light needs to be deleted so that a white line does not appear above and below the "transparent" areas.

SELECT THE WHITE BEAM
WHERE IT GOES OFF THE PAGE

15] Save your work.

Your drawing should now look like the following illustration.

BLENDING MULTIPLE SHAPES

Your next task is to create the water needed for the illustration. Using a template for assistance, you will blend three shapes.

1] Open the document Water.ft7 from the Start folder within the folder for Lesson 6.

The Water.ft7 document has the three shapes in the background that you will need to trace. You will then blend these three shapes together to create the water.

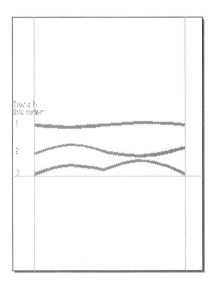

2] With the Zoom tool, zoom in to the left side of the page.

It is important that the closed shapes are traced in the order indicated.

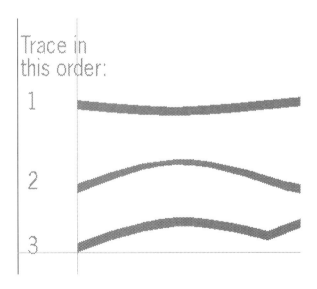

3] Using either the Bezigon or Pen tool, trace the closed shapes in the suggested order, from top to bottom.

Make sure that you end up with three separate closed shapes. You can verify that a shape is closed by checking the information displayed in the Object Inspector. If you get stuck, refer to the illustration for the placement of points.

4] In the Color Mixer, click the CMYK button. You will create two colors that will be added to the Color List. In the Color Mixer, enter the values to create a color that is 80 percent cyan, 70 percent magenta, 0 percent yellow, and 40 percent black. Add this color to the Color List. Then enter the values to create a color that is 90 percent cyan, 80 percent magenta, 50 percent yellow, and 60 percent black. Add this color to the Color List as well.

Two shades of blue have now been added to the Color List.

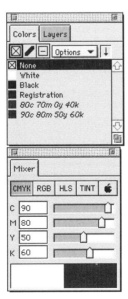

5] With the Pointer tool, select the top two closed shapes and fill them with 80c70m0y40k. Change the stroke to None.

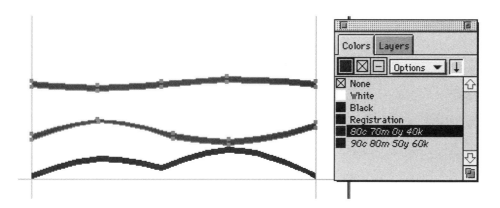

6] With the Pointer tool, select the bottom closed shape and fill it with 90c80m50y60k. Change the stroke to None.

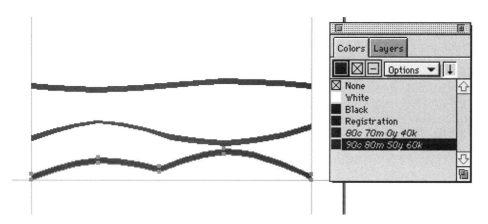

Now blend the three shapes.

**7] With the Pointer tool, select all three closed shapes. Choose Modify ›
Combine › Blend.**

This creates a blend from all three closed shapes. You can also find the Blend
command by choosing Xtras > Create > Blend.

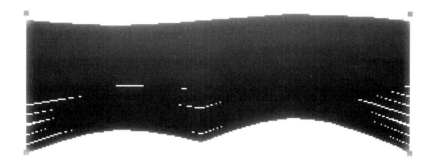

8] In the Object Inspector, change the number of steps for the blend to 100.

By increasing the number of steps, you create a smooth, continuous blend.

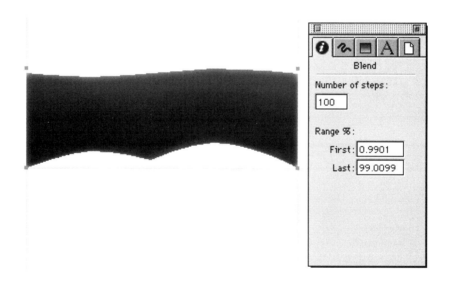

Now copy the blend to your document.

**9] With the Blend selected, choose Edit › Copy. Switch to the MyBeacon document
by choosing Window › MyBeacon. With the MyBeacon document activated, choose
Edit › Paste.**

This copies your completed water blend from the template to the lighthouse illustration. Notice that it also pasted a Foreground layer as the top layer in the Layers panel.

10] Activate the template by choosing Window › Untitled-2. Close this document without saving it.

11] In the MyBeacon document, use the Pointer tool to position the water so it is flush with the left and right edges of the sky. Make sure the top of the water covers the bottom of the sky so that no gap exists between the two. Zoom in to verify your placement.

If you need to nudge the water, remember to use the arrow keys on the keyboard.

12] In the Layers panel, double-click the layer named Foreground. Enter *Water* as the new name for this layer and press Enter to complete the name change. Reorder the layers so the Water layer is beneath the Lighthouse layer.

To reorder the layers, drag a layer name in the Layers panel and drop it above or below another layer name.

tip *Giving your layers descriptive names helps during the organization and editing of an illustration.*

13] Save your work.

Your illustration should now look like the one shown here.

BLENDING SHAPES TO CREATE A REFLECTION

To create the reflection that the lighthouse casts on the water, you will blend two ovals.

1] Activate the Lighthouse layer in the Layers panel. With the Ellipse tool, draw a narrow oval at the base of the lighthouse.

Make sure that the width of the oval does not exceed the width of the base of the lighthouse. The height of the oval should be fairly small.

2] In the Color Mixer panel, click the Tint button. Add 10 percent of the color 0c0m100y0k to the Color List panel. With the oval selected, change its fill color to 10% 0c0m100y0k.

3] **Using the Ellipse tool, draw another extremely small oval in the upper-left portion of the water.**

This second oval should be smaller than the first one. Make sure that this second oval does not overlap into the sky area or off the left edge of the water.

4] **Using the Color List panel, change the fill color of the second oval to 80c70m0y40k.**

The second oval is now the same color as the water that is beneath it.

5] **Using the Pointer tool, select both of the ovals. Choose Modify › Combine › Blend. In the Object Inspector, change the number of steps for the blend to *16*.**

Because you chose the water color for the second oval, the resulting blend gradually fades away.

6] Create a new layer by choosing New from the Options menu in the Layers panel. With the oval blend still selected, double-click the name for the new layer, Layer-1, and enter *Reflection* as the new name for this layer. Press Enter to complete the name change.

This also puts the oval blend onto the Reflection layer. Remember: If an element is selected when you rename a layer, you will not only rename the layer, but you will also move the selected element to that layer.

7] Reorder the layers so that the Reflection layer is beneath the Lighthouse layer and above the Water layer.

This will appropriately place the reflection behind the lighthouse and on top of the water.

8] Save your work.

USING A TEMPLATE TO ADD A SHAPE

You still need to create the ground in front of the lighthouse. You will use a template to help you create this shape.

1] Open the template, *Ground.ft7,* in the Start folder within the folder for Lesson 6.

This template contains in the background the shape needed to create the ground for the illustration.

2] Using the Zoom tool, zoom in on the shape. Using the Bezigon or Pen tool, trace the shape.

Make sure that you end up with a closed shape so it can be filled later. If you get stuck, refer to the picture for the placement of points. Verify in the Object Inspector that you indeed have a closed shape when you are finished tracing.

3] In the Color Mixer, click the CMYK button. You will create two colors that will be added to the Color List. In the Color Mixer, enter the values to create a color that is 30 percent cyan, 70 percent magenta, 90 percent yellow, and 90 percent black, and add this color to the Color List. Then enter the values to create a color that is 50 percent cyan, 70 percent magenta, 80 percent yellow, and 30 percent black, and add this color to the Color List as well.

This adds two shades of brown to the Color List.

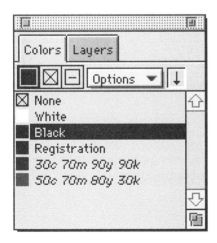

4] With the ground shape selected, display the Fill Inspector. Change the fill type from Basic to Gradient. Set the top color to 50c70m80y30k and the bottom color to 30c70m90y90k. Set the control angle to 270 degrees.

The puts a gradient with brown at the top and darker brown at the bottom of the ground shape.

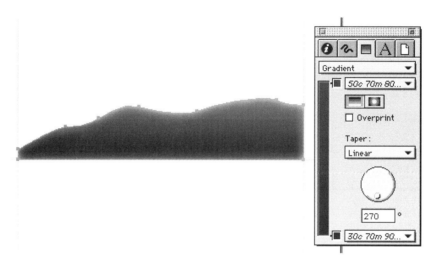

5] With the ground shape selected, choose Edit › Copy. Switch to the MyBeacon document by choosing Window › MyBeacon. With the MyBeacon document activated, choose Edit › Paste.

This copies your completed ground shape from the template to the lighthouse illustration. Notice that it also pasted a Foreground layer as the top layer in the Layers panel.

6] In the Layers panel, double-click the Foreground layer. Enter *Ground* as the new name for this layer. Press Enter to complete the name change.

The Ground layer should be the topmost layer in the document.

7] Activate the template by choosing Window › Untitled-3. Close this document without saving it.

8] With the Ground still selected, display the Object Inspector.

To position the ground accurately, you need to use coordinates. However, when you have a path selected as you do now, the Object Inspector does not list the coordinates of the shape.

9] Choose Modify › Group.

Notice that now the Object Inspector indicates that you have a grouped element selected, and therefore, the coordinates for this shape are now available.

10] In the Object Inspector, set the *x* and *y* dimensions to 0.25 inch.

This positions the bottom-left corner of the ground so it is 0.25 inch from the left side of the page and 0.25 inch from the bottom of the page.

11] Save your work.

The lighthouse illustration looks terrific. Who would guess you imported two graphics, used two templates, and blended a variety of elements to create it?

WHAT YOU HAVE LEARNED

In this lesson you have:

Imported a JPEG image [*page* **225**]

Traced an image using the Trace tool [*page* **227**]

Placed artwork on multiple foreground layers [*page* **230**]

Imported a three-dimensional graphic [*page* **231**]

Used FreeHand's Transparency path operation on text and two objects [*page* **237**]

Created a blend between two shapes and another among three shapes [*page* **239**]

Practiced combining artwork from different documents with Copy and Paste [*page* **250**]

custom fonts

creating

Macromedia Fontographer, one of the four FreeHand Graphics Studio applications, provides tools that enable you to create new typefaces and modify existing ones for use in print, multimedia, and Internet projects.

The use of digital type has brought many changes to the old terms that have described typesetting through the ages. When working with Fontographer, you should be aware of the old meanings as well as the new. Traditionally, a *typeface* is a set of characters that share a similar appearance (such as News Gothic T). A *font* is a complete set of characters that share the same size and style (12 point News Gothic T Regular). And a *font family* refers to all the type sizes and styles of one typeface (all sizes of News Gothic T Light, Regular, Medium, Demi, and Bold).

This logo, and the characters used to make it, are part of a special font you will create with Fontographer, the professional-level font-creation program included with FreeHand Graphics Studio.

Thanks in large part to programs like Fontographer, which make it easy to create fonts that can be manipulated like any other kind of PostScript art, the definition of a font has become much broader. Now a font can be any collection of shapes that are assigned to the keys of a computer keyboard and manipulated via the font controls of a graphics software package. They are not limited to characters in the alphabet or numerals. As you'll see in this lesson, you can create a font that includes not only text characters, but also logos, graphics, and other intricate PostScript artwork.

In this lesson, you will create a custom font and install it on your system. In the lessons that follow, you will use this font in FreeHand artwork for a logo, import that artwork into Extreme 3D, use xRes to add a painted texture and soft shadow, and incorporate the resulting image into a layout in FreeHand.

If you would like to review the final result of this lesson, open Fgslogo.ttf in the Complete folder within the Lesson07 folder.

WHAT YOU WILL LEARN

In this lesson you will:

Create a new document in Fontographer

Import artwork as a character in a new font

Generate a custom font

Install your custom font for use in other applications

APPROXIMATE TIME

It usually takes about 30 minutes to complete this lesson.

LESSON FILES

Media Files:

Lesson07\Media\Fgs.eps

Lesson07\Media\F.eps

Lesson07\Media\G.eps

Lesson07\Media\S.eps

Lesson07\Media\Sample.ttf

Starting Files:

None

Completed Project:

Lesson07\Complete\Fgslogo.ttf

CREATING A NEW DOCUMENT IN FONTOGRAPHER

In this lesson, you will create a font containing the three characters of the FGS logo plus the logo itself.

1] Open the Fontographer application by double-clicking the Fontographer icon.

The Fontographer menu bar appears, without an open document window.

Depending upon the memory available, you may need to quit other open applications to open Fontographer.

2] Create a new document by choosing File › New Font (Windows Ctrl+N, Macintosh Command+N).

The Font Window appears, showing an empty character grid. There are no characters assigned in this new Fontographer document.

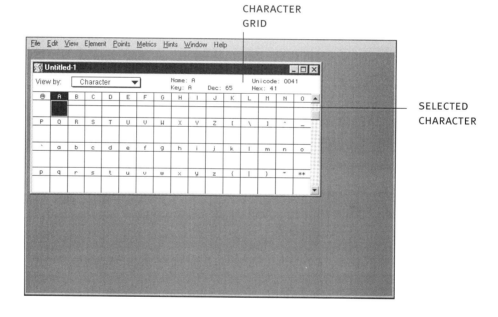

CHARACTER
GRID

SELECTED
CHARACTER

3] Choose Element > Font Info > General (Windows) or Element > Font Info (Macintosh) to open the Font Information dialog box. Enter *MyFont* as the family name and click OK.

This is the name you want to appear in the Font menu when this font is installed on your system.

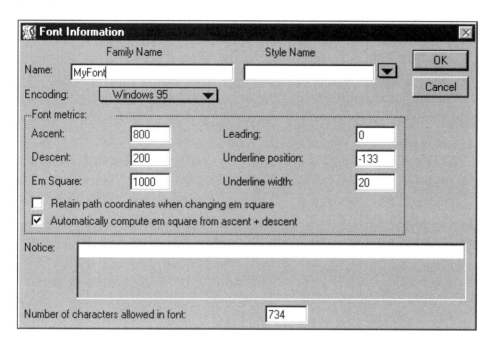

4] Choose File > Save to display the Save As dialog box (Windows Ctrl+S, Macintosh Command+S). Locate your MyWork folder on the hard drive, enter *MyFont* as the name, and click OK.

You have not yet created the font; you have only saved a Fontographer document that can be opened later to continue work on this file.

IMPORTING EPS ARTWORK

You will import Encapsulated PostScript format graphics as characters in this new font. You will import each graphic into a slot on the character grid; then when you generate this font, you will be able to enter the letter by typing the corresponding character on your keyboard.

You will start by importing the FGS logo. You will place this graphic in the *L* slot (for Logo) on the grid.

1] Click the uppercase *L* in the character grid. Choose File › Import › EPS. Open the Lesson07 folder in the Lessons folder and then locate and open Fgs.eps in the Media folder.

The FGS artwork appears in the grid for the character *L*. This artwork was created in FreeHand, by drawing four paths and exporting the artwork as an EPS file.

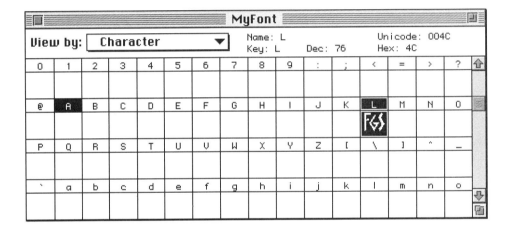

2] Double-click the FGS artwork that appears in the *L* slot to open the Outline window.

You can use this editing window to adjust the outlines of the characters shapes, which are actually paths, just as in FreeHand graphics.

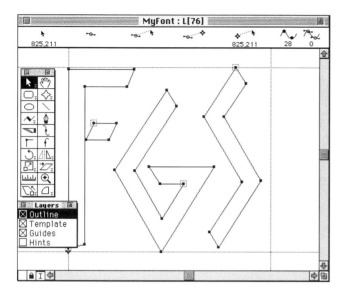

3] Choose Metrics › Equalize Sidebearings.

Sidebearings are the guides on the left and right that indicate the normal spacing around this character. You can reposition the artwork manually with the Pointer tool or the arrow keys on the keyboard, or you can adjust the right sidebearing with the Pointer tool. (The left sidebearing cannot be adjusted.) You can also use the Equalize Sidebearings command, as you did here, to tell Fontographer to automatically balance the space on the left and right sides of this artwork.

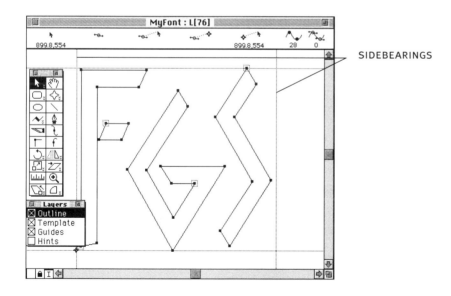

SIDEBEARINGS

4] Choose File › Close to close the Outline window. Then choose File › Save.

The *L* slot now contains this FGS logo. Next you will import artwork for a few more characters.

5] Select the uppercase *F* in the character grid. Choose File › Import › EPS and import F.eps.

The letter *F* artwork will appear in the character grid under the uppercase *F*.

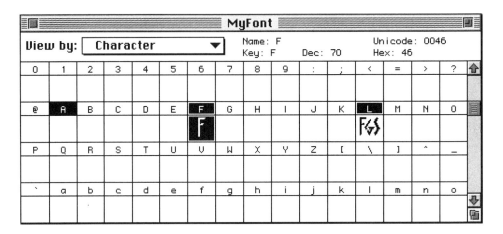

6] Select the uppercase *G* and import the EPS file G.eps in the same fashion. Then select the uppercase *S* and import S.eps.

The artwork for the logo letters *G* and *S*, respectively, appears in these two slots in the character grid.

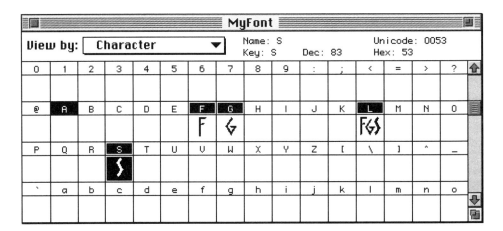

7] Click the *F* character once to select it. Hold down the Shift key and click the *G* and *S* characters.

Holding the Shift key allows you to select multiple characters at the same time.

MyFont																

View by: [**Character** ▼]   Name: Unicode:
                                Key: Dec: Hex:

0	1	2	3	4	5	6	7	8	9	:	;	‹	=	›	?
@	**A**	B	C	D	E	**F**	**G**	H	I	J	K	**L**	M	N	O
						F	G					FGS			
P	Q	R	**S**	T	U	V	W	X	Y	Z	[	\	]	^	_
			S												
`	a	b	c	d	e	f	g	h	i	j	k	l	m	n	o

8] Choose Metrics › Equalize Sidebearings.

Although you cannot see the results of this command when you are not viewing the Outline window, the character spacing for all three selected characters was adjusted.

9] Save your work.

You have defined four characters for this font. Because you positioned the artwork in the uppercase grid, you will need to enter uppercase characters when using this font—that is, you will need to hold down the Shift key when you type the corresponding letter on your keyboard.

GENERATING THE FONT

Now you are ready to create the font file.

1] Choose File › Generate Font Files.

A dialog box appears, where you can specify the type of font you wish to generate.

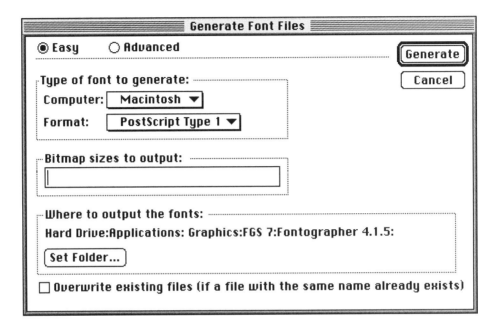

2] Click Easy at the top of the dialog box. Choose your computer from the Computer menu and choose TrueType as the font format.

Fontographer can create fonts for several different computer platforms and can also generate PostScript Type 1 and Type 3 fonts, if desired. Refer to the *Using Fontographer* guide that accompanies the FreeHand Graphics Studio for more information about type formats and options.

TrueType fonts do not require bitmaps, so you can leave the Bitmap sizes to output field empty.

3] Click the Set Folder button and select your MyWork folder on the hard drive.

It is important to know where to find the font once you create it!

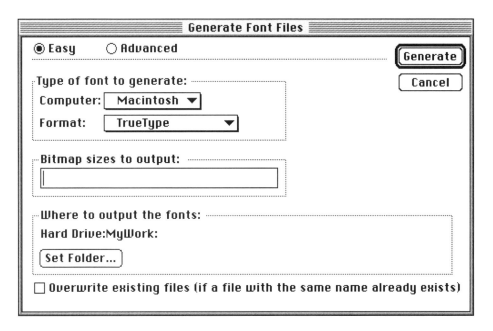

4] Click the Generate button.

Fontographer will generate the font, saved in the MyWork folder, as MyFont.ttf (Windows) or MyFont.suit (Macintosh).

5] Save and close this document.

Your custom font is now ready to be installed on your system, so the FGS logo and characters will be available at the touch of a key.

MODIFYING AN EXISTING FONT

Fontographer can also be used to modify existing fonts, so you can create lighter or heavier versions of fonts, adjust spacing, or simply print samples of characters and keyboard layouts. Here you will learn how to create a new version of an existing font.

1] To create a variation based on an existing font, choose File › Open Font. Locate Sample.ttf in the Media folder for Lesson07 and click the Open button.

The character grid appears for this font.

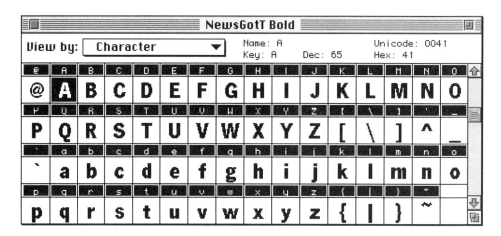

2] Double-click the uppercase *A*.

This opens the Outline window.

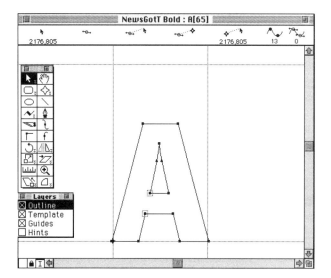

3] Choose Element › Change Weight.

You can quickly create a heavier or lighter version of this character by using the Change Weight command.

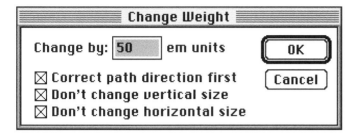

4] Enter *50* as the value, turn on Don't change vertical size and Don't change horizontal size, and click OK.

Fontographer will automatically increase the weight of the character, without increasing its width or height. Entering a positive number makes the character heavier, while a negative number will make a thinner version of the character.

You can apply this technique to other individual characters, or you can Shift+click to select several characters at once in the character grid.

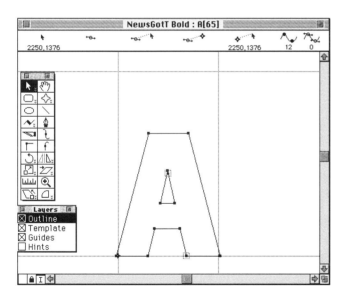

You do not need to change all of the characters at this time, since you will not be actually generating a font in this example.

5] Choose Element › Font Info. Change the Style Name to –Heavy by selecting this name from the menu at the right side of the entry box. Then click OK.

Name your font appropriately in the Font Information dialog box before saving a Fontographer document or generating a font. Be sure you don't duplicate the name of an existing font.

```
┌───────────────────────── Font Information ─────────────────────────┐
│                                                                     │
│              Family Name            Style Name                      │
│   Name: │NewsGotT          │    │–Heavy            │▼│  ┌───OK───┐  │
│                                                        │ Cancel  │  │
│   Encoding:  │   Macintosh      ▼│                                  │
│   ┌─Font metrics:──────────────────────────────────────────────┐   │
│   │ Ascent:     │2058│     Leading:            │0   │           │   │
│   │ Descent:    │400 │     Underline position: │-209│           │   │
│   │ Em Square:  │2048│     Underline width:    │198 │           │   │
│   │  ☐ Retain path coordinates when changing em square         │   │
│   │  ☐ Automatically compute em square from ascent + descent   │   │
│   └────────────────────────────────────────────────────────────┘   │
│   Notice: │URW Software, Copyright 1993 by URW              │       │
│           │                                                 │       │
│           │                                                 │       │
│                                                                     │
│   Number of characters allowed in font: │283│                      │
└─────────────────────────────────────────────────────────────────────┘
```

6] Choose File › Close without saving the changes to this font.

To actually create a usable font, your next step would be to choose File > Generate Font Files to create the font. This task was designed to explore some of the possibilities available using Fontographer with existing fonts. You will not need to generate a font from this exercise.

QUITTING FONTOGRAPHER

You are finished with Fontographer.

1] Select File › Exit (Windows) or File › Quit (Macintosh) to quit the application.

After installing your new font, you will be returning to FreeHand to put this font to use.

INSTALLING A CUSTOM FONT

Now it is time to install your new font. Once it is installed, you will be able to use this font in projects with other applications.

If you did not complete the tasks in this lesson, you can use the complete font provided as Fgslogo.ttf in the Complete folder for Lesson07.

1] Install MyFont by dragging the font file you just created from your MyWork folder to the Fonts folder in the Control Panel (Windows) or on the System Folder icon (Macintosh).

Macintosh users, be sure to drag the font file onto the closed System Folder not to an open System Folder.

You may have to quit and reopen any open applications to make the font available.

WHAT YOU HAVE LEARNED

In this lesson you have:

Created a new Fontographer file [*page* **256**]

Imported EPS artwork into a font file [*page* **258**]

Generated a custom font [*page* **262**]

Edited characters in an existing font [*page* **264**]

Installed a font on your system for use in other applications [*page* **267**]

Extreme 3D

preparing art for

Over the next few lessons, you will be combining the powers of all the programs in the FreeHand Graphics Studio to create a complete logo for the Furniture Gallery Showcase. You will create the basic artwork in FreeHand, add dimension to that artwork in Extreme 3D, and create a drop shadow and background texture for it with xRes. You will also incorporate a character from the Fontographer font you created in the previous lesson.

This logo for the Furniture Gallery Showcase was created in FreeHand, using the font you created in Lesson 7. In the next lessons, you will use the other programs in the FreeHand Graphics Studio to enhance this basic design.

In this lesson, you will create the logo elements and prepare them for use in Extreme 3D.

If you would like to review the final result of this lesson, open Logo1.fh7 in the Complete folder within the Lesson08 folder.

WHAT YOU WILL LEARN

In this lesson you will:

Modify points on a polygon

Attach text to a circle

Combine paths with path operations

Convert text to paths

Prepare FreeHand artwork for Extreme 3D

APPROXIMATE TIME

It usually takes about 30 minutes to complete this lesson.

LESSON FILES

Media Files:

Lesson08\Media\Fgs.fh7

Starting Files:

None

Completed Project:

Lesson08\Complete\Logo1.fh7

USING THE POLYGON TOOL

Your first task is to create the wavy starburst shape that will surround the FGS logo character in the artwork. You will use the Polygon tool to create this multisided shape.

1] Open FreeHand and choose File > New. Choose View > Magnification > 100% and then select View > Info Bar to display the Info Bar. Change the measurement units from Points to Inches using the Measurement menu at the bottom of the screen.

The page is now ready for you to create a starburst.

The Info Bar displays information about the selected FreeHand element.

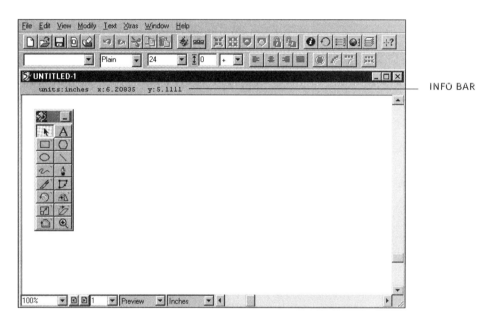

2] Double-click the Polygon tool in the toolbox and set the number of sides to 12. Set the Shape to Star, drag the slider slightly toward Acute, and click OK.

The Polygon tool is another tool that lets you customize its settings before you use it.

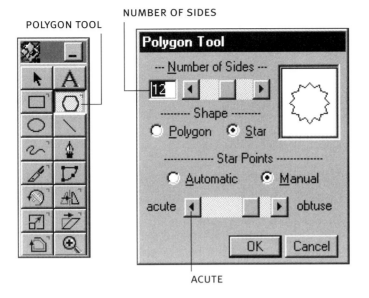

ACUTE

3] Watching the Info Bar at the top of the screen, draw a starburst shape with a radius of about 0.9 inches.

The radius is the distance from the center to the outermost point along the starburst. The information bar displays this value as you draw. Approximate this measurement—it is not important to be absolutely precise.

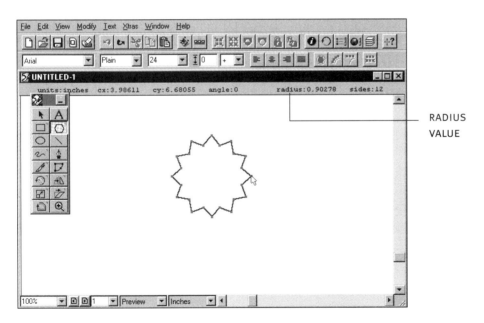

RADIUS
VALUE

4] Save this document as *MyLogo1* in the MyWork folder on your hard drive.

MODIFYING A STAR POLYGON BY CHANGING ITS POINTS

The path created by the Polygon tool has sharp points. You will change these to create a wavy starburst.

1] With the Pointer tool, drag around the entire starburst to select all of the points.

These are all corner points and once you release the mouse they will appear as outlined squares when selected.

2] In the Object Inspector, change the point type to Curve and check the Automatic box to select this option.

This changes all of the points to curves and automatically adjusts each point to the position of the others.

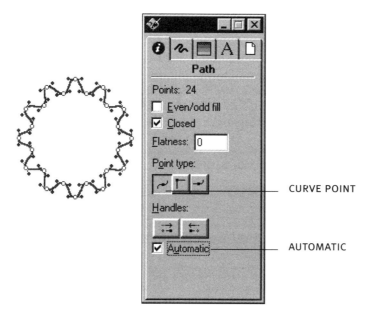

CURVE POINT

AUTOMATIC

3] Choose Modify › Group.

This groups the starburst element, which will make it easier to move without accidentally modifying it in the upcoming tasks.

4] Save your work.

Your wavy starburst is completed.

ATTACHING TEXT TO A CIRCLE

Next create an element with text attached to a circle.

1] With the Ellipse tool, draw a circle with a width and height of 2 inches.

Use the Shift key to constrain the ellipse to a circle and watch the Info Bar to determine the dimensions. You can also verify and adjust the size of an element using the Object Inspector after the element appears on the page.

The circle should position the type close to the border of the starburst, so make it about 2 inches in diameter.

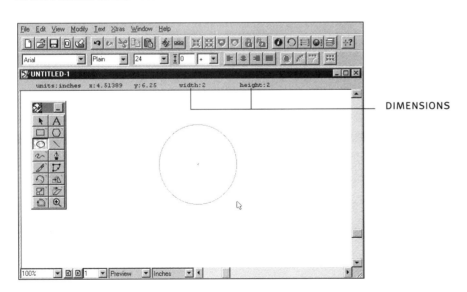

DIMENSIONS

2] With the circle selected, choose Type › Attach to Path. Type *FURNITURE* (in all caps), press Return, and type *GALLERY SHOWCASE*.

Text typed after pressing Return is automatically added along the bottom of the circle.

3] With the Pointer tool, click one of the words to select the entire text block. Set the font to News Gothic T, the style to Bold, and the size to 30 points.

Changing characteristics when a text block is selected with the Pointer tool changes all of the text in the block.

The text looks nice, but it's a little loose.

4] Display the Text Inspector by choosing Window > Inspectors > Text. Change Range Kerning to –5.

Range Kerning changes the space between the selected characters. In this case, entering a negative value tightened the letterspacing for the entire text block.

ENTER A NEGATIVE VALUE
HERE TO TIGHTEN THE
LETTERSPACING

5] While the text block is still selected with the Pointer tool, choose Text > Convert to Paths.

This changes the text into graphic paths, which prepares it for use in Extreme 3D.

6] Save your work.

USING PATH OPERATIONS TO COMBINE PATHS

Now you will create the four corner pieces that surround the circle of text. Instead of creating an individual corner piece and then duplicating and rotating it to create the other three, you will use FreeHand's Path Operations to simplify this task.

1] Draw a perfect square with sides of 2.75 inches and then draw a circle with a diameter of 3 inches.

Be sure to draw the square first. Use the Shift key to constrain the shapes and watch the Info Bar to see the dimensions as you draw the shapes on the page.

(Alternatively, you can use the Object Inspector to adjust the sizes of the elements once you create them.)

2] Select the circle, hold down the Shift key, and select the square with the Pointer tool. Use the Align panel to center these elements over one another horizontally and vertically (Windows Ctrl+Alt+A, Macintosh Command+Opt+A).

Remember that you can click in the center of the Align panel grid to set both horizontal and vertical alignment to Align Center. The circle should protrude slightly from the sides of the square.

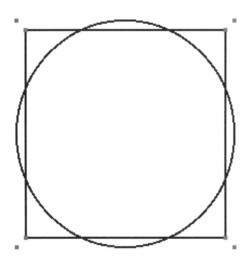 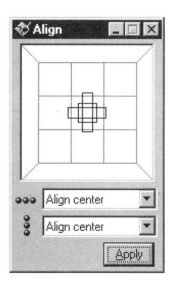

3] With the circle and square still selected, choose Modify > Combine > Punch.

This punches the front item (the circle, since you created it after the square) out of the rear item (the square), leaving just the corner elements.

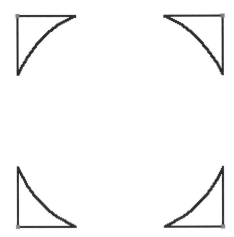

4] Center the starburst, text, and corner elements over one another by choosing Select All and using the Align panel.

Your artwork is almost complete.

5] Save your work.

ADDING A CHARACTER FROM A CUSTOM FONT

To complete the artwork, you will add an element from the Fontographer font you created in the previous lesson.

1] Select the Text tool and type an uppercase _L_ on a blank area of the page. Then select the character with the Pointer tool. Change the font to MyFont and the size to 126 points.

Because this is a character in a font, not a graphic, you manipulate it using FreeHand's text tools. This is how fonts you create can be used in any application with the touch of a key, making it easy to access frequently used artwork.

If you have not completed the previous lesson, you can import the Fgs.fh7 file from the Media folder for this lesson. Position the imported graphic anywhere on the page and continue with step 3.

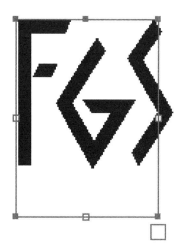

2] Select the character with the Pointer tool and choose Text › Convert to Paths.

You have the same capabilities with your custom font as you have with any other font.

3] Move the FGS element to visually position it over your existing logo elements.

It is better to position this element manually rather than to use the Align panel because of the visual differences between the left and right sides of this character.

4] Save your work.

Your logo artwork is complete.

PREPARING ARTWORK FOR EXTREME 3D

You have already converted your type to paths—an important step in preparing graphics for use in Extreme 3D. In this task you will make a few more adjustments to your FreeHand document that will make it easier to see the imported FreeHand artwork in the Extreme 3D workspace.

1] Choose Edit › Select › All (Windows Ctrl+A, Macintosh Command+A) and group the elements together with the Group command (Windows Ctrl+G, Macintosh Command+G).

Grouping the elements makes it easier to move them without altering the alignment of individual items.

2] Choose View › Fit To Page. Use the Pointer tool to move the artwork to the extreme lower-left corner of the page. Press the Tab key to deselect the group.

The artwork is correctly positioned for Extreme 3D. The next step is to move the page to the lower-left corner of the pasteboard.

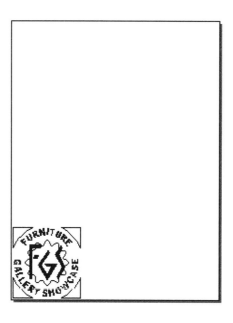

3] In the Document Inspector, drag the page icon against the lower-left corner of the pasteboard. Then double-click the page icon to see the page again.

The page will disappear when you move the page icon in the Document Inspector, so double-clicking that page icon will adjust the view so you can see your page again.

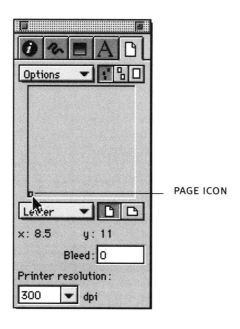

PAGE ICON

4] Save the document.

Now when this FreeHand document is imported into Extreme 3D, it will appear in the workspace without your having to scroll up and to the right to find it. (Your FreeHand page used to be positioned farther up and to the right on the pasteboard.)

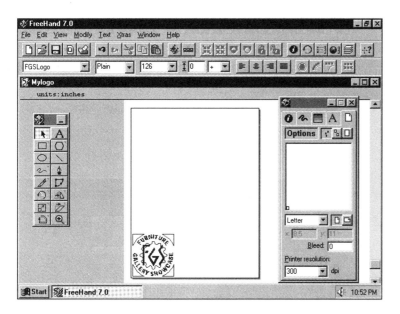

5] Quit FreeHand.

You are finished with FreeHand for now. In the next lesson you will add dimension to this logo in Extreme 3D.

WHAT YOU HAVE LEARNED

In this lesson you have:

Automatically created a starburst-shaped polygon [*page* **270**]

Modified the points on a polygon [*page* **272**]

Attached text to a circle [*page* **273**]

Practiced changing the letterspacing of text [*page* **275**]

Practiced converting text to paths [*page* **275**]

Combined paths with the Punch command [*page* **276**]

Used a character from a custom font [*page* **278**]

Prepared FreeHand artwork for Extreme 3D [*page* **279**]

dimension

Extreme 3D enables you to create artwork, both still images and animations, in three dimensions for print, multimedia, or Web delivery. You can use Extreme 3D to create new artwork to include in your FreeHand projects, such as the lighthouse and robot illustrations incorporated into previous lessons. As you will see in this lesson, you can also use Extreme 3D to add dimension to FreeHand artwork and prepare a rendered image that can be further enhanced in xRes.

The basic paths you created in Lesson 8 become exciting 3D shapes when they are manipulated in Extreme 3D.

The process of creating artwork in Extreme 3D is to first create three-dimensional elements, or *models*; next arrange your models to compose a scene or create an animation; then customize lighting and apply surface materials. The final step is to *render* the finished image, which creates a two-dimensional image from the three-dimensional geometry, lights, and materials.

This lesson builds upon the projects you completed in Lessons 7 and 8. If you would like to review the final result of this lesson, open Logo2.e3d in the Complete folder within the folder for Lesson 9. Note that you will see the completed model in Extreme 3D, not the completed rendering.

WHAT YOU WILL LEARN

In this lesson you will:

Create several types of 3D elements

Navigate in 3D space

Import artwork from FreeHand

Apply materials to surfaces

Render a finished image

APPROXIMATE TIME

It usually takes about 1 hour and 30 minutes to complete this lesson.

LESSON FILES

Media Files:

Lesson09\Media\Logo1.fh7

Starting Files:

None

Completed Project:

Lesson09\Complete\Logo2.e3d

Lesson09\Complete\Logo3.tif

GETTING STARTED WITH EXTREME 3D

Your first task is to get acquainted with the controls and capabilities of Extreme 3D.

1] Launch Extreme 3D by double-clicking the application icon.

When the program opens, you are presented with a new document window called the Extreme 3D **workspace**. This is your window into the 3D **world**, which is the simulated 3D space in which Extreme 3D models are built and scenes are created. The grid in the workspace window is the **working plane**. This working plane is a visible portion of an infinite grid that extends throughout the 3D world. Everything you draw or import is added to the world on the working plane. You can show, hide, and reposition the working plane as you work.

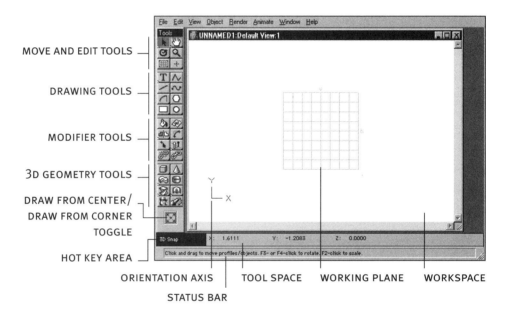

MOVE AND EDIT TOOLS

DRAWING TOOLS

MODIFIER TOOLS

3D GEOMETRY TOOLS

DRAW FROM CENTER/
DRAW FROM CORNER
TOGGLE

HOT KEY AREA

ORIENTATION AXIS   TOOL SPACE   WORKING PLANE   WORKSPACE

STATUS BAR

2] Choose Object › Auto Working Plane to View (Windows Ctrl+Shift+Z, Macintosh Command+Shift+Z) to turn off this feature.

This turns off the default setting, which repositions the working plane as you change your view. Now you can change your view, and the working plane will remain at the position shown here in the Extreme 3D world.

If you use the default setting, the working plane will always remain parallel to your computer screen. Therefore, when you change the view, the working plane will be reoriented so it is parallel to the screen.

In this lesson, you want Auto Working Plane to View toggled off so you can more clearly see the three dimensions you are working with. There should now be no checkmark next to this command in the Object menu.

To visualize the 3D space you are working in, you will now adjust your view so that instead of looking at an object head-on, you see the object turned to provide a three-quarters view.

3] Choose View › Three-Quarters (Windows Ctrl+9, Macintosh Command+9).

Your view of the world changes, and now you can see all three dimensions represented in the workspace. The orientation axis displayed in the lower left of the workspace identifies the direction of each dimension—x is the horizontal axis, y is vertical axis, and z is the axis representing depth.

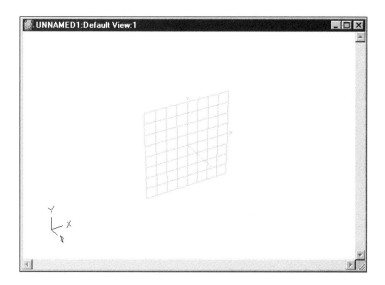

4] Change the perspective applied to your view of the world by choosing View › Perspective › Moderate.

In the real world, objects appear to get smaller the farther away they move from you. This is known as **perspective**. To more accurately simulate a three-dimensional workspace, Extreme 3D lets you specify the distance from which you view the world. Wider perspective settings accentuate the apparent size changes as objects move toward or away from you.

Changing the perspective to Moderate makes only a slight change in the appearance of the working plane at this time, but it will help you to see the objects in space more clearly in the next few steps.

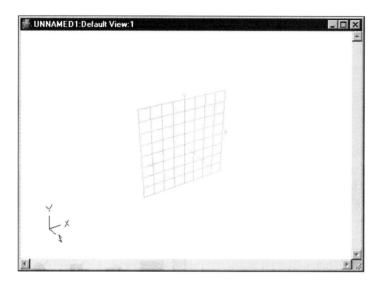

Now draw an object on the working plane to see how Extreme 3D works.

5] Click once on the Circle tool in the toolbox and position your cursor at the center of the working plane. Drag downward two rows on the grid and release.

As you draw, the object **snaps** to the units on the working plane grid. Extreme 3D offers both 2D and 3D snaps to help you create and position elements precisely (for snapping to two-dimensional elements or three-dimensional objects, respectively).

The circle you just created sits directly on the working plane. This circle is similar to those you can create in FreeHand in that it is a two-dimensional object, called a **profile** in Extreme 3D. A profile is the fundamental unit of all models in Extreme 3D. The difference between this profile and a path in FreeHand is your view of the object. Although this is a perfect circle, it appears elliptical because of the perspective and angle of your view.

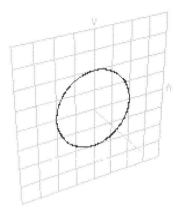

6] With the Pointer, grab the outline of the circle. Move the circle around the workspace by dragging it in any direction.

As you drag, you are moving the profile in just two dimensions: horizontally and vertically along the working plane. (Remember that this plane extends beyond the edges of the visible portion, throughout the world.)

If you watch closely, the circle seems to shrink when you move it down and to the right. As you drag up and to the left, it appears to get larger. The circle actually never changes in size, but it appears to change size as you move it closer or farther away from the screen. This is perspective in action.

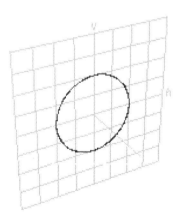

7] Move the circle so it is back on the working plane. Choose Edit › Copy to make a copy of the circle for later use.

Now you are ready to use the 3D geometry tools to create a surface object from this profile.

8] Click the Pointer tool on an empty spot in the workspace to deselect the circle profile. Then select the Extrude tool in the toolbox.

The Extrude tool pulls a profile along a depth line to create objects.

The Status bar will display the name of the tool your cursor is over to help you select the tool you want. It will also show you instructions on how to use that tool once you select it and move the cursor back onto the workspace.

All of the tools in the toolbox that have a black mark in the lower-right corner are members of a **tool group**. You can select from the tools in those groups by holding down the mouse on the visible tool to display the menu for that tool group.

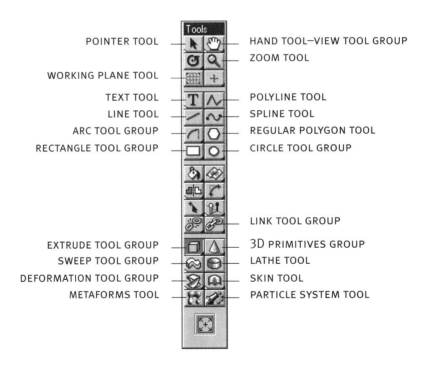

POINTER TOOL — HAND TOOL–VIEW TOOL GROUP
— ZOOM TOOL
WORKING PLANE TOOL —
TEXT TOOL — POLYLINE TOOL
LINE TOOL — SPLINE TOOL
ARC TOOL GROUP — REGULAR POLYGON TOOL
RECTANGLE TOOL GROUP — CIRCLE TOOL GROUP

— LINK TOOL GROUP
EXTRUDE TOOL GROUP — 3D PRIMITIVES GROUP
SWEEP TOOL GROUP — LATHE TOOL
DEFORMATION TOOL GROUP — SKIN TOOL
METAFORMS TOOL — PARTICLE SYSTEM TOOL

9] Following the instructions in the Status bar at the bottom of the screen, click once on the outline of the circle and then drag a line approximately 2 inches long anywhere on the page.

The profile is extruded to a depth that matches the length of the line you drew.

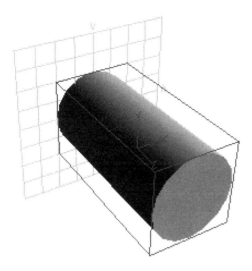

10] Move the object off of the working plane using the Pointer tool.

When you move an element, Extreme 3D moves it parallel to the current working plane. Notice that the Status bar displays keys you can press to make other changes with the Pointer tool.

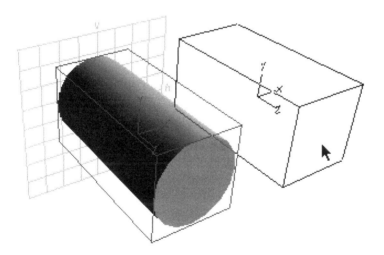

11] Choose Edit › Undo to return the object to its previous position.

The Undo command will undo the last step taken. You can choose Edit > History Backward to go back up to 10 steps, one at a time.

12] Using the Pointer tool, point to the object and hold down the F2 key (Windows) or Control key (Macintosh) and drag upward to reduce the size of the element, or downward to enlarge the element.

Using modifier keys enables you to perform several actions in a single step using the same tool.

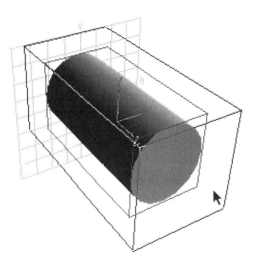

13] Hold the F4 key (Windows) or Command key (Macintosh) while dragging the element with the Pointer tool to rotate the element.

This rotates the element around the x and y axes. Holding F3 (Windows) or Option (Macintosh) rotates the object around the y and z axes. You can hold down both rotation keys while you drag to rotate in both directions at the same time.

With practice, you can perform several actions on the object without releasing the mouse.

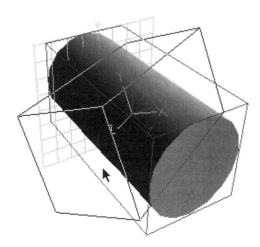

14] Point to the object with the Pointer tool and hold down the mouse button. Drag upward to move the element up a bit and then, without releasing the mouse, press and hold down the F2 (Windows) or Control (Macintosh) key and drag up or down to change the size of the element. Still keeping the mouse button down, release the F2 or Control key and then press F4 (Windows) or Command (Macintosh) and drag to rotate the item. Continuing to keep the mouse button down, release the F4 or Command key and move the object back on the working plane. Now release the mouse button.

This procedure may seem awkward at first, but with practice you will find it a very fluid way to work with elements in the workspace.

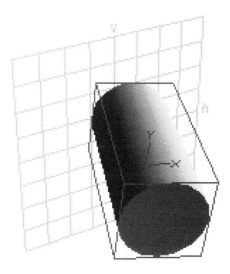

15] Save this document as *MyObjects* in the MyWork folder.

Now that you can move and manipulate elements in 3D space, you will experiment with different 3D geometry tools to create a variety of 3D objects.

CREATING OTHER KINDS OF 3D OBJECTS

The different 3D geometry tools can create different objects from the same profile, as you will see over the next several steps.

1] Move the extruded shape into the upper-right corner of your workspace window. Click the Pointer on an empty part of the workspace to deselect the object. Then choose Edit › Paste to paste a copy of the original circle back onto the working plane.

It is important to deselect objects before choosing Paste. When you paste an item with an object selected, Extreme 3D replaces the selected item with the pasted element; the pasted shape will have the same position and orientation as the selected item it replaces.

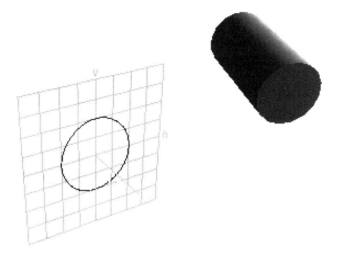

2] Select the Lathe tool in the Toolbox. Click on the circle in your workspace to select the profile to lathe. Point to the top-left corner of the working plane and drag a line to the bottom-left corner, then release the mouse.

The lathe tool rotates the circle profile around the axis you defined by drawing the line—in this case, the left edge of the working plane. By default, the Lathe tool rotates elements 360 degrees, but you can change that value in the Tool Space at the bottom of the screen before performing the lathe.

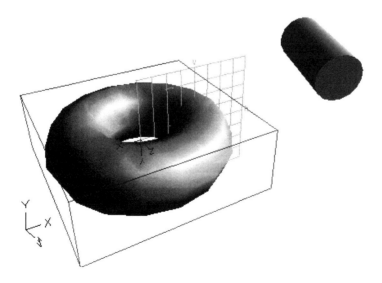

3] Move the lathe object into the lower-right corner of the workspace window. Click on an empty part of the workspace to deselect all elements.

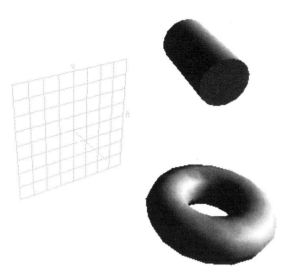

Next you will **sweep** an object, which pulls a profile along a path. To sweep an object, you must have a profile to sweep along a path, plus a path to sweep it along.

4] Use the Circle tool to create a small circle to the left of the working plane. Then select the Regular Polygon tool. Position the cursor on the center of the working plane and drag down to the bottom center of the working plane and release.

The Regular Polygon tool defaults to drawing a six-sided profile. To draw a polygon with a different number of sides, select the Regular Polygon tool and change the value in the Tool Space at the bottom of the workspace window before you draw a profile.

You can now sweep the small circle along the path of the hexagon.

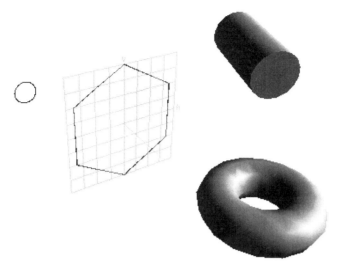

5] Select the Sweep tool in the toolbox. Click once on the circle to select it as the profile to sweep. Then click once on the hexagon to select it as the sweep path.

The circle becomes the cross-section of the hexagon object. You can sweep profiles along open, closed, straight, and curved paths.

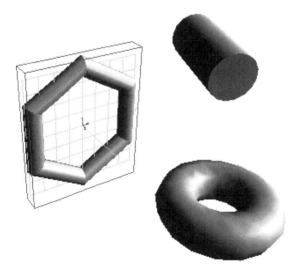

6] Point to the 3D Primitives tool group in the toolbox. Hold down the mouse, select the Sphere tool, and release. Draw a sphere by positioning the cursor in the workspace and dragging in any direction.

The 3D Primitives tools draw basic 3D objects—cones, spheres, and cubes.

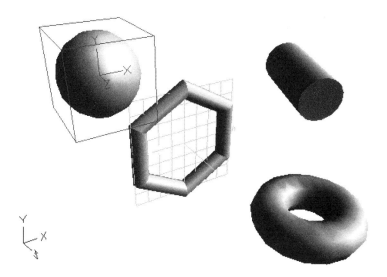

7] Move elements off of the working plane and out of the way (and reduce the size of the elements if necessary) so you can create one more 3D object. Using the Circle tool, position the cursor at the center of the Working plane. Drag two units down and release the mouse to draw a circle. Then draw a another circle that is slightly larger than the first, starting from the same center point.

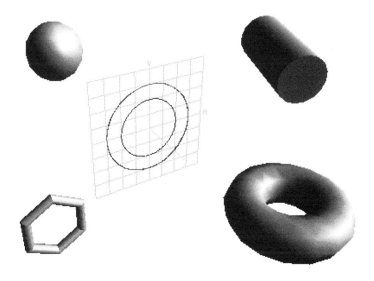

8] Select both circles with the Pointer tool by holding down the Shift key to add the second profile to the selection. Select the Extrude tool from the toolbox, and drag a line about an inch long anywhere in the workspace.

Selecting two profiles with one inside the other extrudes a hollow pipe rather than a closed cylinder. The line you drag with the Extrude tool defines the depth of the extrusion.

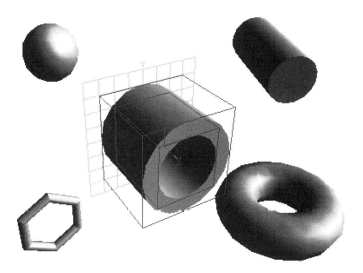

9] Save and close your document.
Now that you have explored the tools and techniques for creating 3D shapes, you will apply those skills to add dimension to profiles that you will import from FreeHand.

ON YOUR OWN
Experiment with these tools to create different kinds of 3D objects. Then use the modifier keys with the Pointer tool to move, rotate, and scale the objects as desired. Extreme 3D opens up an entirely new three-dimensional world of possibilities!

IMPORTING FREEHAND ARTWORK
Now you are ready to begin working on the Furniture Gallery Showcase logo.

1] Create a new document by choosing File › New (Windows Ctrl+N, Macintosh Command+N). Save this document as *MyLogo2* in the MyWork folder on your hard drive.
A new workspace window appears.

2] Choose File › Import › FreeHand and select the MyLogo1 document from your MyWork folder.

The FreeHand artwork is imported as individual elements into the workspace. Do not be alarmed if you cannot see all or even part of the logo. You will locate the artwork and move it in the next steps.

If you did not complete the preceding projects, you can import Logo1.fh7 in the Media folder for Lesson 9 to continue working.

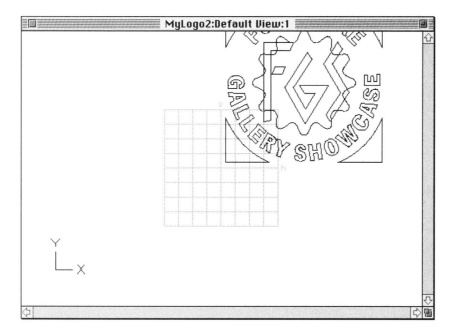

3] If you do not see all of the artwork (or cannot see it at all), change the view by choosing View › Fit to Window.

The last task in the previous lesson moved the FreeHand page to the lower-left corner of the pasteboard and the logo artwork to the lower-left corner of the page. This was done so that the artwork appears closer to the working plane when the document is imported into Extreme 3D.

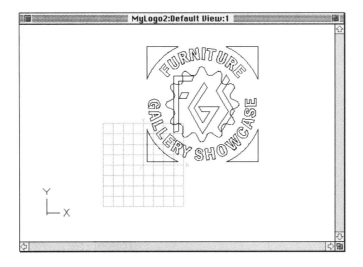

4] Using the Pointer tool, position the mouse above and to the left of the logo artwork. Drag to surround all of the artwork with the selection marquee, and release the mouse.

Even though these elements were grouped in FreeHand, they have been imported as individual elements into Extreme 3D, so you must select all of the elements to move them together. You can surround elements to select them just as you can in FreeHand.

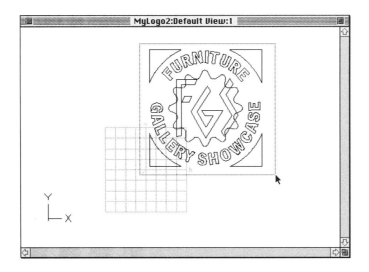

5] Pointing to the edge of one of the selected elements, move the artwork down and to the left to visually center it on the working plane. Then choose View › Home to return to the original view.

Make sure that you position the Pointer tool on one of the profiles, and not on a **bounding box**, to move the artwork. (A bounding box is a selection outline that appears when an element is selected.)

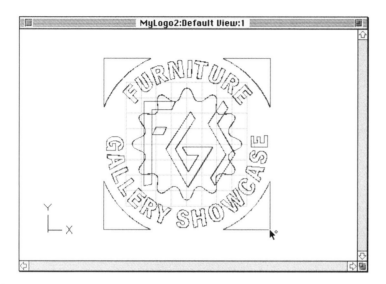

6] Choose View › Perspective › Orthographic. Then choose Object › Show Working Plane.

Changing to an **orthographic** view displays the artwork without any perspective, which is desired for this particular project.

The working plane is very helpful when you are creating elements, but sometimes it can actually interfere with your work. For example, it can be difficult to select small elements without selecting the working plane instead. The Show Working Plane command allows you to turn the display of the working plane on and off as needed. (The working plane always exists in the world—this feature allows you to choose whether or not it is visible.)

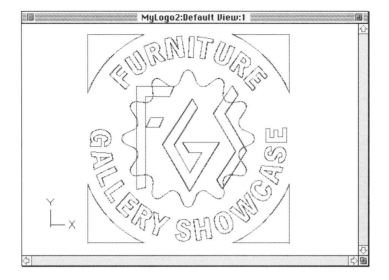

7] Click the Pointer on an empty part of the workspace to deselect all elements. Then save your work.

Your next task will be to link profiles to one another.

LINKING ELEMENTS TOGETHER

Extreme 3D offers powerful linking controls that you can use to tie elements together, similar to the Group command in FreeHand. When you link one object to another, one object becomes the **parent** and the other becomes the **child**. The type of link determines the relationship between the parent and child. For example, a lock link will ensure that if either the parent or child elements are moved, the other linked elements will move as well.

1] Hold down the Link tool group button in the toolbox and choose the Lock Link tool (the second option in the Link tool group).

The Status bar instructs you to click the child object and drag a line to its parent. First you will link the FGS characters in the center of the artwork to one another.

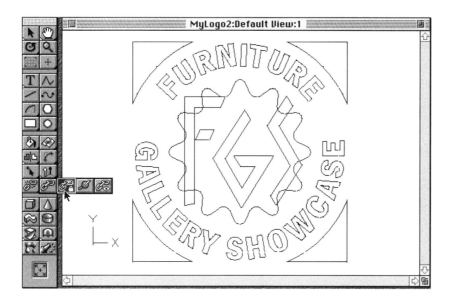

2] Point to the large *S* profile and drag a line to the *G*.

A small outlined shape appears next to the tool cursor to let you know when you are pointing to a profile.

When you have finished this step, the *G* appears selected in color, while the *S* is gray. This indicates that *G* is the parent of *S*. A lock link locks the two objects together in their current positions—neither element can move without the other.

tip *Profiles are two-dimensional outlines. To create the link, you must point to the outline of the child and drag onto the outline of the parent. Watch the cursor to see when you are in the right position.*

3] Choose the Lock Link tool again and link the two pieces of the *F* together by dragging a line from the small profile (the small piece) to the larger profile (the main part of the letter).

The large profile in the *F* will be the parent of the smaller profile.

4] Choose the Lock Link tool again and link the large profile of the *F* to the *G*.

All of the pieces that make up the FGS characters are now linked to the large *G* profile. As the parent of the other elements, the *G* appears selected in color, while the *S* and the two pieces of the *F* are gray.

5] Save the document.

Now link all the corner profiles together.

6] Use the Pointer tool to select the corner element at the top left of the artwork. Then hold down the Shift key and click on the three other corner profiles, one at a time, to select all four together. Choose the Lock Link tool and click on the profile at the top left to link all selected profiles to this one. Save the document.

When you click a Link tool on a selected object, all of the other selected objects are linked to the element you clicked on. This is an excellent way to easily link multiple elements at the same time.

7] To link all of the *Furniture Gallery Showcase* text together, choose Edit › Select All. Using the Pointer tool, hold down the Shift key and click the upper-left corner profile, the wavy starburst shape, and the large *G* in the center.

This deselects everything except the text. Deselecting the parent elements (the top-left corner and the G profiles), deselects all of the child objects as well. Only the *Furniture Gallery Showcase* characters should remain selected.

THIS TEXT SHOULD
BE SELECTED

8] With the Lock Link tool, click once on the *F* in *Furniture*.

You have linked all of the selected elements to the first character profile.

9] Check your links by selecting the parent elements one at a time with the Pointer tool.

The four corner elements should be linked to the one at the upper left. The curved type should all be linked to the small *F* character in *Furniture*. The FGS elements should all be linked to the large *G* in the center.

10] Save the document.

These links will make the next several tasks much easier to perform.

EXTRUDING THE TEXT CHARACTERS

In this task you will control the way the Bevel Extrude tool is applied by entering specific values into the Tool Space near the bottom of your screen. You will extrude all of the text characters in the drawing.

1] Select the small *F* with the Pointer tool.

Selecting this parent object also selects the child objects linked to the parent—in this case, all the text around the circle.

2] Point to the Extrude tool in the toolbox, hold the mouse button down, and slide to the right to select the Bevel Extrude tool.

Two fields appear in the Tool Space at the bottom of the screen. You can enter and change values in the Tool Space to control the tool operations.

The Bevel Extrude tool creates 3D shapes with rounded corners. You can also create shapes with angled corners by double-clicking the Bevel Extrude tool in the toolbox to display the tool preferences dialog box and choosing Hard Bevel before you bevel an object.

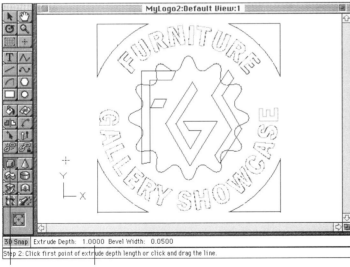

BEVEL   TOOL SPACE
EXTRUDE TOOL

3] In the Tool Space, enter an Extrude Depth value of 0.15 inch and a Bevel Width value of 0.02 inch. Then press Enter.

The selected object and all of the child objects now appear as three-dimensional objects, with beveled edges.

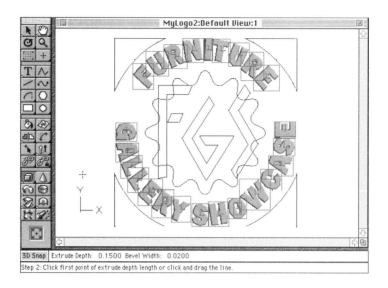

4] While all of the 3D characters are selected, click the Lock Link tool on the _F_ in _Furniture_. Save your work.

Links on 2D profiles are not transferred to 3D elements created from those profiles. By lock linking the 3D objects immediately, you save yourself the step of having to repeat the selection process to link these objects later.

5] Using the Pointer, select the large *G* in the center, which is the parent of the FGS character profiles. Choose the Bevel Extrude tool, change the Extrude Depth value to 0.20 inch, leave the Bevel Width value at 0.02 inch, and press Enter.

The FGS elements now appear as 3D extruded elements.

6] While all of the FGS elements are selected, click the Lock Link tool on the *G* in the center to link the 3D elements together. Then save your work. Choose View › Three-Quarters to see these elements from an angle.

The characters have been extruded forward; the back of the elements and the remaining 2D profiles all sit on the same plane (the working plane). Because of the values entered, the FGS characters extend a bit farther out from the working plane.

7] Choose View › Front to return to the previous view.

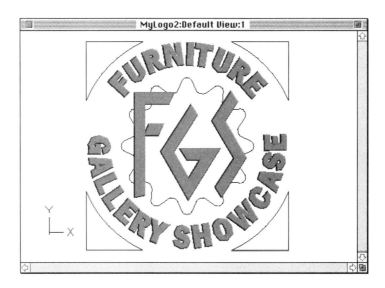

SWEEPING PROFILES ALONG A PATH

Next you will turn the remaining two-dimensional elements in this logo—
the corner pieces and wavy starburst profiles—into three-dimensional objects
with the Sweep tool.

**1] Select the Circle tool in the toolbox. In the Tool Space, enter a Radius value
of *.03*, and press Enter.**

A very small circle appears in the center of the workspace window.

A CIRCLE APPEARS HERE

2] Select the Sweep tool in the toolbox. Click once on the small circle and then click on the upper-left corner element to perform the sweep.

The circle is swept along the path defined by the corner element, turning the two-dimensional path into a three-dimensional element.

Notice that unlike the extrusions you just performed, sweeps are not automatically applied to the child objects when a parent object is swept. You will need to sweep each corner element individually.

In addition, notice that the circle you used as the sweep profile has disappeared—it is incorporated into the swept object—so you will need to create an additional circle for each of the remaining paths you wish to sweep.

tip　*When you need to use the same profile to sweep several items, you can copy the profile (Edit > Copy) before performing the first sweep operation. Then after you sweep the first object, make sure to deselect all elements by clicking the Pointer tool on an empty spot in the workspace. Choose Edit > Paste to add a duplicate of the original profile to the page. Perform the next sweep and then paste again as needed. You can continue to paste duplicates of the original item until you cut or copy something else. Be sure, though, that nothing is selected when you paste. Extreme 3D will replace any selected item with the item you paste on the page.*

3] Select the Circle tool and press Enter.

The Circle tool retains the values you entered in the Tool Space for the previous circle, so selecting the tool and pressing Enter creates a new circle of the same size.

A NEW CIRCLE APPEARS HERE

4] Sweep one of the other corner elements with the new circle.

You can always follow the instructions displayed in the Status Bar at the bottom of the screen if you need help.

5] Create another circle by selecting the Circle tool and pressing Enter and then sweep another corner element. Repeat this operation for the last corner element and again for the wavy starburst in the center.

All of the two-dimensional FreeHand artwork has been transformed into three-dimensional objects.

6] Using the Pointer tool and the Shift key, select all five sweep objects (the four corner elements and the wavy starburst). Click the Lock Link tool on the corner element in the upper left.

The sweep objects are now linked together.

THIS WILL BE RED TO SHOW THAT IT IS THE PARENT

7] Save your work.

APPLYING MATERIALS TO 3D OBJECTS

Extreme 3D provides a wide variety of materials—marble, chrome, textures, and more—you can apply to your objects to give them a more exciting look than the gray plastic default material currently assigned. In this next task you will change the surface materials applied to the elements in your drawing.

First you will apply a marble material to the FGS character.

1] Select the large _G_ in the center of the artwork to select this parent object. Open the Materials browser by selecting Window › Materials.

Selecting a parent object will enable you to apply a material to the child objects at the same time as you apply it to the parent.

The left side of the Materials browser shows that Gray Plastic is the only material currently used in the scene. For this lesson you will select from the collection of preset materials supplied with Extreme 3D.

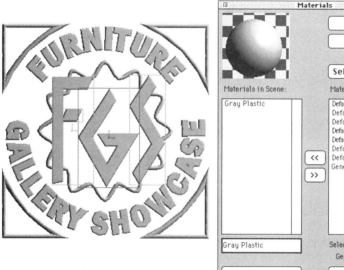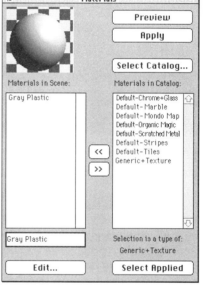

2] Click the Select Catalog button at the upper right of the Materials browser. Locate the folder containing Extreme 3D and open the Presets folder. You will apply the Marble_Green material, so open the Marble folder to see the contents. Then open the next Marble folder: on Windows systems, click OK; on the Macintosh, click the Select "Marble" button.

These preset materials are imported into the Materials in Catalog list on the right side of the Materials browser.

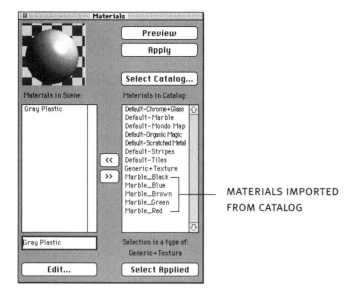

MATERIALS IMPORTED
FROM CATALOG

3] In the Materials browser, double-click Marble_Green in the list on the right to add that preset to the Materials in Scene list on the left.

Now this material can be used in this scene.

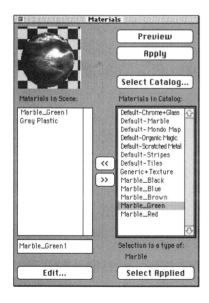

4] Select Marble_Green1 on the left and click Apply.

You can tell that the material is applied in the workspace because the shading changes to indicate a different material. However, you will not see the detail of the marble material until the scene is rendered.

You have applied the material to the selected object only, not to the child objects of the parent.

5] With the *G* still selected, hold down the F2 key (Windows) or Control key (Macintosh) and click Apply.

This applies the material down the family tree (**down-tree**)—all of the child objects now have the same material applied as the parent.

6] Save your work.

Next you will apply a Brass finish to the sweep objects.

7] Select the parent of the sweep objects, the corner element at the top left. Click the Select Catalog button in the Materials browser and import the Brass presets from the Metal folder located in the Presets folder. Add Brass_Smooth to the scene and apply it to the selected parent object while holding F2 (Windows) or Control (Macintosh).

The sweep objects all display a yellowish color, which indicates that this material has been successfully applied down-tree.

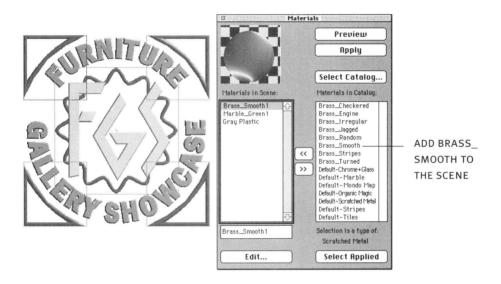

ADD BRASS_
SMOOTH TO
THE SCENE

8] Select the small *F*, which is the parent of the remaining text objects. Use the Select Catalog button in the Materials browser to import the Wood presets from the Solid directory. Add Wood_Oak to the scene and apply the material down-tree.

All of the objects have new materials applied.

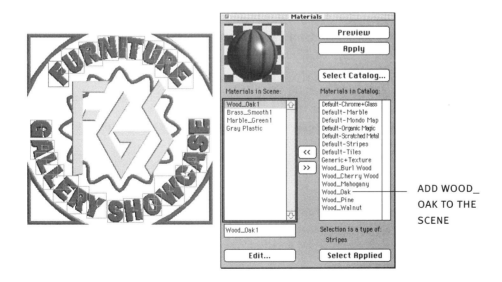

ADD WOOD_
OAK TO THE
SCENE

Remember to hold down the F2 (Windows) or Control (Macintosh) key when you click Apply in the Materials browser to apply the materials to both the child objects and the selected parent object at the same time.

9] Click the Pointer tool on an empty spot in the workspace to deselect all elements. Close the Materials browser and save your work.

The modeling is complete; now it is time to render the image.

RENDERING A SCENE

You should set several options before you render a scene in Extreme 3D.

Now that the artwork is complete, you can enhance the three-dimensional effect of the logo by applying a small amount of perspective.

1] Change the perspective of the view by choosing View › Perspective › Narrow.

Notice that the curved text now appears to radiate out from the center slightly.

Your view of the scene determines what will be rendered, so always adjust your view to display the scene as desired in your final image.

2] Choose Edit › Select All and choose Render › Adaptive Smoothing. Click Final Render Settings, adjust the slider to about 0.80, with Render Edges Sharper turned on, and click OK. Then click the Pointer tool on an empty spot in the workspace to deselect all elements.

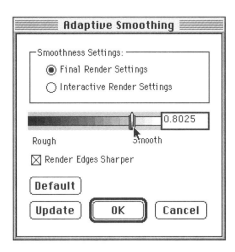

The Final Render Settings option determines the smoothness settings for the selected elements in the final rendering. The other option in the Adaptive Smoothing dialog box is Interactive Render Settings, which controls the display of elements on the screen as you work. This allows you to work quickly with lower-quality rendering displayed on the screen. This sometimes results in round objects that appear to have flat spots as you work. The image will be rendered using the Final Render Settings option, thus delivering high quality where it is needed most, but without forcing you to work slowly all of the time.

3] Choose Render › Final Render Setup and select the Better Quality setting. Save the document.

This setting improves the anti-aliasing capability, which smoothes the edges between pixels, but it also lengthens rendering time. Leave the other options as shown here.

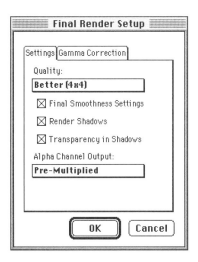

4] Choose Render › Render to Disk. In the dialog box, choose TIFF as the Output File Format. Then click Render.

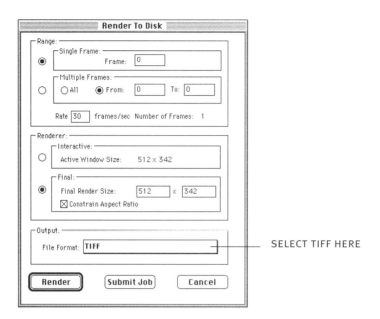

SELECT TIFF HERE

A dialog box will appear asking for a name for the rendered image.

5] Save the rendered image as *MyLogo3* in the MyWork folder. Select 32-bit with Alpha in the TIFF Options dialog box and click OK.

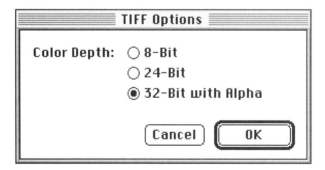

The various file formats offer options specific to that format. A color depth of 32 bits offers the highest-quality rendering, and *with Alpha* means that Extreme 3D will create a custom alpha channel as it renders the document. When you open the rendered image in xRes or Photoshop, you will be able to use this channel as a mask to knock out the background.

Rendering progress is displayed in the Status bar at the bottom of the screen, and you can see the progress visually as the rendered image is also displayed on the screen as it is drawn.

6] When the rendering process is complete, save your work.
Your final effects are rendered in the separate document MyLogo3, but you will want to save this Extreme 3D document in case you want to work with the geometry or render with different materials or settings.

7] You are finished with Extreme 3D, so quit the program.
The next step requires xRes. You will work with this application in the next lesson.

WHAT YOU HAVE LEARNED

In this lesson you have:

Adjusted the view and manipulated elements in the workspace [*page* **284**]
Created objects with the extrude, lathe, and sweep tools [*page* **288**]
Imported FreeHand artwork and transformed it into 3D objects [*page* **296**]
Created parent and child relationships between objects [*page* **300**]
Practiced extruding and sweeping objects along a path [*page* **305**]
Applied surface materials to objects [*page* **312**]
Set up and rendered an image [*page* **316**]

and textures

creating shadows

LESSON 10

Macromedia xRes is a powerful tool for creating, editing, and combining bitmap images. You can create digital paintings working with a variety of natural, textured brushes, including charcoal, oil, and pencil, or you can customize your own brush settings and textures. xRes also allows you to manipulate and combine digital images in new ways, with precise control over the outcome.

The bitmap image editing features of xRes add a textured background and soft drop shadow to the logo image you rendered in Extreme 3D.

In this lesson, you will import the logo image you rendered in Extreme 3D and enhance it by adding a drop shadow and background texture in xRes. You will then export the completed logo for use in a FreeHand layout.

If you would like to review the final result of this lesson, open Logo4.mmi in the Complete folder within the Lesson 10 folder.

WHAT YOU WILL LEARN

In this lesson you will:

Paint with xRes brushes to achieve special effects

Apply textured brush strokes

Import images into xRes documents

Combine images using xRes objects

Use a channel as a mask

Create a drop shadow

APPROXIMATE TIME

It usually takes about 1 hour to complete this lesson.

LESSON FILES

Media Files:

Lesson10\Media\Logo3.tif

Starting Files:

None

Completed Project:

Lesson10\Complete\Logo4.mmi

Lesson10\Complete\Logo5.tif

GETTING STARTED WITH XRES

Your first task is to get acquainted with the controls and capabilities of xRes.

1] Launch xRes by double-clicking the application icon.

When the program opens, the toolbar, toolbox, and many of the panels you will use are displayed. xRes is now ready for you to open an existing image file or create a new document.

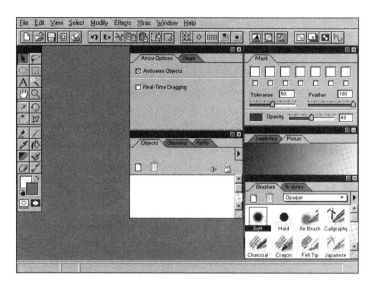

2] Close each of the panels that are currently displayed on the screen. Choose File › Preferences › Memory and change the number of Undo Levels to 3. Then click OK.

After working in FreeHand and Extreme 3D, one level of undo would seem very limiting. Increasing the undo levels in xRes increases the memory requirements of the program.

xRes creates a temporary file on your disk (which it calls the **swap disk**), allowing disk space to act as memory for the application. This allows you to work with large, high-resolution images with a minimum amount of RAM (which is typically more limited and expensive than hard disk space). You can specify in the Memory Preferences dialog box which storage devices you want xRes to use as primary and secondary swap disks. xRes defaults to using your Startup disk as the primary and secondary swap disks. xRes needs about 20 megabytes of swap-disk space to process operations. If the disk you have designated as the swap disk has less than 20 megabytes free, either designate another disk to use as a secondary swap disk or reduce the number of undo levels.

You must quit and relaunch xRes to apply any changes to the swap disk settings. Changing the number of undo levels does not require you to relaunch the program.

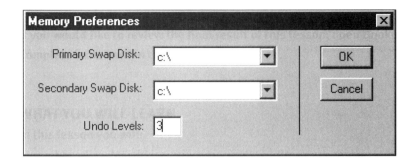

Now create a new document.

3] Choose File > New to display the New Image dialog box.

In xRes, a dialog box appears for you to specify the size, resolution, and other characteristics of a new image.

DIMENSIONS   UNITS MENU

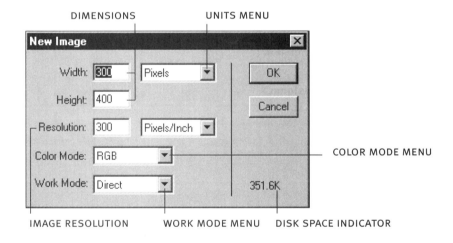

COLOR MODE MENU

IMAGE RESOLUTION   WORK MODE MENU   DISK SPACE INDICATOR

4] Use the Units menu in the dialog box to change the measurement units to inches, and enter a width of 5 inches and a height of 5 inches for the new document. Change the resolution to 72 pixels/inch. Make sure that Color Mode is set to RGB and Work Mode is set to Direct.

RGB color space is the native working mode for xRes. All of the tools and features are available when you work with RGB images. In this lesson, you will prepare the artwork as an RGB image and then convert it to CMYK before exporting the image for use in FreeHand.

Direct mode allows you to interact with the pixels directly, so the changes you make are applied immediately. Direct mode is a good choice for creating and editing smaller files (less than 10 to 20 megabytes in size). The xRes mode offers outstanding speed and flexibility for larger, high-resolution images.

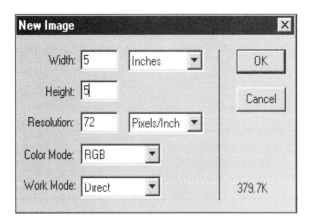

5] Click OK to create a new document with the specified settings.

A new window appears displaying an empty image document.

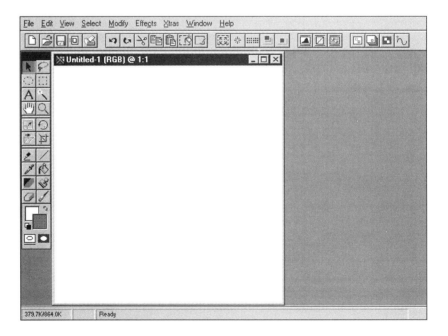

In xRes, you need to choose a brush and color before you begin to paint.

6] Choose the Brush tool in the Toolbox.

Unlike FreeHand, which creates paths and other elements that are easily modified later on, xRes creates images by changing the pixels in a document. Once paint has been applied, you cannot change the color without painting over it or applying a new color with a different tool.

Therefore, you will want to select the desired color and brush settings before you paint a stroke on the image. (Stroke here refers to *brush stroke*, not the object outlines called strokes in FreeHand.)

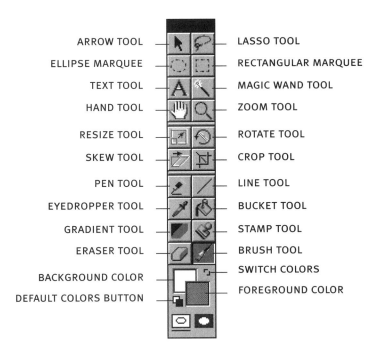

ARROW TOOL	LASSO TOOL
ELLIPSE MARQUEE	RECTANGULAR MARQUEE
TEXT TOOL	MAGIC WAND TOOL
HAND TOOL	ZOOM TOOL
RESIZE TOOL	ROTATE TOOL
SKEW TOOL	CROP TOOL
PEN TOOL	LINE TOOL
EYEDROPPER TOOL	BUCKET TOOL
GRADIENT TOOL	STAMP TOOL
ERASER TOOL	BRUSH TOOL
BACKGROUND COLOR	SWITCH COLORS
DEFAULT COLORS BUTTON	FOREGROUND COLOR

7] Double-click the Brush tool in the toolbox to display the Brush Options and Brushes panels.

As in FreeHand, these are tabbed panels that are located in panel groups by default. The Brush Options panel controls the way paint is applied by the Brush tool. Many of these settings are automatically adjusted when you select a different brush type in the Brushes panel.

The Brushes panel displays a variety of brush types, ranging from the smooth and flat look of the Hard brush to the textured effect of Charcoal and the delicate strokes of Calligraphy.

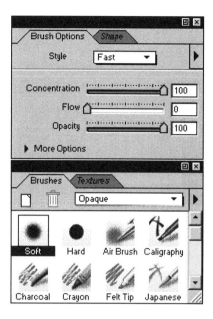

8] Click the Charcoal brush in the Brushes panel.

You have selected the type of brush you wish to paint with, but now you must specify the color you want to use.

9] Double-click the Foreground color swatch in the toolbox to display the Picker panel.

You can click any color in the Picker panel to change the foreground color. Click within the color spectrum across the bottom of the Picker to display that part of the spectrum in the larger Picker window.

By default, the Picker is grouped with the Swatches panel.

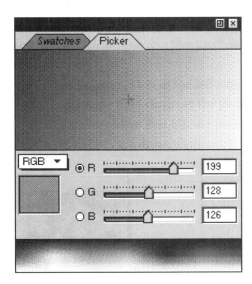

10] **Click the Swatches tab at the top of the panel group to display the Swatches panel. Enlarge the panel to see more color swatches, if desired. Click any color swatch in the panel to select that color as the foreground color.**

Now you are ready to use the Brush tool you selected.

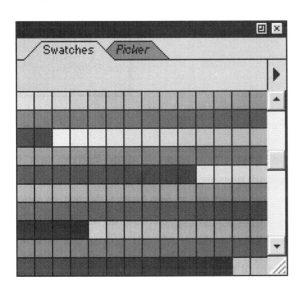

11] Move your mouse onto the page and drag around to put paint on the image. Release the mouse to finish the stroke.

Notice the texture that the Charcoal tool applies to your strokes.

12] Click the Shape tab at the top of the panel group containing the Brush Options panel. Drag the Size slider right to about the middle of the range to increase the size of the brush. Select a different color by clicking a swatch in the Swatches panel and paint a new stroke on the page.

In xRes, you will always want to specify the settings for a tool before you use that tool in your document.

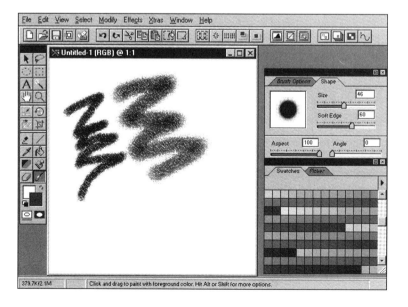

13] Close this document. Do not save your changes.

Now that you have a brief introduction of the way xRes works, you will begin to work on the Furniture Gallery Showcase artwork.

IMPORTING AN IMAGE RENDERED IN EXTREME 3D

You will be enhancing the logo artwork you have been developing over the last few lessons. First you need to import the rendered image you created in Extreme 3D.

1] Choose File › New to display the New Image dialog box.

All of the settings from the previous document are displayed again. Your settings should be the same as the ones shown here.

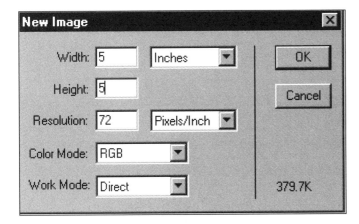

2] Choose File › Import. Select the MyLogo3 document from the MyWork folder and press Enter.

You may not be able to see all of the logo initially, since the workspace window you rendered in Extreme 3D was rectangular, and you have imported the artwork into a square image.

If you did not complete the previous projects, you can complete this lesson by importing Logo3.tif from the Complete folder within the folder for Lesson 10.

3] Save this document as *MyLogo4* in the MyWork folder on your hard drive.

The file format for this document is set to Macromedia Image (MMI), which is the
xRes file format that supports multiple objects (or images) in a single document.
Since this document contains two objects (as you will learn in the next task), it is
automatically saved as an MMI file.

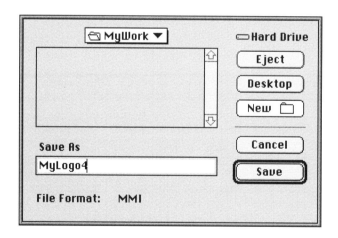

WORKING WITH XRES OBJECTS

Objects in xRes are independent image elements that you can freely move and edit, akin to the layers you have worked with in FreeHand. These objects stack up on top of one another in your documents and can be edited at any time without altering the artwork on other objects.

Every new xRes document has one object in it. When you import new objects, as you did when you imported the logo into xRes in the last task, the new element is imported as a new object, on top of any objects already in the document. The xRes file you just saved in the multiple-object format because it already had two objects in it.

1] Choose Window › Objects to display the Objects panel.
The MyLogo3 object is above Object 1 in the panel, indicating that the logo is in front of Object 1.

Only one object can be active at a time. The active object is indicated by a gray background behind the object name in the Objects panel.

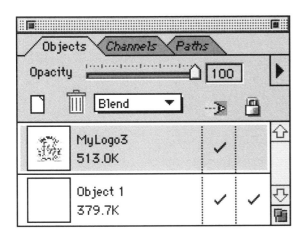

2] Center the logo artwork by choosing Modify › Align › Center to Page.

Since the MyLogo3 object was active, the logo artwork is now centered in the document window.

3] Save the document.

Now you will apply paint to Object 1, behind the MyLogo3 object.

PAINTING WITH TEXTURES

In this task, you will create a textured background that will appear behind the three-dimensional logo artwork.

1] Click once on Object 1 in the Objects panel to make that the active object.

Object 1 is now displayed with a gray background in the Objects panel. An object must be active for you to add paint or change the artwork on that object.

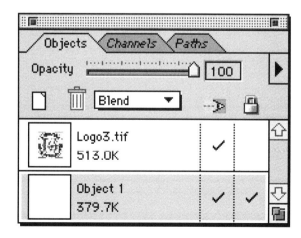

2] Hide the MyLogo3 object by clicking the check mark in the View column of the Objects panel.

This will temporarily make the artwork on the MyLogo3 object invisible. To display this object again, click its View column in Objects panel, and it will reappear.

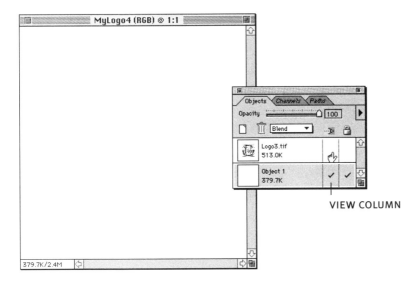

VIEW COLUMN

Now begin work on Object 1.

3] Pick a color to paint with by double-clicking the Foreground color swatch in the toolbox to display the Picker panel. Select a light color from the panel.

Too dark a background will make it difficult to see the logo clearly, so try to work with pastels or other light colors. If you prefer, you can select a color using the Swatches panel.

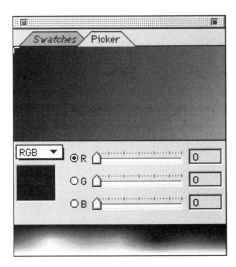

4] Choose the Brush tool from the toolbox. (If the Brushes panel is not visible on your screen, double-click the Brush tool in the toolbox.) Click once on the Air Brush icon in the Brushes panel to select that type of brush. Then choose Textured from the menu at the top of the panel.

The Brushes menu allows you to change the way a particular tool will apply color. Selecting Textured makes the Air Brush tool use a texture as it applies paint to the image.

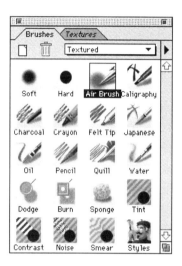

5] Click the Textures tab at the top of the panel group that contains the Brushes panel. In the Textures panel, choose the surface texture you wish the Air Brush tool to use.

xRes provides many textures—scroll down through the textures in this panel to see them all. The texture used to create the original image is Grain.

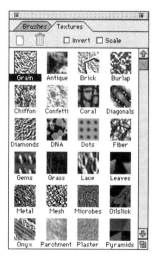

6] Drag in the document window to paint broad, textured strokes. If the brush makes very light strokes, increase the amount of paint applied by increasing the Concentration and Flow values in the Brush Options panel.

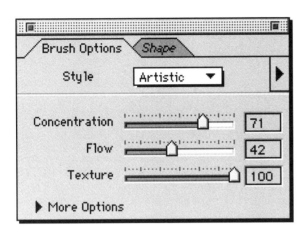

Increasing the concentration and flow in the Brush Options panel allows more paint to be applied with each stroke of the brush. You can also reduce the soft edge amount in the Shape panel which determines the softness of the brush edge.

This object will be a textured background behind the 3D logo artwork. Cover as much of the document as desired.

tip   *Remember that you have three levels of undo to work with. (That is the number of undo levels you specified in the Memory Preferences dialog box.)*

7] Choose a different color or texture (or both) and apply more paint. Experiment until you are pleased with the texture.

Since this texture is on a separate object, you can come back and change this background at any time.

8] Save your work.

The background for the artwork is complete.

CREATING A SOFT DROP SHADOW

A drop shadow is a special effect you can apply when working with multiple objects.

1] Display the MyLogo3 object by clicking its View column in the Objects panel. Activate the MyLogo3 object by clicking its name once in the Objects panel.

Notice that the logo object, with its white background, hides almost all of the beautiful texture you just created.

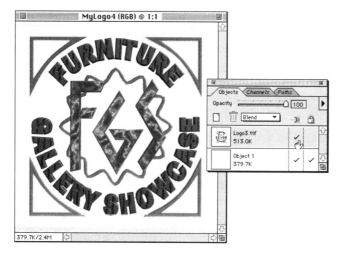

2] Click the Channels tab at the top of the Objects panel group to display the Channels panel (or choose Window > Channels).

When rendering the scene as a TIFF file in Extreme 3D, you specified that the file should contain an alpha channel for the image. (Remember that in the TIFF Options, you selected 32-bit with Alpha.) Alpha channels store intermediate channel operations and special effects.

xRes imported that alpha channel along with the visible artwork, so you can use that channel as a mask—a feature built into xRes's Channels panel.

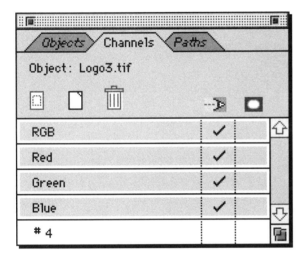

3] Click the right column for channel 4 to activate this channel as a mask.

This will mask out the area in the active object where no artwork exists, allowing the texture to show wherever the logo does not.

The top channel in the Channels panel, represented by the name RGB, is called the composite channel. Clicking the composite channel makes all of the primary channels editable and viewable. The Channels panel also displays the red, green, and blue channels, followed by one alpha channel, #4.

A mask channel determines which sections of an object are transparent and which are translucent. You create a mask channel by clicking the mask checkbox in the Channels panel.

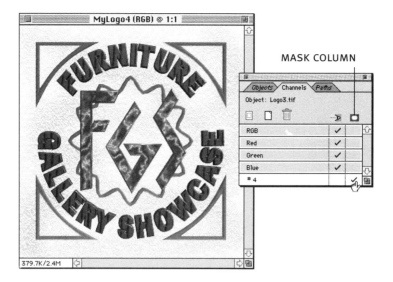

MASK COLUMN

Now you will create the drop shadow.

4] Return to the Object panel and duplicate the MyLogo3 object by choosing Edit › Duplicate.

A duplicate of the active object appears in the Object panel directly above the original. In the document window, the new object is offset to the right, just as the logo object had been when it was imported. You will reposition it in a moment.

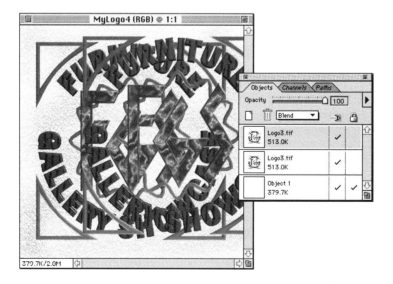

5] Rename the new object by double-clicking the object in the Objects panel to access Object Options. Enter the name *Shadow* and click OK.

Naming the objects in this way makes it very clear which object is the shadow and which is the logo, even though right now they look exactly the same.

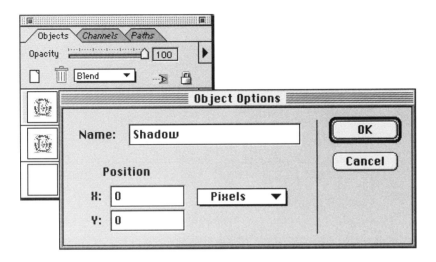

6] Click the Default Colors button near the color swatches in the toolbox to reset black and white as the foreground and background colors.

This is a quick way to reset colors to black and white.

DEFAULT COLORS BUTTON

CREATING SHADOWS AND TEXTURES

7] Fill the Shadow object with 100 percent opacity of the foreground color by selecting Edit › Fill and then sliding the Opacity slider all the way to the right.

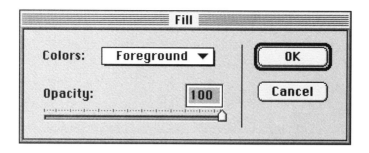

The artwork in the Shadow object is replaced with a solid black fill. However, the shadow artwork is still in the wrong position, and it is in front of the 3D artwork.

8] Select the Arrow tool in the toolbox. Choose Modify › Align › Center to Page to center the shadow artwork. Then click the Right Arrow key on the keyboard six times to move the shadow artwork 6 pixels to the right. Use the Down Arrow key on the keyboard to move the artwork down 6 pixels.

You want the shadow to be just slightly offset from the logo. Using the arrow keys to nudge artwork into position is easy and precise.

9] Move the shadow behind the logo by dragging the Shadow object below your MyLogo3 object in the Objects panel.

Watch for a heavy line to indicate that the Shadow object will be positioned as desired when you release the mouse.

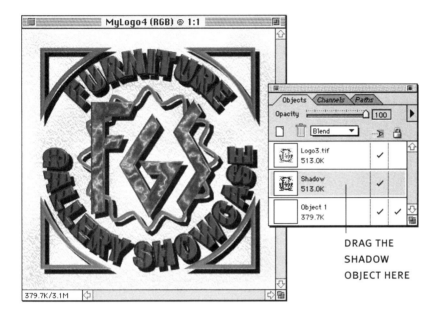

DRAG THE
SHADOW
OBJECT HERE

The shadow artwork is now behind the 3D logo. Next you will soften the shadow.

10] Display the Channels panel by clicking its tab at the top of the panel group containing the Objects panel. Click channel 4 to activate that channel.

Activating channel 4 deactivates and hides the RGB channels, which hides the color components of this artwork. That is why the shadow now appears white.

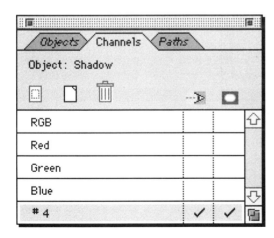

11] Display the RGB channels by clicking the View column of the RGB channel.

Turning on the display of the RGB composite channel automatically displays
the individual red, green, and blue channels, which displays the black artwork
in your image.

tip *To achieve the desired results, make sure that channel 4 is active (it has a gray
background behind it) and the other channels are not (they appear with white behind the
channel name).*

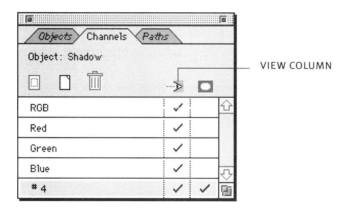

VIEW COLUMN

**12] Soften the shadow using a Gaussian Blur effect by choosing Effect › Blur ›
Gaussian. Enter an amount of *10* and click OK.**

This slightly blurs the edges to soften the shadow. A Gaussian Blur is a smooth blur.
You chose a radius for the blur of 10 pixels.

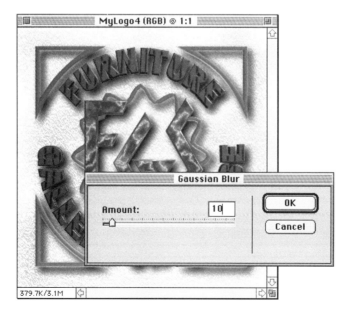

13] Go back to the Objects panel. With the Shadow object active, change the opacity at the top of the panel to 40 percent.

You can adjust the opacity of your shadow as desired.

14] Save the document.

The artwork is complete.

CHANGING THE COLOR MODE TO CMYK FOR PROCESS COLOR OUTPUT

In the next lesson, you will incorporate the completed logo image into a layout in FreeHand that you will prepare for process color output. You will need to convert this image to CMYK before exporting the file.

1] Select Modify > Color Mode > CMYK.

The only visible difference is that the colors in the image may appear to lose some of their brilliance, since very bright colors cannot be reproduced with process color inks.

2] Save the document.

This updates the xRes MMI file. The individual objects will be available the next time you open this file. To prepare the file for use in other applications, use the Export command.

3] Choose File › Export › TIFF. Save this TIFF file in your MyWork folder with the name *MyLogo5*. In the Tiff Options dialog box that appears, select your computer platform and click OK.

This creates a new single-object TIFF file, ready to be imported into FreeHand or other applications.

xRes offers a wide variety of export formats, including the most popular formats for print, multimedia, and Internet projects. xRes also imports and exports Photoshop files, automatically converting between xRes objects and Photoshop layers.

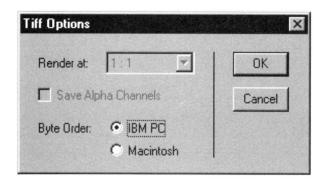

4] You are finished with xRes, so quit the program.

In the next lesson, you will return to FreeHand.

WHAT YOU HAVE LEARNED

In this lesson you have:

Chosen colors from the Color Picker and Swatches panels [*page* **327**]

Used and modified xRes brushes [*page* **328**]

Imported an Extreme 3D rendering into an xRes document [*page* **329**]

Combined xRes objects to create a composite image [*page* **331**]

Created an artistic background using the brush and texture controls [*page* **332**]

Used an alpha channel as a mask [*page* **337**]

Created a drop shadow by duplicating an object and applying a filter [*page* **338**]

Changed the color mode for process color output [*page* **343**]

together

putting it all

Now you will see the full power of the FreeHand Graphics Studio. Over the previous four lessons, you have used all four FreeHand Graphics Studio applications— FreeHand, Fontographer, Extreme 3D, and xRes—to create a logo image. In this lesson, you will bring all of that work together by incorporating the logo you exported from xRes into a layout for a bookmark in FreeHand. As you prepare the layout, you will put to use many of the concepts you learned in the earlier lessons in this book, such as formatting, blending, and applying colors.

**Furniture
Gallery
Showcase
2000**

The Annual National
Furniture Exhibit

Coming soon to a city near you!

In this lesson, the logo you created using all four FreeHand Graphics Studio applications will be incorporated into a bookmark layout. In creating this bookmark, you will return to many of the concepts you learned in the earlier lessons in this book.

If you would like to review the final result of this lesson, open Bookmark.fh7 in the Complete folder within the folder for Lesson 11.

WHAT YOU WILL LEARN

In this lesson you will:

Assemble a FreeHand layout incorporating an xRes image

Apply paragraph formatting to text

Apply colors from imported images to other elements

Join a blend to a path

Center text and graphics on the page

APPROXIMATE TIME

It usually takes about 30 minutes to complete this lesson.

LESSON FILES

Media Files:

Lesson11\Media\Logo5.tif

Starting Files:

None

Completed Project:

Lesson11\Complete\Bookmark.fh7

SETTING UP THE PAGE

The bookmark layout does not fit a standard page size, so your first task is to create a new document with a custom page size.

1] Launch FreeHand and create a new document. Change the measurement units to Picas. In the Document Inspector, set a custom page size of 16P0 x 42P0, select Portrait (tall) orientation, and set the Printer resolution to 600 dpi. Change the view to Fit to Window (Windows Ctrl+Shift+W, Macintosh Command+Shift+W).

The page is now the correct size for the bookmark you are creating.

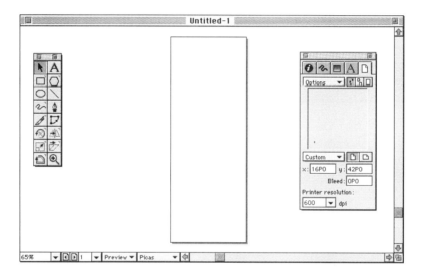

2] Save the document as *MyBookmark* in the MyWork folder on your hard drive.

IMPORTING THE XRES FILE

The FGS logo you completed in the previous lesson will be the first element of the bookmark.

1] Choose File > Import. Locate the MyLogo5 image in your MyWork folder and click Open.

The import cursor appears, ready to add the image to your page.

If you did not complete the projects in the previous lessons, you can open Logo5.tif in the Complete folder within the folder for Lesson 11 to continue with this lesson.

2] Position the import cursor at the top-left corner of the page and click.

The logo you created in the previous four lessons appears on your page, although it is much larger than you need for this layout.

Next you will resize this image using Shift+Alt (Windows) or Shift+Option (Macintosh). Holding down Shift keeps the image in proportion, and holding down Alt (Windows) or Option (Macintosh) snaps the artwork to the optimum sizes for the output resolution you specified.

3] Hold down Shift and Alt (Windows) or Option (Macintosh) and drag the lower-right corner handle up and to the left. Release the mouse when the logo is sized to fit on the page.

The logo snaps to predetermined sizes as you drag.

4] Move the logo to visually center it on the top of the page. Save your document.

You will use the Align controls to accurately center this on the page in a few moments.

5] Use the Color Mixer to create a color containing 0 percent cyan, 100 percent magenta, 100 percent yellow, and 27 percent black. Add this color to the Color List.

All the colors in this document will be process colors.

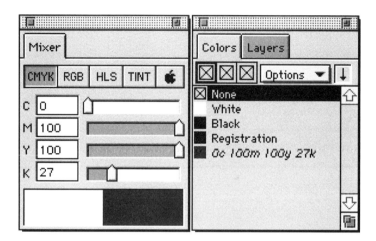

6] Using the Eyedropper tool, pick up a medium shade of green from the logo image and add it to the Color List. Then pick up a light shade of blue (or any light color in the background of your logo) and add it to the Color List as well.

The Eyedropper tool can be found by choosing Window > Xtras > Xtra Tools. The three process colors will be applied to the text you are about to enter.

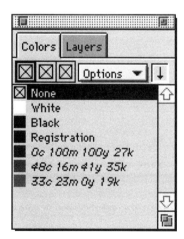

7] Save the document.

CREATING A TEXT BLOCK AND ENTERING TEXT

Next you will create one text block to hold all of the text in this layout.

1] With the Text tool, start at the left edge of the page, just below the logo, and drag to the bottom-right corner of the page.

This creates a text block that fills the page from the left to the right edge. Centering text in this text block will automatically center the text on the page.

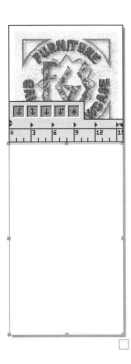

2] Type the first paragraph, *Furniture Gallery Showcase*, without pressing Enter (Windows) or Return (Macintosh) between the words. When you have typed the entire paragraph, press Enter or Return.

Don't worry that the words do not appear on separate lines. After you format the text it will flow properly within the text block.

Just as in a word processor, press Enter or Return only at the end of a paragraph.

3] Type *2000* and press Enter (Windows) or Return (Macintosh).

This puts the number in a paragraph by itself.

4] Type the next paragraph, *The Annual National Furniture Exhibit,* and press Enter (Windows) or Return (Macintosh).

Use the Backspace or Delete key as needed if you make a mistake.

5] Type the last line of text, *Coming soon to a city near you!*

This is the last paragraph, so you do not need to press Enter or Return at the end of this text. All of the text should appear on the page, but it is not formatted correctly.

6] Save the document.

After all that typing, you don't want to lose your work!

FORMATTING THE TEXT

In addition to FreeHand's character formatting and alignment controls, you will also use the paragraph formatting controls.

1] Select all of the text by clicking the Text tool anywhere in the text and choosing Edit > Select All (Windows Ctrl+A, Macintosh Command+A). Change the view to 100%.
Select All in a text block selects all of the visible text in a block as well as any text that did not fit into the text block or the continuation of this story that flows into other text blocks throughout the document.

Zooming in to actual size allows you to clearly see the type as you apply formatting.

2] Change the font to URWGaramondTDemi and set the text to Align Center by clicking the toolbar button or choosing Text > Align > Center.

Each paragraph requires a different type size, so you must format each one individually.

3] Select _Furniture Gallery Showcase_ and set the type size to 30 points. Select _2000_ and change the type size to 50 points. Apply your green color to the number. Save your work.

Once the words in the first paragraph are large enough, they each require their own line and are now positioned as you want them.

Remember that to change the color of specific characters within a text block (without changing the others), you must first select the characters—in this case, *2000*—with the Text tool. Then drag a color swatch from the Color List and drop it on the selected text. (If you chose colors other than green from your logo, apply the color of your choice to this character.)

tip *In situations where the text does not automatically wrap as you would like in a text block, position your insertion point where you want the text to break and press Shift+Enter. This inserts a line break within the current paragraph, moving the text that follows the insertion point to the next line.*

4] Select the next paragraph (The Annual National Furniture Exhibit), change the type size to *16* points, and apply your red color from the Color List. Change the following paragraph (Coming soon to a city near you!) to *12* points and apply the blue color to the last line of text.

If you chose different colors from your logo image, apply a color you have not used yet to the last line in the text.

The characters are formatted properly, but the positioning of the text needs adjustment.

APPLYING PARAGRAPH FORMATTING

The Text Inspector offers additional ways to control the behavior of paragraphs of text.

1] Select the third paragraph (The Annual National Furniture Exhibit). Display the Text Inspector, and activate the Paragraph subpanel by clicking the ¶ button at the top of the Inspector. Change the Space Above Paragraph value to 3P0 and press Enter.

The selected paragraph moves 3 picas down, away from the preceding paragraph.

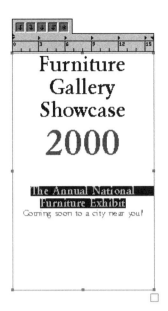
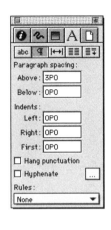

2] Select the next paragraph (*Coming soon to a city near you!*). Change the Space Above Paragraph value to 7P0 and press Enter.

Paragraph formatting applies only to the selected paragraph.

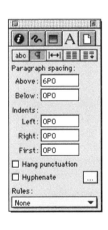

3] Save your work.

Now your text is positioned properly.

ADDING A BLEND JOINED TO A PATH

In previous lessons you created blends between elements. In this task, you will create the same type of blend and then join it to a path to add a star design to the bottom of the bookmark.

1] Double-click the Polygon tool in the toolbox. Change the shape to Star, specify 5 sides, and click OK.

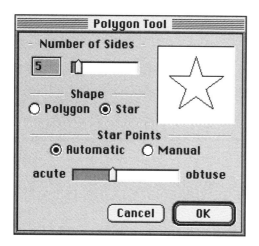

2] In the space between the last two paragraphs of text, draw a small star and then another star just a bit larger.

These should be located in the open space near the bottom of the bookmark page and should be similar in size to the ones shown here.

3] Fill one of the stars with red and another with blue (or any two colors you have in the Color List). Set the stroke to None.

Now you will blend the two shapes.

4] Select both stars by holding the Shift key to select the second star, and choose Modify › Combine › Blend.

FreeHand creates a blend with the optimum number of steps for the printer resolution you defined earlier—assuming that you want a smooth blend that completely fills the distance between the original shapes. However, this is not what you want.

5] In the Object Inspector, enter *8* as the number of steps in this blend.

The blend now contains 8 stars between the original two shapes.

6] Use the Ellipse tool to draw an ellipse that fits between the lower two paragraphs of text, as shown here.

The ellipse can overlap the stars. This is the path you will attach the blend to in the next step.

7] Use the Pointer tool and the Shift key and select both the ellipse and the blend. Choose Modify › Combine › Join Blend to Path.

You can blend two or more elements, and you can also join blends to open or closed paths.

tip *The Join Blend to Path feature is a great tool for creating custom borders.*

8] Save your work.

CENTERING EVERYTHING ON THE PAGE

There is one more detail to complete before the layout is finished. The text and graphic elements are not quite centered on the page.

1] To accurately center the elements horizontally on the page, choose Edit › Select All. Use the Align panel to center these two element horizontally.

The text block extends slightly farther to the left and the right than the logo and blend graphic. Centering these three items horizontally leaves the text block in its current position (extending from the left to the right edge of the page) and repositions the graphics so they center align with the text. In this case, since the text block fits the width of the page perfectly, the elements are already centered horizontally on the page.

You may not be able to see much difference in the position of elements on the page, depending upon how your graphics were originally positioned, but now you are certain that all of the elements are centered on this page.

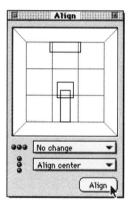

tip *When you need to center a graphic on your page, you can temporarily create a rectangle that matches the size of the page exactly. (FreeHand will even help you snap it in to the page edges.) Align your element(s) to this page rectangle and then delete the rectangle.*

2] Save your work.
You have combined artwork created in each of the four individual FreeHand Graphics Studio applications together to create your completed bookmark.

WHAT YOU HAVE LEARNED

In this lesson you have:

Imported and resized an xRes image [*page* **348**]

Practiced creating new process colors [*page* **350**]

Practiced selecting colors from a bitmap image [*page* **350**]

Used paragraph formatting to add space between text paragraphs [*page* **356**]

Created a blend and joined it to a path [*page* **358**]

Accurately centered text and graphics on the page [*page* **361**]

for the web

shocking artwork

Shockwave is Macromedia technology that allows users to interact with and view dynamic media and graphics over the World Wide Web. Shockwave comes in many forms, including Shockwave Multimedia for Macromedia Director movies, Shockwave Graphics for FreeHand artwork, and Shockwave Imaging for high-resolution xRes images. Shockwave elements provide a high-impact way to communicate your ideas by enhancing a standard Web page with dynamic graphics.

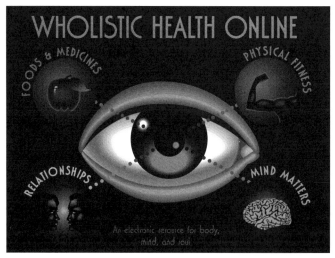

FreeHand illustrations like this one can be posted on the Web with Shockwave Graphics. xRes images can be posted with Shockwave Imaging.

LESSON 12

Designed by Julia Sifers of Glasgow & Associates.

In this lesson, you will see how Shockwave Graphics enables you to display FreeHand graphic files within standard HTML Web pages. You will also see how you can use Shockwave Imaging to publish and view high-resolution image files on the Web, without having to download the entire image file.

You create artwork for use with Shockwave and the World Wide Web the same way you create any other graphic or image. After the artwork is completed, you simply "shock" it to prepare it for the Web.

The best way to start your study of Shockwave is by viewing examples of Shockwave elements in a Web browser—so that's how you'll begin here. Note that you will need a Shockwave-enabled browser to see these examples.

WHAT YOU WILL LEARN

In this lesson you will:

Learn about Shockwave Graphics and Shockwave Imaging

Learn what a browser is and why you need one

Prepare FreeHand artwork for display on a Web page

Prepare an xRes image for distribution on a Web page

APPROXIMATE TIME

It usually takes about 1 hour to complete this lesson.

LESSON FILES

Media Files:

Lesson12\Media\Health.fhc

Lesson12\Media\Healthy.htm

Lesson12\Media\Whodunit.swx

Lesson12\Media\Mystery.htm

Starting Files:

Lesson12\Start\Zoo.fh7

Lesson12\Start\Mystery.tif

Completed Project:

Lesson12\Complete\Zoo.fhc

Lesson12\Complete\Mystery.swx

OBTAINING SHOCKWAVE AND THE BROWSER SOFTWARE

Shockwave includes two distinct functional parts: **Afterburner**, the developer tools that allow you to create Shockwave elements from your FreeHand, xRes, or Director artwork; and the Shockwave **plug-ins**, which allow shocked elements to be incorporated and viewed on a Web page. (Once a graphic or image is processed with Afterburner, it can be referred to as a 'shocked' graphic or image.)

You will experiment with two different Shockwave technologies in this lesson. Shockwave Graphics includes an Afterburner Xtra for FreeHand and a plug-in for your browser that enables the display of FreeHand artwork within a Web page. Shockwave Imaging utilizes an Afterburner utility that compresses xRes images along with another plug-in for the browser.

The most up-to-date versions of Afterburner and the Shockwave plug-ins can always be downloaded for free from Macromedia's Web site (http://www.macromedia.com). A Shockwave developer's kit, which includes information on server configuration, tips and techniques, troubleshooting, and more, can also be downloaded from the Web site.

tip *Before using Shockwave or Afterburner, you should visit Macromedia's Web site to be sure you have the latest version of the software.*

1] If you don't already have Afterburner and Shockwave for both FreeHand and xRes on your computer, install the files from the CD-ROM now.

You will not be able to follow the steps in this lesson if you do not have the software installed on your computer.

2] If you don't already have a Web browser that supports the Shockwave plug-ins, download that now.

A Web browser is software that is used to navigate around the World Wide Web and view files published there. Netscape Navigator versions 2.02 and later and Microsoft Internet Explorer versions 3.0 and later are two popular browsers that support Shockwave. Both are available for downloading from the Web. To download Netscape Navigator, go to http://www.netscape.com. To download Internet Explorer, go to http://www.microsoft.com.

VIEWING AN EXAMPLE OF SHOCKWAVE GRAPHICS

To better understand how Shockwave works for FreeHand documents, you first will look at an example document in a Web browser. If you do not have a Shockwave-enabled browser, read through these steps in order to learn about the features offered by Shockwave Graphics.

1] Quit any other applications that may be open. Drag the Healthy.htm document located in the Media folder within the folder for Lesson 12 and drop it on the icon for your Web browser.

This launches your browser and opens this sample Web page containing "shocked" FreeHand artwork and displaying the Shockwave Graphics toolbar across the top. (The toolbar can be shown at the top or bottom of the graphic, or not at all, if you prefer.)

Keyboard commands for the toolbar functions are displayed below the graphic on the Web page. You may have to scroll down to find them.

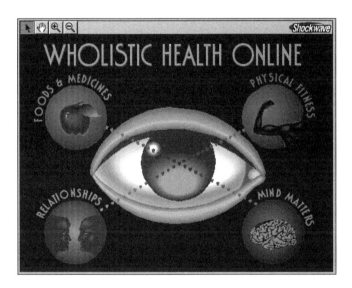

2] Zoom in to any part of the artwork using the Zoom tool. Then zoom in on the text.

Just as when you are working in FreeHand, you can zoom in (up to 26,500 percent) and out without losing detail.

The fonts used in this document are not installed on your system, yet the type looks great. Shockwave Graphics can embed the font information and anti-alias the characters in the graphic, which blends the edges to make the text look smoother.

3] Click the Shockwave name on the toolbar to return to the original view of the document. Select the Pointer tool from the toolbar.

Shockwave Graphics also enable you to assign a **URL**, or universal resource locator, to any element in the artwork. The URL is the standard address for anything on the Internet. Assigning a URL turns an element into a button that will take your viewers to the assigned address when they click the element.

4] Without clicking, point to any of the four regions identified by the circles in the artwork.

The cursor will change from a pointer to a pointing hand, indicating that this element is a button. Some Web browsers also display the URL of this button in the bar across the bottom of the browser screen.

If you click one of these buttons, the browser will attempt to find the page to which the button is linked. Since these buttons are for illustration purposes only and are not actually linked to anything, the browser will display a Not Found error. Simply click the Back button in the browser window to return to the Shockwave Graphics example.

5] Close this Web page.

Next you will experiment with a sample of an xRes image on a Web page.

VIEWING AN EXAMPLE OF SHOCKWAVE IMAGING

Most graphics currently displayed on Web pages are 72-pixel-per-inch images which do not permit you to zoom in to see a portion of these images in greater detail. If you want to show a larger version of the image or more detail in a particular area of the image, you must prepare a separate graphic and link its location to the small original (**thumbnail**) view. Shockwave Imaging for xRes eliminates that process.

New Shockwave technology enables you to include a high-resolution image on your Web page, and the server will download only enough image data to display the image at the zoom level that the viewer selects. If the viewer zooms in to get a closer look, the server delivers the image data needed to display the image at that magnification.

In this task, you will see the results of this process. If you do not have a Shockwave-enabled browser, read through these steps in order to learn about the features offered by Shockwave Images.

1] In your Web browser, open the Mystery.htm document located in the Media folder within the folder for Lesson 12.

A Web page appears displaying an xRes image along with the Shockwave toolbar.

2] Select the Zoom tool and click any part of the image to see more detail.

This Shockwave Image updates without changing to a different Web page, zooming it to see the portion of the graphic you clicked on at greater magnification. Additional detail is loaded as needed when you zoom in or out or pan around the image with the Grabber Hand tool.

3] Quit the browser application.

In the next tasks, you will learn how to shock graphics and images yourself. You will be working in FreeHand and xRes.

SHOCKING A FREEHAND DOCUMENT

In this task, you will be using FreeHand to shock an illustration you completed in an earlier lesson.

1] Launch FreeHand and open the MyZoo document you saved in the MyWork folder on the hard drive.

This artwork includes five wildlife figures at the bottom of the page, which will make excellent buttons on a Web page!

A completed Zoo.fh7 is available in the Start folder within the folder for Lesson 12.

2] Choose Window > Xtras > URL Editor. Choose New from the Options menu at the top of the URL Editor and click OK to accept the default URL that appears. Then drag the new item from the panel and drop it on the wolf figure to assign this URL to the wolf.

The URL Editor panel enables you to define URLs then drag and drop them onto elements on the page. FreeHand always suggests the Macromedia Web site when you create a new URL.

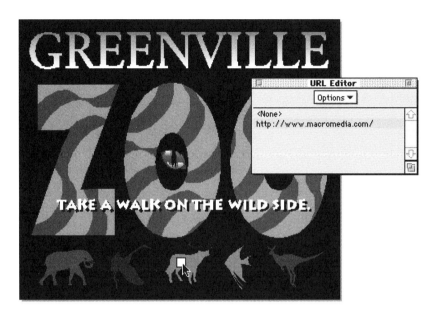

3] Create a few more URLs and apply them to other figures at the bottom of the page.
Any FreeHand element can have a URL assigned.

You are just about ready to compress this file with Afterburner.

4] Choose File > Save As. Enter *MyZoo2* as the name and save this file in your MyWork folder.
The file must be saved before you compress it with Afterburner.

5] Choose Xtras > Afterburner > Compress Document.
You can lock this item so others with FreeHand will not be able to open it to make changes. Embed Outline Fonts enables the Shockwave graphic to display text accurately without requiring the viewer to have the fonts loaded on his or her computer. Shockwave Graphics supports all Type 1 PostScript and TrueType fonts and will anti-alias the text in your Shockwave graphic, blending the edges to make the characters appear smoother.

All of the text in this graphic has been converted to paths, so there are no fonts in this layout to embed.

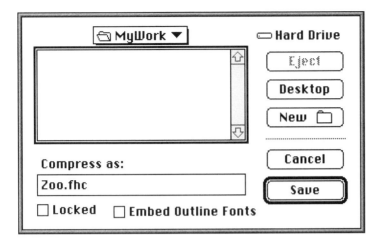

6] Enter the name *Zoo.fhc,* leave Locked and Embed Outline Fonts turned off, and save this document in the MyWork folder on your hard drive.

The FHC extension on the name means FreeHand Compressed, and indicates to the browser plug-in what type of file it is. The original FreeHand document takes up approximately 63 kilobytes on the disk. After converting it with Afterburner, the FHC file takes up only 25 kilobytes—and on the Web, the smaller your file is, the faster your viewers will be able to see it!

This Shockwave element is ready for the Web. Before returning to the browser to see your results, however, you will learn how to shock an xRes image.

SHOCKING AN XRES IMAGE

Next you will explore the process of preparing an image file for presentation as a Shockwave image on a Web page.

1] Quit FreeHand and launch xRes. Open Mystery.tif, located in the Start folder within the folder for Lesson 12.

In traditional Web graphic preparation, the resolution of an image is reduced to 72 pixels-per-inch (ppi). If this Mystery.tif were reduced to 72 ppi, it would take up approximately 176 kilobytes on a disk. With Shockwave Imaging, high-resolution images will allow users to zoom in on a portion of the image for greater detail. This Mystery.tif graphic is four times the resolution of a standard Web graphic, and takes up approximately 2.7 megabytes on the disk.

2] Choose File › Save As. Change the file format to LRG and the name to *MyMystery*. Then press Enter to save this document in the MyWork folder.

If your document contains more than one object, use the File > Export command instead.

xRes images must be saved as LRG files in order to be converted to Shockwave images. LRG is the format used for the xRes work mode (as opposed to the Direct mode you have used in these lessons).

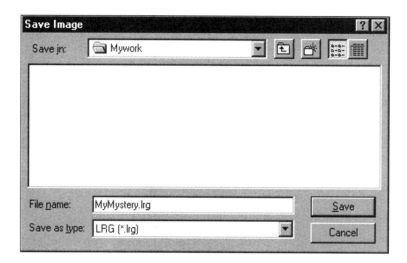

3] Quit the xRes application.

Afterburner for Imaging is a separate utility application, so you are finished with xRes at this time.

4] Open Afterburner for xRes and choose File › Open. Select your MyMystery document and press Enter.

The LRG file is converted to SWX format, the Shockwave Imaging format.

The original TIFF file for this image is approximately 2.7 megabytes, and the LRG file is 4.7 megabytes, but the Shockwave image (SWX file) is only 272 kilobytes—using the default compression settings. (You can customize the compression settings with the Compression menu before opening an LRG image.) This incredible compression is one part of the magic of Shockwave Imaging.

5] Quit Afterburner.

Now you are ready to see your results!

VIEWING YOUR SHOCKWAVE ARTWORK

Now you will open the Web browser application and see how your Shockwave elements turned out.

1] Drag the Zoo.fhc document located in your MyWork folder and drop it on the icon for your Web browser.

A completed Zoo.fhc file is also available in the Complete folder within the folder for Lesson 12.

This is an easy way to view the document in the browser. No toolbar will appear on this artwork.

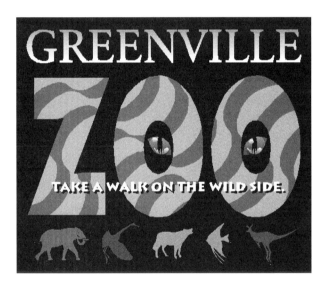

In Windows, hold down the Ctrl key and click the left mouse button to zoom in; hold down Ctrl+Alt and click to zoom out. Return the view to the original magnification by holding down Ctrl+Shift and clicking. Hold down the spacebar to display the Grabber Hand and drag to pan around the document.

On the Macintosh, hold down the Command key and click your mouse button to zoom in; hold down Command+Option and click to zoom out. Return to the original magnification by holding down Command+Shift and clicking. Hold down Ctrl to display the Grabber Hand and drag to pan around the document.

Now look at the other document.

2] Drag your MyMystery.swx document onto the icon for the browser application and release.

The xRes image appears in the browser window. Use the same keyboard controls as described in the previous step to zoom and pan in the image.

EMBEDDING SHOCKWAVE ELEMENTS IN HTML PAGES

Now that you can create Shockwave elements, you need to learn how to incorporate them into Web pages. The steps here will only get you started. For more information on how to create web pages and incorporate Shockwave elements, visit the *Shockwave Developer's Guide* at Macromedia's World Wide Web site: http://www.macro-media.com.

1] Open the text file Healthy.htm located in the Media folder within the folder for Lesson 12 and review the contents.

This file is a pure text file and can be opened in any text editor or word processor.

The text you see is in **HTML**, the hypertext markup language that is used to create Web pages.

2] Locate this line in the document:

<A><EMBED SRC="health.fhc" WIDTH=452 HEIGHT=332 TOOLBAR=TOP></A>

The <EMBED> tag is the instruction that tells the browser to include a shocked graphic. Within this tag are the dimensions of the graphic (in pixels) and an instruction to display the toolbar at the top of the graphic.

The toolbar can be set to Top or Bottom, or it can be left out of the <EMBED> tag if you don't want the toolbar to be displayed. If you do use a toolbar, add 20 pixels to the height of the graphic when entering the dimensions in the tag, as was done here.

Use this form of embed command to incorporate FreeHand graphics as Shockwave elements in your Web pages.

3] Quit the application without saving any changes.

The <EMBED> tag for xRes images is a bit more complex, since the technology requires that the system hosting the Web pages must be configured to provide Shockwave Imaging capability. Refer to Macromedia's Web site at http://www.macromedia.com for detailed information about incorporating Shockwave Images into your Web pages.

WHAT YOU HAVE LEARNED

In this lesson you have:

Worked with examples of Shockwave Graphics [*page* **367**]

Viewed Web pages and graphics in a Web browser [*page* **367**]

Converted a FreeHand document into a Shockwave graphic [*page* **369**]

Converted an xRes file into a Shockwave image [*page* **371**]

Learned how to embed a Shockwave graphic into an HTML page [*page* **374**]

CONCLUSION

Congratulations! You have just completed all the lessons in the FreeHand Graphics Studio Authorized book. In these lessons, you have created simple and complex graphics and designed single- and multiple-page layouts containing text, graphics, and imported images. You've also used FreeHand's tracing tools to create paths, organized your documents using layers and styles, pasted artwork inside other paths, and created blends between paths.

You have learned how to combine the four FreeHand Graphics Studio applications on projects, and been introduced to Shockwave Graphics and Imaging. We hope you enjoyed learning about the FreeHand Graphics Studio, and most of all, we hope the techniques in these lessons will help you in your own graphic design, page layout, and illustration projects.

windows shortcuts

FreeHand offers lots of keyboard shortcuts that, once you learn them, will make your work easier. Many are described in the lessons in this book. This appendix list's FreeHand's keyboard shortcuts for menu commands, for some other common tasks, and for displaying FreeHand's panels and tools on Windows computers.

APPENDIX A

FILE MENU

Command	Shortcut
New	Ctrl+N
Open	Ctrl+O
Close	Ctrl+F4
Save	Ctrl+S
Save As	Ctrl+Shift+S
Import	Ctrl+R
Export	Ctrl+Shift+R
Print	Ctrl+P
Preferences	Ctrl+Shift+D
Exit	Alt+F4

EDIT MENU

Command	Shortcut
Undo	Ctrl+Z
Redo	Ctrl+Y
Cut	Ctrl+X
Copy	Ctrl+C
Paste	Ctrl+V
Cut Contents	Ctrl+Shift+X
Paste Inside	Ctrl+Shift+V
Copy Attributes	Ctrl+Shift+Alt+C
Paste Attributes	Ctrl+Shift+Alt+V
Duplicate	Ctrl+D
Clone	Ctrl+Shift+C
Select All	Ctrl+A
Select All in Document	Ctrl+Shift+A
Find and Replace Text	Ctrl+Alt+Z
Find and Replace Graphics	Ctrl+Alt+E

VIEW MENU

Command	Shortcut
Fit Selection	Ctrl+0 (zero)
Fit to Page	Ctrl+Shift+W
Fit All	Ctrl+Alt+0 (zero)
Magnification 50%	Ctrl+5
Magnification 100%	Ctrl+1
Magnification 200%	Ctrl+2
Magnification 400%	Ctrl+4
Magnification 800%	Ctrl+8
Preview or Keyline	Ctrl+K
Panels	Ctrl+Alt+H
Info Bar	Ctrl+Alt+J
Page Rulers	Ctrl+Alt+M
Text Rulers	Ctrl+Shift+Alt+T
Snap to Point	Ctrl+Shift+Z
Snap to Guides	Ctrl+Alt+G

MODIFY MENU

Command	Shortcut
Object	Ctrl+I
Stroke	Ctrl+Alt+L
Fill	Ctrl+Alt+F
Text	Ctrl+T
Document	Ctrl+Alt+D
Transform	Ctrl+M
Transform Again	Ctrl+Shift+G
Bring to Front	Ctrl+F
Move Forward	Ctrl+Shift+F
Move Backward	Ctrl+Shift+K
Send to Back	Ctrl+B
Align	Ctrl+Alt+A
Align Again	Ctrl+Shift+Alt+A
Join	Ctrl+J
Split	Ctrl+Shift+J
Blend	Ctrl+Shift+B
Lock	Ctrl+L
Unlock	Ctrl+Shift+L
Group	Ctrl+G
Ungroup	Ctrl+U

TEXT MENU

Command	Shortcut
Smaller Size	Ctrl+Alt+1
Larger Size	Ctrl+Alt+2
Type Style Plain	F5 or Ctrl+Shift+Alt+P
Type Style Bold	F6 or Ctrl+Alt+B
Type Style Italic	F7 or Ctrl+Alt+I
Type Style Bold Italic	F8 or Ctr.l+Shift+Alt+O
Effect None	Ctrl+Shift+Alt+N
Effect Highlight	Ctrl+Shift+Alt+H
Effect Strikethrough	Ctrl+Shift+Alt+S
Effect Underline	Ctrl+Alt+U
Align Left	Ctrl+Shift+Alt+L
Align Right	Ctrl+Shift+Alt+R
Align Center	Ctrl+Shift+Alt+M
Align Justified	Ctrl+Shift+Alt+J
End of Line	Shift+Enter
Non-Breaking Space	Ctrl+Shift+H
Em Space	Ctrl+Shift+M
En Space	Ctrl+Shift+N
Thin Space	Ctrl+Shift+T
Discretionary Hyphen	Ctrl+_ (underscore)
Editor	Ctrl+Shift+E
Spelling	Ctrl+Alt+S
Run Around Selection	Ctrl+Alt+W
Flow Inside Path	Ctrl+Shift+U
Attach to Path	Ctrl+Shift+Y
Convert to Paths	Ctrl+Shift+P

378

WINDOW MENU

Command	Shortcut
New Window	Ctrl+Alt+N
Text Toolbars	Ctrl+Alt+T
Toolbox	Ctrl+7
Object Inspector	Ctrl+I
Stroke Inspector	Ctrl+Alt+L
Fill Inspector	Ctrl+Alt+F
Text Inspector	Ctrl+T
Document Inspector	Ctrl+Alt+D
Layers Panel	Ctrl+6
Styles Panel	Ctrl+3
Color List Panel	Ctrl+9
Color Mixer Panel	Ctrl+Shift+9
Halftones Panel	Ctrl+H
Align Panel	Ctrl+Alt+A
Transform Panel	Ctrl+M
Xtras Operations	Ctrl+Alt+O
Xtra Xtra Tools	Ctrl+Alt+X
Cascade	Shift+F5
Tile	Shift+F4

DRAWING AND EDITING COMMANDS

Command	Shortcut
Clone	Ctrl+Shift+C
Cut Contents	Ctrl+Shift+X
Thinner Stroke	Ctrl+Shift+1
Deselect All	Tab
Grabber Hand	Spacebar
Group	Ctrl+G
Thicker Stroke	Ctrl+Shift+2
Paste Inside	Ctrl+Shift+V
Preview or Keyline	Ctrl+K
Select All in Document	Ctrl+Shift+A
Select All on Page	Ctrl+A
Snap to Guides	Ctrl+Alt+G
Snap to Point	Ctrl+Shift+Z
Increase Variable Stroke or Calligraphic Pen Size	Left Arrow or 1
Decrease Variable Stroke or Calligraphic Pen Size	Right Arrow or 2
Ungroup	Ctrl+U

GENERAL COMMANDS

Command	Shortcut
Close Document	Ctrl+F4
Close All Open Documents	Ctrl+Shift+F4
Export	Ctrl+Shift+R
Help Cursor	Shift+F1
Import	Ctrl+R
Next Page	Ctrl+Page Down
New Window	Ctrl+Alt+N
Previous Page	Ctrl+Page Up
Zoom In Magnification	Ctrl+Spacebar+click
Zoom Out Magnification	Ctrl+Alt+Spacebar+click

DISPLAYING PANELS AND TOOLS

To display this	Use
Align	Ctrl+Alt+A
Arrowhead Editor Arrowhead	Alt+Select
Bezigon tool	8
Blend	Ctrl+Shift+B
Color List	Ctrl+9
Color Mixer	Ctrl+Shift+9
Columns and Rows Inspector	Ctrl+Alt+R
Copyfit Inspector	Ctrl+Alt+C
Document Inspector	Ctrl+Alt+D
Ellipse tool	3
Fill Inspector	Ctrl+Alt+F
Freehand tool	5
Grabber Hand tool	Spacebar
Halftones panel	Ctrl+H
Hide or Show All Open Panels	Ctrl+Alt+H
Knife tool	7
Layers panel	Ctrl+6
Line tool	4
Object Inspector	Ctrl+I
Operations panel	Ctrl+Alt+O
Paragraph Inspector	Ctrl+Alt+P
Pen tool	6
Pointer tool	0 (zero)
Polygon tool	2
Rectangle tool	1
Page Rulers	Ctrl+Alt+M
Spacing or Horizontal Scale Inspector	Ctrl+Alt+K
Stroke Inspector	Ctrl+Alt+L
Styles panel	Ctrl+3
Text tool	. (period) or A
Text Toolbar	Ctrl+Alt+T
Toolbox	Ctrl+7
Transform	Ctrl+M
Xtra Tools panel	Ctrl+Alt+X

macintosh shortcuts

APPENDIX B

FreeHand offers lots of shortcuts that, once you learn them, will make your work easier. Many are described in the lessons in this book. This appendix lists FreeHand's keyboard shortcuts for menu commands, for some other common tasks, and for displaying FreeHand's panels and tools on Macintosh computers.

FILE MENU

Command	Shortcut
New	Command+N
Open	Command+O
Close	Command+F4
Save	Command+S
Save As	Command+Shift+S
Import	Command+R
Export	Command+Shift+R
Print	Command+P
Preferences	Command+Shift+D
Exit	Option+F4

EDIT MENU

Command	Shortcut
Undo	Command+Z
Redo	Command+Y
Cut	Command+X
Copy	Command+C
Paste	Command+V
Cut Contents	Command+Shift+X
Paste Inside	Command+Shift+V
Copy Attributes	Command+Shift+Option+C
Paste Attributes	Command+Shift+Option+V
Duplicate	Command+D
Clone	Command+Shift+C
Select All	Command+A
Select All in Document	Command+Shift+A
Find and Replace Text	Command+Option+Z
Find and Replace Graphics	Command+Option+E

VIEW MENU

Command	Shortcut
Fit Selection	Command+0 (zero)
Fit to Page	Command+Shift+W
Fit All	Command+Option+0 (zero)
Magnification 50%	Command+5
Magnification 100%	Command+1
Magnification 200%	Command+2
Magnification 400%	Command+4
Magnification 800%	Command+8
Preview or Keyline	Command+K
Panels	Command+Option+H
Info Bar	Command+Option+J
Page Rulers	Command+Option+M
Text Rulers	Command+/
Snap to Point	Command+'
Snap to Guides	Command+\
Snap to Grid	Command+;

MODIFY MENU

Command	Shortcut
Object	Command+I
Stroke	Command+Option+L
Fill	Command+Option+F
Text	Command+T
Document	Command+Option+D
Transform	Command+M
Transform Again	Command+,
Bring to Front	Command+F
Move Forward	Command+[
Move Backward	Command+]
Send to Back	Command+B
Align	Command+Option+A
Align Again	Command+Shift+Option+A
Join	Command+J
Split	Command+Shift+J
Blend	Command+Shift+B
Lock	Command+L
Unlock	Command+Shift+L
Group	Command+G
Ungroup	Command+U

TEXT MENU

Command	Shortcut
Smaller Size	Command+‹
Larger Size	Command+›
Type Style Plain	F5 or Command+ Shift+Option+P
Type Style Bold	F6 or Command+ Option+B
Type Style Italic	F7 or Command+ Option+I
Type Style Bold Italic	F8 or Ctr.l+Shift+ Option+O
Effect None	Command+Shift+ Option+N
Effect Highlight	Command+Shift+ Option+H
Effect Strikethrough	Command+Shift+ Option+S
Effect Underline	Command+Option+U
Align Left	Command+Shift+ Option+L
Align Right	Command+Shift+ Option+R
Align Center	Command+Shift+ Option+M
Align Justified	Command+Shift+ Option+J
Special Characters Em Space	Command+Shift+M
Special Characters En Space	Command+Shift+N
Special Characters Thin Space	Command+Shift+T
Special Characters Discretionary Hyphen	Command+_ (underscore)
Editor	Command+Shift+E
Spelling	Command+Shift+G
Run Around Selection	Command+ Option+W
Flow Inside Path	Command+Shift+U
Attach to Path	Command+Shift+Y
Convert to Paths	Command+Shift+P

WINDOW MENU

Command	Shortcut
New Window	Command+Option+N
Text Toolbars	Command+Option+T
Toolbox	Command+7
Object Inspector	Command+I
Stroke Inspector	Command+Option+L
Fill Inspector	Command+Option+F
Text Inspector	Command+T
Document Inspector	Command+Option+D
Layers Panel	Command+6
Styles Panel	Command+3
Color List Panel	Command+9
Color Mixer Panel	Command+Shift+C
Halftones Panel	Command+H
Align Panel	Command+Option+A
Transform Panel	Command+M
Xtras Operations	Command+Shift+I
Xtra Xtra Tools	Command+Shift+K

DRAWING AND EDITING COMMANDS

Command	Shortcut
Clone	Command+=
Close a Cut Path	Control+Knife Tool
Cut Contents	Command+Shift+X
Deselect All	Tab
Grabber Hand	Spacebar
Group	Command+G
Paste Inside	Command+Shift+V
Preview or Keyline	Command+K
Select All in Document	Command+Shift+A
Select All on Page	Command+A
Snap to Guides	Command+\
Snap to Point	Command+'
Variable Stroke or Calligraphic Pen Size Down	Left Arrow or 1 or [
Variable Stroke or Calligraphic Pen Size Up	Right Arrow or 2 or]
Ungroup	Command+U

GENERAL COMMANDS

Command	Shortcut
Export	Command+Shift+R
Help Cursor	Help
Import	Command+R
Next Page	Command+Page Down
New Window	Command+Option+N
Pause Screen Redraw	Command+.
Previous Page	Command+Page Up
Zoom In Magnification	Command+Spacebar+click
Zoom Out Magnification	Command+Option+Spacebar+click

DISPLAYING PANELS AND TOOLS

To display this	Use
Align	Command+Option+A
Arrowhead Editor	Option+Select Arrowhead
Bezigon tool	8 or Shift+8
Blend	Command+Shift+B
Color List	Command+9
Color Mixer	Command+Shift+C
Columns and Rows Inspector	Command+Option+R
Copyfit Inspector	Command+Option+C
Dash Editor	Option+Select Dash pop-up
Document Inspector	Command+Option+D
Ellipse tool	3 or Shift+F3
Fill Inspector	Command+Option+F
Freehand tool	5 or Shift+F5
Grabber Hand tool	Spacebar
Halftones panel	Command+H
Hide or Show All Open Panels	Command+Shift+H
Knife tool	7 or Shift+F7
Layers panel	Command+6
Line tool	4 or Shift+F4
Object Inspector	Command+I
Operations panel	Command+Option+O
Paragraph Inspector	Command+Option+P
Pen tool	6 or Shift+F6
Pointer tool	0 (zero) or Shift+F10
Polygon tool	2 or Shift+F2
Rectangle tool	1 or Shift+F1
Page Rulers	Command+Option+M
Spacing/Horizontal Scale	Command+Option+K
Stroke Inspector	Command+Option+L
Styles panel	Command+3
Text tool	. (period) or A or Shift+F9
Text Toolbar	Command+Option+T
Toolbox	Command+7
Transform	Command+M
Xtra Tools panel	Command+Shift+K

index

Macromedia tech support number: 415-252-9080

LICENSING AGREEMENT